Transformation Fast and Slow

Higher Education: Linking Research, Policy and Practice

The titles published in this series are listed at *brill.com/eair*

Transformation Fast and Slow

Digitalisation, Quality and Trust in Higher Education

Edited by

Bruno Broucker, Rosalind Pritchard, Clare Milsom and
René Krempkow

BRILL

LEIDEN | BOSTON

All chapters in this book have undergone peer review.

The Library of Congress Cataloging-in-Publication Data is available online at https://catalog.loc.gov
LC record available at https://lccn.loc.gov/

Typeface for the Latin, Greek, and Cyrillic scripts: "Brill". See and download: brill.com/brill-typeface.

ISSN 2666-7789
ISBN 978-90-04-52089-9 (paperback)
ISBN 978-90-04-52090-5 (hardback)
ISBN 978-90-04-52091-2 (e-book)

Printed by Printforce, the Netherlands

Contents

PART 1
Digitalisation

PART 2
Quality

PART 3
Trust

Figures and Tables

Figures

Tables

Notes on Contributors

Stephanie Albrecht

is Executive Coordinator to the Vice-President for Studies, Teaching & International Affairs at Hochschule für Technik und Wirtschaft (HTW) Berlin. Her main areas of interest are the internationalisation of higher education and sustainability concepts.

Tony Armstrong

Is Director of Postgraduate Research Degrees in the field of Education & Social Work at Birmingham City University. His research and professional interests are in doctoral learning and development including supervision and the history of supervision.

Victoria Birmingham

is a research assistant in the School of Education and Social Work at Birmingham City University. She recently completed her PhD in Education. Her doctoral research explored the impact of government policy reform on the assessment of primary school children.

Victor M. H. Borden

is Professor of Higher Education at Indiana University Bloomington. He previously directed institutional research offices at three different institutions. From 2015 to 2022, he directed the Carnegie Classification of Institutions of Higher Education. His research focuses on evidence-informed methods for improving the effectiveness of higher education programmes and institutions. He is a past President of the Association for Institutional Research and a Fulbright Scholar serving the University of KwaZulu-Natal in Durban, South Africa.

Bruno Broucker

is Guest Professor at the KU Leuven and Higher Education Policy Advisor at the Institute of Tropical Medicine. He is member of the executive committee of EAIR and Editor-in-Chief of the book series "Higher Education. Linking Research, Policy and Practice".

Uwe Cantner

is Professor of Economics at Friedrich Schiller University Jena and at the University of Southern Denmark, Odense, Denmark. At Friedrich Schiller University Jena, he is Vice President for Young Academics and Diversity

Management. Since 2019, he has been chairman of the German government's Commission of Experts on Research and Innovation (EFI). He publishes widely and internationally in the fields of economics of innovation, evolutionary economics, and empirical economics.

Helge Dauchert
heads the office of the Commission of Experts on Research and Innovation (EFI) in Berlin. He supports the Commission of Experts in analysing the strengths and weaknesses of the German innovation system and in developing recommendations for action for the Federal Government. Before jumping into scientific policy advising, he managed the office of a member of the German Bundestag.

Harry de Boer
is a Senior Research Associate at the Center for Higher Education Policy Studies, University of Twente. His research focuses on governance and funding issues, public management, policy analysis and thematic policy-oriented studies, mainly in the field of higher education, about which he publishes regularly both nationally and internationally.

Caterina Fox
teaches online at IU Internationale Hochschule, Germany, and has been working as an Adjunct Associate Professor (Communication) at the University of Maryland (Global Campus).

Amanda French
is a Reader in Education at Birmingham City University in the School of Education and Social Work. She has an established track record in research and development employing creative methodologies, related to academic/professional literacies, HE policy and pedagogies and professional development with a particular focus on Equality, Diversity and Inclusion.

Gunnar Grepperud
is Professor Emeritus at UiT The Artic University of Norway in the Center of Education, Learning and Technology.

Katharina Hölzle
is Professor for Technology Management and Industrial Engineering at the University of Stuttgart. She is Deputy Chair of the Commission of Experts for Research and Innovation (EFI) and former member of the German government's High-Tech Forum. She is Editor-in-Chief of the journal *Creativity and*

Innovation Management (Wiley). Her research focuses on digital entrepreneurship, digital innovation and transformation, and digital ecosystems.

Seonmi Jin

is a Project Associate for the Charting the Future while in the PhD program in Higher Education and Student Affairs at Indiana University Bloomington. She also serves as a data specialist intern for the American Democracy Project (ADP), a nonpartisan initiative of the American Association of State Colleges and Universities (ASSCU). Her professional experiences include faculty development and academic program assessment.

Ben Jongbloed

is a Senior Research Associate in the Center for Higher Education Policy Studies (CHEPS) at the University of Twente. He has worked at CHEPS for almost 30 years and published extensively on governance and resource allocation in higher education. His recent work is on performance-based funding, the public funding of research, and embedding entrepreneurship and sustainability in higher education.

Alex Kendall

is Professor of Education and Associate Dean Research in the Faculty of Health, Education and Life Sciences at Birmingham City University. Her research interests focus on teacher development across sectors with a particular focus on literacies, creative research methods and the education of marginalised groups.

Cindy Konen

is a lecturer for business administration and a scientific assistant for innovation management as well as innovative teaching concepts at the University of Applied Sciences in Dortmund (Germany). She has a doctoral degree in business administration and is currently researching with a focus on the innovative ability of Higher Education Institutions.

René Krempkow

is Senior Manager and Researcher at HU Berlin (D). He is editorial board member of the journals *Qualität in der Wissenschaft* (Quality in HE) and *Zeitschrift für Hochschulentwicklung* (Journal for HE Development).

Anne-Kristin Langner

is Professor for Social Media at IU Internationale Hochschule, Germany. She is the director of the degree programme Social Media (BA).

Theodor Leiber

is Scientific Advisor and Higher Education Researcher with Evaluation Agency Baden-Wuerttemberg, Mannheim (Germany) and Associate Professor of Philosophy at University of Augsburg (Germany). He received a Diploma in Theoretical Physics, PhD degrees in Theoretical Physics and Philosophy and a habilitation in Philosophy. His research focuses on evaluation, impact studies, performance measurement and governance, quality management and organisational development, learning and teaching spaces and transformative digitalisation in higher education. His publications relate to physics, epistemology, philosophy of science, ethics and higher education research.

Oddlaug Marie Lindgaard

is a senior adviser and a researcher at the Centre for Learning and Technology (KOLT) at Nord University. Fields of interest are change management, teaching and learning combined with ICT.

Silke Masson

is a research associate and educational developer at the Center for Quality Assurance and Development (ZQ) at Johannes Gutenberg University in Mainz, Germany. Her research focuses on the development of teaching quality especially through teacher communities.

Clare Milsom

is currently the interim Registrar and Chief Operating Officer at Liverpool John Moores University. She is National Teaching Fellow of the UK's Higher Education Academy. A palaeontologist by background Clare has worked in higher education for over 30 years. Known for her work on the evaluation of large scale qualitative data. Clare has spent the last decade working in professional services with responsibilities for the Academic Registry, Teaching and Learning Academy and Student Support.

Jessica Nooij

is Senior Researcher at the Department of Institutional Research, part of the Expert Center for Learning and Innovation at Avans University of Applied Sciences. She has a PhD in sociology and behavioural psychology and is a board member of the Dutch Association for Institutional Research (DAIR). Her current research focusses on the role and development of data-feedback tools in higher education learning and policy.

Mark O'Hara

is a National Teaching Fellow and Principal Fellow of the UK's Higher Education Academy. He works as Associate Pro Vice Chancellor (Education) at Aston University, Birmingham. His academic interests include student enablement and learner development, teaching enhancement, and the development of more inclusive educational practices. He is an Executive Committee member of both the European Association of Institutional Research (EAIR) and the UK's Forum for Access and Continuing Education (FACE) and also chairs AHE's Collaborative Award for Teaching Excellence Network (CATE-Net).

Matt O'Leary

is Professor of Education and Director of the education research centre CSPACE at Birmingham City University, UK. He is well known internationally for his extensive body of work on the use of classroom observation in understanding and improving teaching and learning. His recent research has explored the topic of teaching 'excellence' and 'quality' in higher education.

Pascale Stephanie Petri

is psychologist and researcher as well as lecturer at JLU Giessen (D). She earned her PhD for her research on freshmen's experiences in HE. Her research is situated in the area of psychological assessment (in HE).

Rosalind Pritchard

is Emeritus Professor of Education and Distinguished Scholar of Ulster University. Her PhD was on comparative education. She is a member of the Royal Irish Academy and Secretary of the European Association of Institutional Research (EAIR).

Christopher Stolz

is researcher at the Fraunhofer Institute for Systems and Innovation Research (ISI) in Karlsruhe. Before joining ISI the worked as research associate in the office of the Commission of Experts for Research and Innovation (EFI) in Berlin. There he supported the Commission in analysing the strength and the weaknesses of the German innovation system and in developing recommendations for the Federal Government.

Elisabeth Suzen

is an Associate Professor at Nord University and Inland Norway University of Applied Sciences. She holds a PhD in Pedagogy and her research interest is on quality in higher education.

Sara-I. Täger

is an advisor in the quality management department at HTW Berlin. She is responsible for HTW's Monitoring of Study Programmes and works on data analyses and reporting.

Daniel Thiemann

is data warehouse architect at HTW Berlin. He works in the Information Technology Centre and is responsible for the design and maintenance of data management systems and reporting for several departments.

Lieke van Berlo

is researcher at the Department of Institutional Research, part of the Expert Center for Learning and Innovation at Avans University of Applied Sciences. She holds a MSc degree in Sociology and has broad experience in coordinating and conducting research among students.

Lotte J. van Dijk

is researcher and data scientist at the department of Institutional Research, part of the Expert Center for Learning and Innovation at Avans University of Applied Sciences. She holds a BSc in educational science, a BEd and two MScs degrees in Computer Science and Interaction Technology.

Katy Vigurs

is a Reader in Education in the Centre for the Study of Practice and Culture in Education at Birmingham City University, UK. Katy is a critical higher education researcher with a particular interest in stratification and its relationship to university access, student experience and graduate outcomes. She is primarily concerned with issues of inclusion, equity and social justice. Katy specialises in narrative, visual and participative research methods and has expertise in creative pathways to public engagement.

Tilo Wendler

is Professor for Quantitative Methods. His research areas are the application of multivariate statistical methods and data mining. He is vice-president for studies, teaching and international affairs at HTW Berlin.

Tamara Zajontz

is a research associate at the Centre for Quality Assurance and Development (ZQ) at Johannes Gutenberg University in Mainz, Germany, in the field of teaching and learning. Her research interests comprise teaching and learning research as well as higher education research.

Transformation Fast and Slow

Digitalisation, Quality and Trust in Higher Education

Bruno Broucker, Rosalind Pritchard, Clare Milsom and René Krempkow

Abstract

This volume is based upon a selection of papers that were presented at the online EAIR Forum in 2021. The book brings together scholars, practitioners and policymakers in higher education, and sets out the theme of transformation in three key areas: digitalisation, quality and trust. Herewith this volume presents a stimulating and careful analysis of the opportunities and associated challenges of transformation in higher education systems and institutions.

Keywords

higher education transformation – quality – trust – digitalisation – COVID-19 – higher education

1 Introduction

2020 will go down in history as the year where the whole world was again exposed to the rapid pace of societal, economic and political transformation. The global COVID-19 pandemic has accelerated change in the higher education sector across the globe and has required huge efforts and commitments on the political, institutional and individual levels. During this period higher education was considered, maybe more than ever, as an essential sector. Providing critical information and, contributing to the delivery of scientifically based solutions to help societies overcome this global crisis, universities also simultaneously maintained core educational activities to secure the academic future of the next student generation. This required, as in many other sectors, a high level of innovation, adaptivity and creativity.

It is therefore little wonder that the concepts of change and transformation in higher education were central at the 2021 conference of the European

DOI:10.1163/9789004520912_001

Association for Institutional Research (EAIR) – the European Higher Education Society. This book is the outcome of that annual conference. It is the third volume of the series "Higher Education: Linking Research, Policy and Practice" and it brings together a collection of papers that were presented at the online EAIR Forum 2021. In line with the philosophy of the series, the book presents a range of well-selected topical chapters and a rich diversity of perspectives: academic investigations by reputed scholars, critical evidence-based papers of third space professionals, and/or policymakers' perspectives on the daily practice and management of higher education institutions and systems. In line with the history of EAIR, this third volume crosses boundaries between educational activities and caters for a mix of contributors.

2   Three Central Concepts

This volume is centred on three main themes linked to transformation and change in higher education: digitalisation, quality and trust. Obviously, transformation entails more than those concepts, but in the current context they are at the core of the debate: the transformative power of the pandemic has raised concerns and questions of each of them.

2.1   *Digitalisation*

When it comes to digitalisation, there is no question about the significant value that digitalisation added during long periods of quarantine and national lockdowns: because of the potential of digitalisation, higher education institutions were able to continue with their core activities. Teaching and learning activities pivoted to fully online, and then to hybrid. And then back again. However, digitalisation goes far beyond tools for teaching and learning. How the administration at higher education institutions is affected by digitalisation for instance is maybe less discussed and researched but of profound importance in e.g. back-office processes, student-follow up, learning analytics, and communication and research activities. The development of digital competences of both the administrative and the academic staff takes place through the individual use of digital tools, but also through an in-depth understanding of digital society and its building blocks. The sudden digital shift in the delivery of higher education requires a critical, considered governance structure. It entails the use of data analytics and the application of Artificial Intelligence to create personalised education. All those changes impact the core activities of higher education, but also affect the traditional model of higher education, the way it is run, its organisational culture, and its role in society.

As places of education and reflection, higher education institutions feel particularly committed to the responsible design and use of digitalisation for the purpose of quality knowledge production and knowledge distribution. Furthermore, while digitalisation is generally expected to enable institutions to conduct research, teaching and third mission activities on a higher, more professional level, countries and institutions differ considerably in their expectations of change and in the extent to which they have already implemented change via digitalisation. Dealing with the COVID-19 pandemic has shown that institutions are able to react flexibly and responsibly even under the most difficult of conditions. However, it has also shown that a more systematic approach should be taken to the development. The challenges of digitalisation have become so complex and diverse that, in future, individual institutions will find it increasingly difficult to cope alone. More collaborative working will enable better testing of methods and concepts, including participatory approaches, applied to higher education. Transformation requires active academic participation. Digitalisation transformation is the focus of the first part of the book.

In Chapter 1, Fox and Langner discuss the digital transition that higher education institutions had to make during the COVID-19 pandemic, and the driving (or impeding) factors which lecturers experience in that shift. Interestingly they found out that lecturers who were interested in teaching online, were also more satisfied with it, while the converse was true as well: those who were not interested, were more dissatisfied. Yet, the authors emphasize another important element in this debate: those who were more satisfied experienced more stress and greater risk of having a burn-out. For higher education institutions it might imply that the individual preferences for online teaching might become an important element to take into account when it comes to future employment. Indeed, institutions that are building on the experiences of the COVID-19 pandemic, and willing to further invest in online teaching, will have to make active efforts to further invest in personal development for lecturers, and in the recruitment of lectures with online learning experience – or at least online learning interest.

In Chapter 2, Krempkow and Petri address the question of how precisely digital competences can be assessed. In this they stress the significance of digital competences in the first year of higher education under pandemic conditions. The authors argue that self-efficacy has proven to be a good predictor of study success, satisfaction and dropout intentions. With careful analysis, in their chapter they examine the extent to which digital competences mediate this relationship in the situation where students experience their first year in higher education only in a virtual environment. Their extensive and original data analysis demonstrates that digital competencies have a mediating function in the interplay between self-efficacy in the first year in higher education and study satisfaction, which is an interesting and valuable contribution to the state-of-the art of research. Moreover, in their chapter they provide a ready-to-use questionnaire for HEIs willing to measure the level of digital competencies, also allowing them to differentiate amongst different fields of study.

In the next chapter, Leiber questions why Digital Transformation (DT) in higher education institutions can be of limited success. He discusses how this situation can be overcome and proposes the application of an integrative concept of quality literacy in DT composed of competencies in quality strategies, practice, and culture. In fact, his analysis demonstrates that in higher education digital transformation is still a major topic, and not only because it is about technical innovation, but also because it is about the development of academic, curricular, organisational und structural matters towards digitalisation, including ethical issues as well.

In the last chapter of the digital part, Cantner, Dauchert, Hölzle and Stolz illustrate that Germany is a case in which the development of both digital technologies and the digital university have considerable room for improvement, as German universities seem to find the development of a digital university particularly challenging. The process of digitalisation to the crossing of institutional frontiers requires cultural changes: from the organisation of research activities, structuring of internal communication, to teaching formats and university administration. The authors state that Nordic and Baltic university systems are much further developed and more successful, compared to Germany, which raises the potential opportunity for more peer learning between institutions. While a number of improvements are already visible, such as in online teaching formats, digital exams, and video-conferencing, the authors attest that policy makers and university managers need to take more action to deliver truly digital university experience.

2.2   *Quality*

Pre-COVID-19 handling of digitalisation involved embedding it gradually in a quality-led rationale to enhance teaching and learning.

Post-COVID-19, this was replaced by the need to implement a rapid pivot from face-to-face teaching to online provision. Because of the speed with which this had to be implemented, quality remained an important concern in this shift. Indeed, it is crucial to note that even in a crisis, digitalisation for higher education institutions remains a mean to an end. Not an end in itself. Higher education institutions are driven by quality, in its broadest sense: quality of education, quality of student support, quality in research activities, quality in cooperation, quality in the way they address societal challenges or aim to achieve their institutional goals. Despite its huge usefulness, digitalisation has implications for higher education and for the quality of the student (and staff) experience.

In this context, to the traditional dimensions of quality have been added the technical concerns of stability of internet connections and user-friendliness of video software, which have become essential co-determinants of successful learning and teaching. The crisis has been a unique event and, as highlighted by the European Network for Quality Assurance, it has already had some procedural impact on quality assurance (QA), such as conducting external visits entirely online. In the post-COVID-19 context, pre-corona reflections on digitalisation as a mean of enhancing quality will be back on the agenda – but enriched by the lessons learnt in between. Established quality management approaches in higher education are coming into focus here. These aim to support stakeholders and decision makers both in deriving effective measures systematically in order to maintain and enhance quality and further develop the strategic goals of higher education institutions in learning and teaching. Attention naturally focuses on the determinants of student success and quality in its different dimensions. From that perspective, quality is a key driver for higher education activities on the micro, the meso and the macro level, and goes beyond teaching and learning. Quality is the second part of the book.

In Chapter 5, Nooij, van Berlo and van Dijck discuss the development in their institution of a data-application that works as a "mental compass" for students so that the institute can offer tailor-made support that fits the needs of the students. This policy was developed for enhancing student wellbeing and aimed at helping students become more resilient to stress by teaching them how to better cope with it. In order to achieve that, the institution developed a "positive mind monitor" for students. This innovative tool helps students to reflect on their current wellbeing by answering questions on how they perceive it. These questions are based on multiple underlying aspects of stress and coping. Additionally, the tool provides data-feedback for students with tips on coping strategies that fit their self-reported, current state of wellbeing. In a time where mental wellbeing is high on the agenda across the globe, this tool seems to be highly valuable, not only because of its practicality, but also because it explicitly views mental health as something that can be talked about. It cannot be denied that this is intrinsically linked to quality in its broad sense.

In Chapter 6, Borden and Jin provide a framework for designing and implementing evidence-informed transformations within higher education institutions using techniques that have emerged from equitable, impactful applied research. It was developed as part of an institutional transformation project that seeks to leverage the institution's advanced expertise and technologies for accessing, analysing, and visualising data from traditional (structured) and emerging (transactional) big data systems. This chapter importantly discusses the balance that exists in higher education between resistance to change and responsiveness to change and forms an important debate in the search for increased quality.

In the next chapter, Suzen, Lindgaard and Grupperud review learning experiences among 48 university lecturers at Nord University, Norway, during a three-month pedagogical course. The basic question in the study was which measures have to be considered or adopted to create an arena for pedagogical reflection among academic staff? The authors demonstrated that the lecturers felt a positive recognition of their experiences, they appreciated the observation and learning dialogues with colleagues, demanded a more strategic and holistic approach to academic development and reflected on actions with intention to learn from experiences. When discussing quality, the role of academic development of staff is sometimes forgotten. This is in fact surprising because one could argue that the quality of the learning experience starts with the lecturer. By focusing on this aspect of pedagogical reflections, the institute builds on the development of a quality culture among staff, which eventually will influence not only the quality of student learning, but also the quality of the programs, and even the quality of the organisational climate.

In Chapter 8, Jongbloed and De Boer discuss the use of performance agreements in higher education. In those agreements institutions negotiate with the government the objectives they have to achieve in conjunction with the grants they hold. From the comparative international case-study they conclude that performance agreements can be a policy tool that contributes to a more interactive trust-based type of coordination in the higher education system, and that it has the potential to increase transparency and performance at the system and institutional level. In their conclusion the word "potential" is key: much depends on the design of the performance agreements, the level of freedom that is given to higher education institutions to determine for themselves what they want to achieve, and how the agreements are integrated in the overall policy context. As stated at the beginning of the paragraph, the link with quality is important here: institutions need room for creativity and critical thinking in order to avoid a tick box-mentality when implementing the performance agreements. Developing overall goals for higher education institutions, while maintaining and supporting academic freedom, will eventually lead to higher quality of research, teaching and third mission activities. This is why high-quality performance agreements are necessary.

In the last chapter of this part, Täger, Albrecht, Thiemann and Wendler describe in detail how the Hochschule für Technik und Wirtschaft (HTW) Berlin, a university of applied sciences, used its business intelligence software to gain insights into COVID-19 pandemic related changes in student dropout rates, exam registrations, and credit point gains. Their findings indicate fewer dropouts at the beginning of the pandemic and lower numbers of exam registrations compared to pre-pandemic semesters, but also that there might be delayed effects that are starting to emerge. Interesting is that the institution will use those results to further monitor its study programmes as a quality management tool for continuous improvement. Indeed, the biggest benefit from a transparent system of data collection and monitoring, is that it allows to build in an evidence-based informed policy that supports the overall quality of teaching and learning activities in the institution.

2.3   *Trust*

Often, in transformation processes, trust has been mentioned as a key component of successful implementation. Nowadays, the notion of trust in higher education has often been translated into accountability, responsibility or even resilience. The effort to build trust can be viewed at different levels. At the micro level, it is an issue pertaining to individual academics, teachers, students and academic support staff. At the meso level, it applies to the academic organisation and its sub-units. It is sometimes lacking on the part of State representatives with their detailed control interventions, for example new governance approaches — even if in recent years institutional autonomy has increased overall. Another dimension of trust concerns the support of learning processes and assessment of research via Learning Analytics and Performance Measuring. Here it is a question of trust in and responsible handling of Artificial Intelligence with its concomitant risks and opportunities. Trust is key in higher education, both on the individual level and on the institutional level or even between the meso and the macro-level. Trust is the third part of the book.

In Chapter 10, Pritchard discusses extensively the notion of trust and the impact of the pandemic on trust in British higher education. She provides the reader with a conceptual overview of "trust" and carefully demonstrates its complexity when discussing it in the context of the pandemic. At the same time the author highlights the quite negative impact of the pandemic on the quality of teaching and the wellbeing of students and staff in the United Kingdom. Moreover, emphasis is put on the declining levels of trust towards the British government and its leadership. As the role and importance of higher education in society are very obvious, Pritchard stresses the worryingly limited attention that higher education has received in the British Academy's analysis of the pandemic. Given the low levels of trust and the increase in inequality in British society, Pritchard advocates important and significant reforms by the

British government to re-establish trust, and reaffirm the important position of British higher education within society. For inspiration, a comparison with Finland is made. It has remained the world's happiest country for four years in a row despite the pandemic. It attributes its resilience in considerable measure to education and the overall high level of trust that is so important for societal wellbeing.

In Chapter 11, Konen provides HEIs with a model for assessing their ability for cooperative innovations with enterprises. While previous approaches mainly focus on analysing innovation-supporting frame conditions and, on this basis, try to determine the extent of innovative ability, this contribution looks further. By discussing the role of the individual professor acting as an innovator, a bottom-up perspective which shows that different ideal types can usually be found within one HEI. An interesting conclusion from the chapter is that innovative ability often does not arise due to the combination of supporting frame conditions and the professor acting as an innovator, but simply by the professor acting as one without support. It is obvious that in this approach, trust is needed, as is demonstrated in the chapter as well: acting as an innovator without support or trust leads for a professor to personal dissatisfaction with the HEI and a medium to long-term decline in innovation cooperation activities. Only by analysing both the supporting frame conditions and the person-specific ability as well as their interplay, the HEI gets a realistic picture of its innovative ability. With this analysis, the leadership of the HEI gets into a better position to use its potential to steer the HEIs innovative ability. As a result, leadership can coordinate the innovation-supporting frame conditions in a more targeted manner and better support the professors' willingness and ability to innovate. In the end, this may increase the professors' satisfaction with the HEI and their extent of innovation cooperations. Konen argues that future research has to focus more on the individual perspective and the interplay of innovation-supporting frame conditions and the person-specific innovative ability.

In Chapter 12, Masson and Zajontz discuss the increased demand for continuous staff development and training. Based on evaluation data of six years and a recent survey on digital teaching during the COVID-19 pandemic, this chapter discusses a community-based professional development initiative in higher education at a German university and assesses its features and effects. Through continuous opportunities for dialogue and long-term cooperation, the initiative enables the development of mutual trust amongst participants and provides ways to transform academic teaching whilst ensuring academic freedom and freedom of teaching. However, successful implementation depends on external support and the necessary infrastructure for cooperation. The results of the study suggest that community-based professional developments add value compared to individual formats of staff development, as they improve teachers' readiness to assume collective responsibility for the quality of teaching and student learning as well as for their own professional development.

In the last chapter O'Leary, Armstrong, Birmingham, French, Kendall, O'Hara and Vigurs draw on evidence from three distinct projects undertaken in one university in England, each involving academic staff and students co-researching and collaborating on areas of curriculum, pedagogy and mental health. What links these projects is the participatory approach to rethinking notions of quality and excellence in practitioner education, which empowers students and staff to collaborate in improving the quality of teaching and learning experiences. They share a series of innovations in practitioner education with the aim of opening up critical conversations about "quality" and "excellence" in higher education (HE) and interrogating what these terms might come to mean "in the ruins of humanism and the aftermath of Black Lives Matter". Their research into the student experience and mental health suggests that modern universities, with their diverse student cohorts, need to work harder to make new spaces for all students, which allow them to feel more that they belong within and can relate more positively and with more agency to HE demands and expectations.

3   Some Final Reflections

In the second volume of this book series we emphasised the following (Broucker et al., 2021, p. 7):

> Higher education does not just *do* change, nor does it see change as a process with a start or an end. In reality, higher education *is* change.

That conclusion has become even more important and pertinent now. The present collection of chapters has demonstrated two elements. First, higher education institutions have change, transformation and innovation in their DNA. Researchers, policymakers and practitioners in higher education develop on an almost constant basis new ideas, models and concepts to improve what they are doing or to address identified challenges. In this book, innovative practices have been demonstrated in the field of student wellbeing, staff development and training, digitalisation, cooperative innovations. From that diverse overview, it is clear that transformation in higher education can go relatively fast, certainly when the external pressure increases. The COVID-19 pandemic has only confirmed the speed with which higher education institutions can adapt.

Second, and maybe more important: the picture is not perfect. This book has shown that transformation sometimes is (too?) slow, that resistance can be high or that diversity of opinion might cause difficulties in finding a perfect and consensual way forward. Trust in this respect is crucial, though fragile. A rule of thumb in change literature is that the effectiveness of change is equal to the quality of the change project (or strategy) multiplied by the acceptance of that project or strategy. This equation applies also to higher education institutions, and this has also been shown by the COVID-19 pandemic: while policy measures were (to a varying degree) scientifically based, the acceptance rate fluctuated over time – obviously affecting the effectiveness of, for instance, the vaccination strategy or lockdown measures. While being "locked down" physically, higher education institutions have been reminded that in spirit they cannot be "locked down". They are an integral and recognised part of society. They contribute to change process and innovation, they address challenges and are guardians of social, cultural and economic welfare. But they are also confronted with internal resistance to change, conflicting scientific evidence, or internal tensions that need to be dealt with. From that perspective higher education probably does not differ that much from other sectors in society.

This book has demonstrated the impact the pandemic has had on higher education and the challenge it has caused for students, staff and institutions. But it has also demonstrated the resilience of the sector, and its willingness to continuously address societal challenges and contribute to what is needed. And despite the fact that transformation in higher education is sometimes too slow – or even sometimes too fast – in general it deserves trust in its eagerness to help the world become a better place. The chapters in this book are proof of that unstoppable willingness and drive.

Reference

Broucker, B., Pritchard, R., Melim, G., & Milsom, C. (2021). Introduction. Sustainability of higher education in uncertain times. In B. Broucker, R. Pritchard, G. Melim, & C. Milsom (Eds.), *Sustaining the future of higher education* (pp. 1–7). Brill.

PART 1

Digitalisation

∴

CHAPTER 1

COVID-19: Challenges of the Virtual Classroom

Satisfaction, Motivation and Burnout in Online Teaching

Caterina Fox and Anne-Kristin Langner

Abstract

As all higher education moved online due to COVID-19, some instructors were thrust into the digital environment without preparation. Despite enthusiastic efforts to learn and master new tools, many traditional educators quickly became worn out, disillusioned and dissatisfied. Without the direct feedback from students, they felt their teaching was stifled and ineffective. At the same time, there are highly effective online teachers who thrive in this environment and provide high quality education. Are they simply more used to this format or do they possess specific qualities that make them better suited to teaching online? After all, they made the conscious decision to teach online rather than in a traditional, in-person classroom. The exceptional situation of 2020/2021 presented a unique opportunity to study this question. This study explored the relationships between personal teaching preference, job satisfaction and burnout. A quantitative online survey with 114 instructors at IU Internationale Hochschule was conducted to shed light on this issue. Results indicated that overall satisfaction was very high, yet moderate to high burnout levels were a concern. Both satisfaction and burnout were closely linked to personal preference, which has interesting implications for hiring and developing faculty.

Keywords

online teaching – satisfaction – burnout – preference

1   Introduction

Due to the COVID-19 pandemic, almost all higher education was forced to move online in 2020. Thus, faculty accustomed to teaching exclusively face-to-face had to adapt their approaches to a virtual environment. Without any prior notice or training they had to navigate and master new digital tools and technology. However, many took the challenge head on and with enthusiasm. Yet anecdotal evidence suggests that traditional instructors started encountering problems later in the semester. They reported increased stress levels and less satisfaction with the digital teaching experience. The lack of feedback and interaction seemed to stifle them more than their online-only counterparts who had been teaching virtually even before the pandemic. For instance, traditional educators complained noticeably more about turned-off cameras and missing their colleagues. The lack of student visibility and direct feedback is a typical problem of online education (Wingo et al., 2016), but not all educators describe it as a problematic factor. Research has shown that throughout the COVID-19 pandemic the attitudes of educators towards online teaching and online formats have changed in a positive way as educators developed new routines and realized the long-term perspective and potentials of online formats (Albrecht et al., 2021). Becker et al. (2021) explored that educators as well as students were overall satisfied with the execution of online teaching and the accomplishment of learning targets.

However, the differences and problems addressed in this study were observed within the same institutions and same departments, meaning that many possible intervening factors were controlled for. It stands to reason that while certain instructors thrive in an online-only teaching environment, others are not well-suited to it. However, it is not immediately apparent nor predictable who will succeed in a fully online teaching environment and who will suffer. What drives satisfaction with online teaching?

While research on satisfaction with fully online academic courses exists in abundance, the focus is usually on the student perspective, not that of faculty (Cohen & Baruth, 2017; Göncz, 2017; Kim et al., 2019). To address this gap in the literature, an exploratory study was conducted. The unique situation of 2020/2021 made it possible to gather insight from both traditional face-to-face instructors as well as fully online faculty and compare their satisfaction levels with online teaching. With regard to the construct of job satisfaction in general, research results show that professional recognition and self-determination are essential. Putting one's own ideas into practice and being satisfied with the courses conducted lead to job satisfaction (Krempkow, 2005). Further, a correlation between a strong learning and teaching focus and job satisfaction has been discovered. Academic personnel with a learning and teaching focus are more open to changes and reforms (Krempkow, 2005; Schaeper, 1995).

2   Background of the Study

2.1   *Satisfaction*
Satisfaction with online teaching varies widely (Abe, 2020; Allen & Seaman, 2013; Bollinger, 2014). In general, online faculty may feel isolated from colleagues and

wish for more community (Ferencz, 2017). More specifically, the factors affecting (dis)satisfaction can be categorized into four dimensions (Walters et al., 2017):

– Online environment factors, such as the flexibility and accessibility of the online classes;
– Institutional factors, such as the support and compensation received from the school;
– Personal factors, such as experience, personal feelings, and attitudes;
– Student Engagement, such as student participation and involvement.

Walters et al. (2017) found that the effectiveness of communication tools was a major challenge for online education and a big driver of dissatisfaction among faculty. But they also noted the mediating factor of experience, indicating the need for specific faculty development.

2.2 *Motivation, Self-Determination, and Preference*

The relationship of motivation, self-compassion and self-determination has been studied from a students' perspective and with regard to academic outcome (Breva & Galindo, 2020; Fangfang et al., 2021; Fjelkner et al., 2019; Kotera et al., 2021; Luo et al., 2021; Nishimura et al., 2021). The results can be summarized as follows: a feeling of self-determination and self-compassion has a positive impact on motivation and can help to turn extrinsic motivation into long-lasting intrinsic motivation. This is especially challenging when it comes to online learning environments. Whereas teachers hold different roles here, for example as initiators or administrators, the students are pure users and the question of self-determination is essential (Luo et al., 2021).

However, due to the COVID-19 pandemic all academic teaching personnel had to move online, whether they prefer to teach online or not. Although they might take different roles within an online environment, the question is whether they feel comfortable enough to do so. For those who prefer to teach offline, does the feeling of self-determination translate from offline to online?

The self-determination theory (SDT) was proposed by US psychologists Deci and Ryan (1985a, 1985b). The theory explores human behaviour and personality development related to the natural energy everyone has. The theory investigates which factors facilitate the energy flow and which thwart it. Energy in the SDT is related to three basic psychological needs: autonomy, competence, and relatedness. These needs and the question whether they are satisfied or frustrated determines how people interact with the (online) environment (Tang et al., 2020). Consequently, research exploring the relation of SDT and education has been conducted (Deci & Ryan, 1993). Further, a positive relation of self-determination and intrinsic motivation, social development and well-being has been revealed (Deci & Ryan, 2000).

Therefore, there is a plausible correlation between the degree of perceived self-determination and the chance to teach within an environment the teacher feels most comfortable in. If the teaching environment offers the chance to fulfil the needs of autonomy, competence, and relatedness and enables the teacher to keep the energy level up high, self-determination has a positive correlation with personal preference and teaching philosophy.

2.3   *Burnout*

Unrelated to the challenges of the virtual classroom due to COVID-19, higher education has undergone additional changes in the past few years, such as massification and greater expectations of academic performance (Zaynab et al., 2018). This means that adapting to the new virtual reality is not simply an additional task for faculty, but one that is piled on top of what is already an immense workload. The relationship between increase in workload and faculty burnout has been demonstrated repeatedly in the literature (Catano et al., 2010; Rothmann & Barkhuizen, 2008; Tytherleigh et al., 2005; Watts & Robertson, 2011; Winefield et al., 2003). In fact, there is empirical evidence that faculty burnout is a serious concern (e.g., Blix et al., 1994; Byrne et al., 2013; Ghorpade et al., 2011; Lackritz, 2004; Teven, 2007).

Burnout was first described by Freudenberger (1974) as a state of being physically, mentally, and emotionally exhausted after trying to live up to extreme expectations over a prolonged period of time. Generally, the syndrome is composed of three dimensions: emotional exhaustion, depersonalization, and perception of reduced professional efficacy (Maslach & Jackson, 1981). Emotional exhaustion describes a feeling of fatigue and emotional emptiness and is the most critical dimension (Maslach, Schaufeli, & Leiter, 2001). The second component refers to the tendency to disengage from colleagues and work issues. Finally, reduced efficacy means that employees have low opinions of their own competence and performance.

The Job Demands–Resources model (Demerouti et al., 2001) has proven useful for examining burnout as it conceptualizes both antecedents and consequences. According to this model, job demands are draining factors, while job resources are motivating factors. Unrealistic job demands typically cause

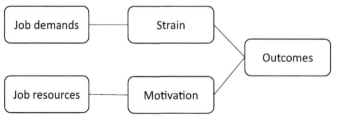

FIGURE 1.1   Simplified job demands–resources model

burnout, but employees can be shielded from this effect by so-called job resources. Those could be an amount of autonomy, support, feedback, rewards, and growth opportunities (Zaynab et al., 2018).

In accordance with the model, job demands – and especially workload – are related to high levels of faculty burnout (e.g., Fernet, Guay, & Senécal, 2004; Zhong et al., 2009). Social support, either from colleagues or the organization as a whole, is related to low levels of faculty burnout (Rothmann, Barkhuizen, & Tytherleigh, 2008; Van Emmerik, 2002).

3 Method and Measures

3.1 *Participants*

A cross-sectional quantitative online survey was conducted among traditional and online instructors at IU International Hochschule. IU has three main models of education: (1) The school offers fully online programs, (2) fully in person programs, and (3) hybrid programs. This means that students and faculty can normally choose the mode of teaching that is most suitable to their own personal preferences. However, at the time of the study, all classes took place online due to COVID-19, regardless of their original format. The link to the survey was distributed in July 2021 via faculty email addresses.

Of the 114 instructors who completed the survey (N = 114), 52.6% were male and 45.6% were female.[1] Two chose not to disclose their gender. The respondents' ages ranged between 32 and 64, with the mean age being 45 years. One third (33.3%) of the respondents had taught online prior to 2020, the other two thirds had been traditional face-to-face instructors before the pandemic. One third (33.3%) was employed part-time at IU, the others were full-time faculty. Most of the respondents had taught online between 1 and 5 years (50%). However, there was also a sizable group of very new online instructors (40.4%). Faculty with more than 5 years of online experience were the exception (9.6%).

3.2 *Measures*

Preference: To assess teaching preferences, respondents indicated on a dichotomous scale which environment (online/offline) they thought to be more suitable for specific requirements. These included, among others, teaching effectiveness, work-life-balance, and personal well-being.

Satisfaction: For an overall assessment, respondents indicated their general satisfaction with online teaching on a 5-point-scale (1 = do not agree at all to 5 = agree completely). The same scale was used for a more differentiated assessment of the four dimensions: online environment, institutional factors, personal factors, and student engagement.

Burnout: To assess the level of burnout, a variation of the Maslach Burnout Inventory (MBI SS KV) was administered (αt1/t2/t3 = .86/.82/.68; 1 = never to 5 = every day). The adaption is a shorter version of the MBI available in German, consisting of three items per dimension (Wörfel et al., 2015). In a study of 9,663 students, this measure had been shown to be reliable and was recommended for studies with multiple concepts of interest. Since the MBI SS KV was originally developed for students, the wording was altered slightly to address the faculty experience.

3.3   *Data Analyses*

To describe the sample and gain preliminary insights, descriptive statistics were used (frequency, percentage, mean, and standard deviation). Internal consistency (Cronbach's alpha) was calculated to check the reliability of each scale used. T-test and analysis of variance (ANOVA) was used to compare means according to teaching environment. For categorical data such as preference, Chi Square was calculated. Finally, a Pearson's correlation analysis was performed to analyse the relationship between socio-demographic and professional factors and online teaching satisfaction and burnout. The significance level was set at 5% for all tests. All data analyses were carried out using the Statistical Package for Social Sciences (SPSS).

3.4   *Results*

3.4.1   Preference

To gain a better understanding of why some instructors prefer face to face teaching while others enjoy teaching online, the survey included various

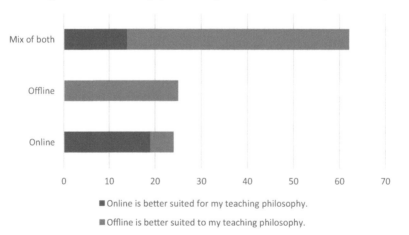

FIGURE 1.2   Preference of teaching environment based on the environment believed to be most conducive for effective teaching (N = 114)

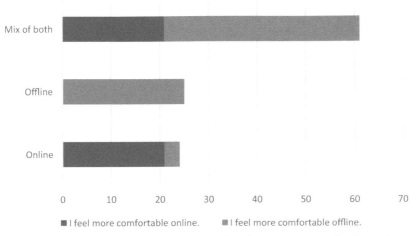

FIGURE 1.3   Preference of teaching environment based on instructor comfort (N = 110)

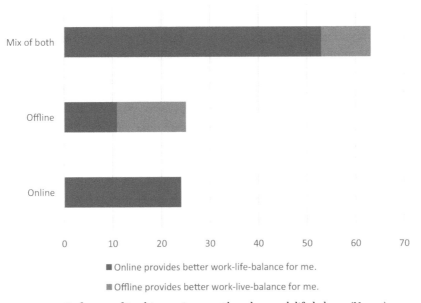

FIGURE 1.4   Preference of teaching environment based on work-life-balance (N = 112)

aspects related to this preference: (1) the environment most conducive for effective teaching, (2) the environment the instructor felt most comfortable in, (3) the environment providing the best work-life-balance and (4) the environment most suited for the instructor's personal teaching philosophy. Each of these aspects emerged as a significant driver of preference (p < 0.001).

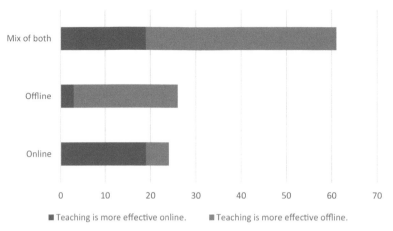

FIGURE 1.5   Preference of teaching environment based on teaching philosophy (N = 111)

3.4.2   Satisfaction

The results indicated that satisfaction overall was very high. No significant differences could be observed between traditionally online or face-to-face faculty. There was also no significant difference based on mode of employment (full- vs. part-time). In addition, no significant differences in satisfaction were found for demographic characteristics. The most satisfied department was IT & Technology, the least satisfied department was Transportation & Logistics. However, a significant difference in satisfaction emerged based on personal preference (p = 0.004). Those instructors who preferred teaching online were significantly more satisfied in this environment than those who preferred teaching face to face.

The individual factors of satisfaction show a more nuanced picture.[2] Instructors were confident in their online teaching abilities and generally happy with the online environment. They also believed that online education was important to and generally supported by their institution.

3.4.3   Burnout

To assess the level of burnout among the respondents, the normative scores of the MBI were adjusted to the shortened version of the instrument used for this study (Michinov & Rusch, 2010).

Based on those scores, the respondents reported moderate to high levels of burnout.

There was a clear and significant (p < 0.001) higher occurrence of burnout among those faculty members who prefer teaching in person. They were more emotionally exhausted and felt more cynical and disengaged from their work than those colleagues who prefer teaching online or enjoy both environments. However, all instructors reported a high self-assessment of personal competence, meaning they did not feel that their efficacy as teachers was diminished.

TABLE 1.1   Overall satisfaction with online teaching

	N		Mean Satisfaction	SD
Overall	114		4.07	0.99
Age	45	45 or younger	4.11	0.94
	47	Over 45	4.04	1.04
Gender	60	Male	3.95	1.03
	52	Female	4.23	0.94
Employment	74	Full-time	4.04	1.04
	38	Part-time	4.13	0.94
Environment according to contract	38	Online	4.21	1.04
	75	Offline	4.0	0.97
Department[a]	40	Health & Social Studies	4.00	1.038
	10	Hospitality, Tourism & Event	(4.10)	0.568
	9	IT & Technology	(4.56)	0.527
	16	Marketing & Communication	(4.00)	1.317
	2	Transportation & Logistics	(2.50)	0.707
	29	Business & Management	4.24	0.786
Personal preference	24	Online	4.54	0.884
	26	Offline	3.62	1.203
	64	Mix of both	4.08	0.860

a   Note that the responses in several departments were insufficient. A minimum of 20 responses are required for a sample of this size (Döring & Bortz, 2016, p. 843). However, they are reported (in brackets) for the sake of completeness.

Interestingly, satisfaction with online teaching emerged as preventer of burnout. Those faculty members who were satisfied with teaching online felt less emotionally exhausted ($r = -0.536$, $p < 0.01$), less cynical ($r = -0.546$, $p < 0.01$), and had a better sense of personal accomplishment ($b = -0.407$, $p < 0.01$).

3.5   *Discussion*
The study results indicated overall high satisfaction with online teaching at IU Internationale Hochschule. Instructors are confident in teaching online and

TABLE 1.2   Satisfaction with different aspects of online teaching

Factor	Aspect of satisfaction (Item)	Pearson r[a]	N	Mean	SD
Personal	I enjoy teaching online.	0.535	114	3.51	1.199
Personal	I am able to build relationships with my online students.	0.524	114	3.85	1.091
Institution	The quality of online courses is important to the university.	0.47	114	3.96	1.163
Personal	I feel confident in my ability to teach online.	0.429	114	4.36	0.667
Personal	I feel that my online persona is an accurate reflection of who I am as a lecturer.	0.427	114	3.43	1.16
Personal	I can reach students who otherwise would not be able to take courses.	0.377	114	3.2	1.332
Institution	Online instruction is valued by my university.	0.364	114	4.09	1.11
Students	My online students are actively engaged in their learning.	0.337	114	3.22	1.011
Personal	I am concerned about data protection issues.	0.307	114	3.5	1.015
Students	Students help each other to learn.	0.275	114	3.11	1.103
Environment	Effectiveness of communication tools.	0.268	114	3.8	0.952
Institution	I receive fair evaluation of online instruction by the school.	0.261	114	2.8	1.284
Institution	Adequate/reliable technical support is provided to instructors.	0.248	114	3.64	1.235
Institution	I receive fair student evaluations for online instruction.	0.243	114	3.14	1.204
Students	There is a low level of student participation in class discussion or learning activities.	−0.329	114	3.28	1.171
Students	It is not easy to motivate my students in the online course.	−0.401	114	3.24	1.154

a   Significant at p < 0.01.

TABLE 1.3   Adjusted normative scores to calculate level of burnout with the
            Maslach Burnout Inventory

Level	Exhaustion	Depersonalization	Efficacy
Low	≤4	≤2.5	≤10
Moderate	5–8	3–5.5	10–12
High	>8	≥6	>12

TABLE 1.4   Levels of burnout in the sample

	N	Mean	SD	Level of burnout
Exhaustion	114	7.3	2.93	Moderate
Depersonalization	114	6	2.89	High
Efficacy	114	5.8	2.28	Low

TABLE 1.5   Levels of burnout according to personal teaching preference

Personal preference	N	Exhaustion	Depersonalization	Efficacy
Online	24	5.2 (SD 2.1)	3.6 (SD 1.1)	4.8 (SD 1.7)
Offline	26	9.2 (SD 3.2)	7.9 (SD 3.1)	7.1 (SD 2.4)
Mix of both	64	7.3 (SD 2.6)	6.1 (SD 2.6)	5.6 (SD 2.2)

feel sufficiently supported by the institution. They understand the benefits of the virtual learning environment (access and flexibility) and believe that the quality of online education is important to their school. At the same time, they are doubtful whether students are stepping up enough and wish for more student motivation and participation.

While demographic or employment-related factors did not affect overall satisfaction, personal teaching preference emerged as a significant predictor of preference. Those instructors who prefer to teach online are much more satisfied with online teaching than those who would rather teach in person. This preference is driven by various reasons, namely personal teaching philosophy, teaching effectiveness, personal comfort level and personal life circumstances. Thus, the results of the study confirm the notion that increased self-determination will improve motivation and well-being (Deci & Ryan, 2000).

Most interestingly, work satisfaction seems to act as a preventer of burnout. Those instructors who were more satisfied with teaching online also reported significantly lower levels of burnout. This finding is consistent with the literature which shows job satisfaction to be consistently and negatively correlated with burnout (Blix et al., 1994; Jamal, 1999; Jamal & Baba, 2001; Li et al., 2013; McClenahan et al., 2007; Siegall & McDonald, 2004; Teven, 2007; Vera et al., 2010; Zhang & Zhu, 2008).

Considering the relationship between personal preference and satisfaction, it is not surprising that personal preference also predicted burnout while teaching online. Those faculty members who were forced to teach online due to COVID-19 reported significantly higher levels of burnout than those educators who preferred to teach online regardless of social distancing. Critically, the results indicated that the amount of online teaching has no effect at all. Even faculty who teach very little online, but simply do not prefer it, are less satisfied and more exhausted. Again, this finding is in line with self-determination theory. Consequently, it is recommended that schools and universities consider and try to cater to their faculty's personal preferences. Work-life-balance seems to be a crucial factor that increases both satisfaction with online teaching and prevents burnout.

Overall, the study has interesting implications for institutions, especially those who offer both online and in-person programs. Matching instructors to teaching assignments could improve faculty well-being and, as an effect, teaching effectiveness and student satisfaction.

Notes

1 At the time of publication, there were 486 professors teaching at IU, 63% of them male and 37% female. 52% of those faculty members had a full-time contract.
2 We proofed the central requirements for regression analysis, particularly normal distribution for the dependent variable satisfaction, not too much autocorrelation, multicollinearity and heteroskedasticity. Because it does not fit we renounced regression analyses.

References

Abe, J. A. A. (2020). Big five, linguistic styles, and successful online learning. *The Internet and Higher Education*, 45. https://doi.org/10.1016/j.iheduc.2019.100724

Albrecht, S., Apostolow, B., & Nguyen, T. T.-U. (2021). Vom Zwang zum Drang? Wie Lehrende die Online-Lehre (zu lieben) lernten. Erfahrungen an der Universität Potsdam während der Corona-Pandemie [From compulsion to urge? How teachers learned to (love) online teaching. Experiences at the University of Potsdam during the

Corona Pandemic]. *Qualität in der Wissenschaft. Zeitschrift für Qualitätsentwicklung in Forschung, Studium und Administration, 15*(2), 30–35.

Allen, E., & Seaman, J. (2017). *Digital learning compass: Distance education enrollment report.* https://onlinelearningsurvey.com/reports/digtiallearningcompassenrollment2017.pdf

Blix, A. G., Cruise, R. J., Mc Beth Mitchell, D., & Blix, G. G. (1994). Occupational stress among university teachers. *Educational Research, 36*(2), 157–169.

Bolliger, D. U., Inan, F. A., & Wasilik, O. (2014). Development and validation of the Online Instructor Satisfaction Measure (OISM). *Educational Technology & Society, 17*(2), 183–195.

Breva, A., & Galindo, M. P. (2020). Types of motivation and eudemonic well-being as predictors of academic outcomes in first-year students: A self-determination theory approach. *PsyCh Journal, 9*(5), 609–628. doi:10.1002/pchj.361

Byrne, A. C., Flood, B., Murphy, E., & Willis, P. (2013). Burnout among accounting and finance academics in Ireland. *International Journal of Educational Management, 27*(2), 127–142.

Catano, V., Francis, L., Haines, T., Kirpalani, H., Shannon, H., Stringer, B., & Lozanzki, L. (2010). Occupational stress in Canadian universities: A national survey. *International Journal of Stress Management, 17*(3), 232–258.

Cohen, A., & Baruth, O. (2017). Personality, learning, and satisfaction in fully online academic courses. *Computers in Human Behavior, 72*, 1–12. http://dx.doi.org/10.1016/j.chb.2017.02.030

Deci, E. L., & Ryan, R. M. (1985a). *Intrinsic motivation and self-determination in human behavior.* Plenum Press.

Deci, E. L., & Ryan, R. M. (1985b). The General Causality Orientations Scale: Self-determination in personality. *Journal of Research in Personality, 19*(2), 109–134. https://doi.org/10.1016/0092-6566(85)90023-6

Deci, E. L., & Ryan, R. M. (1993). Die Selbstbestimmungstheorie der Motivation und ihre Bedeutung für die Pädagogik [The self-determination theory of motivation and its significance for pedagogy]. *Zeitschrift für Pädagogik, 39*(2), 223–238.

Deci, E. L., & Ryan, R. M. (2000). Self-determination theory and the facilitation of intrinsic motivation, social development, and well-being. *American Psychologist, 55*(1), 68–78. doi:10.1037110003-066X.55.1.68

Demerouti, E., Bakker, A. B., Nachreiner, F., & Schaufeli, W. B. (2001). The job demands-resources model of burnout. *Journal of Applied Psychology, 86*(3), 499–512.

Döring, N., & Bortz, J. (2016). *Forschungsmethoden und Evaluation* [*Research methods and evaluation*]. Springer.

Fangfang, Z., et al. (2021). Using a self-determination theory approach to understand student perceptions of inquiry-based learning. *Teaching & Learning Inquiry, 9*(2), 1–19. https://doi.org/10.20343/teachlearninqu.9.2.5

Ferencz, T. (2017). Shared perceptions of online adjunct Faculty in the United States who have a high sense of community. *Journal of Educators Online 14*(2). http://search.ebscohost.com.pxz.iubh.de:8080/login.aspx?direct=true&db=eric&AN=EJ1150582&site=eds-live&scope=site

Fernet, C., Guay, F., & Senécal, C. (2004). Adjusting to job demands: The role of work self-determination and job control in predicting burnout. *Journal of Vocational Behavior, 65*(1), 39–56.

Fjelkner, A., et al. (2019). Do personality traits matter? A comparative study of student preferences for TLAs and assessment modes in two different majors. *Teaching & Learning Inquiry, 7*(1), 78–102.

Freudenberger, H. J. (1974). Staff burn-out. *Journal of Social Issues, 30*, 159–165.

Ghorpade, J., Lackritz, J., & Singh, G. (2011). Personality as a moderator of the relationship between role conflict, role ambiguity, and burnout. *Journal of Applied Social Psychology, 41*(6), 1275–1298.

Göncz, L. (2017). Teacher personality: A review of psychological research and guidelines for a more comprehensive theory in educational psychology. *Open Review of Educational Research, 4*, 75–95.

Jamal, M. (1999). Job stress, type-a behavior, and well-being: A cross-cultural examination. *International Journal of Stress Management, 6*(1), 57–67.

Jamal, M., & Baba, V. V. (2001). Type-a behavior, job performance, and well-being in college teachers. *International Journal of Stress Management, 8*(3), 231–240.

Kim, L. E., Jörg, V., & Klassen, R. M. (2019). A meta-analysis of the effects of teacher personality on teacher effectiveness and burnout. *Educational Psychology Review, 31*, 163–195. https://doi.org/10.1007/s10648-018-9458-2

Krempkow, R. (2005). Arbeitszufriedenheit und Akzeptanz hochschulpolitischer Reformvorhaben an drei ostdeutschen Hochschulen [Job satisfaction and acceptance of higher education policy reform projects at three East German universities]. *Das Hochschulwesen. Forum für Hochschulforschung, -praxis und -politik, 53*(3), 102–108.

Kotera, Y., et al. (2021). Motivation of UK graduate students in education: Self-compassion moderates pathway from extrinsic motivation to intrinsic motivation. *Current Psychology: A Journal for Diverse Perspectives on Diverse Psychological Issues*, 1–14. https://doi.org/10.1007/s12144-021-02301-6

Lackritz, J. R. (2004). Exploring burnout among university faculty: Incidence, performance, and demographic Issues. *Teaching and Teacher Education, 20*(7), 713–729.

Li, Y., Li, J., & Sun, Y. (2013). Young faculty job perceptions in the midst of Chinese higher education reform: The case of Zhejiang University. *Asia Pacific Journal of Education, 33*(3), 273–294.

Luo, Y., et al. (2021). Students' motivation and continued intention with online self-regulated learning: A self-determination theory perspective. *Zeitschrift für Erziehungswissenschaft*, 1–21. https://doi.org/10.1007/s11618-021-01042-3

Maslach, C., & Jackson, S. E. (1981). The measurement of experienced burnout. *Journal of Organizational Behavior*, *2*(2), 99–113.

Maslach, C., Schaufeli, W. B., & Leiter, M. P. (2001). Job burnout. *Annual Review of Psychology*, *52*(1), 397–422.

McClenahan, C. A., Giles, M. L., & Mallett, J. (2007). The importance of context specificity in work stress research: A test of the demand-control-support model in academics. *Work & Stress*, *21*(1), 85–95.

Michinov, E., & Rusch, E. (2010). Job satisfaction, life satisfaction and burnout in French anaesthetists. *Journal of Health Psychology*, *15*(6), 948–958.

Nishimura, M., & Joshi, A. (2021). Self-determination theory and the happiness and academic achievement of students at a women's university. *Psychological Studies*, *66*(2), 139–153. https://doi.org/10.1007/s12646-021-00617-8

Rothmann, S., & Barkhuizen, N. (2008). Burnout of academic staff in South African higher education institutions. *South African Journal of Higher Education*, *22*(2), 439–456.

Rothmann, S., Barkhuizen, N., & Tytherleigh, Y.N. (2008). Model of work-related ill health of academic staff in a South African higher education institution. *South African Journal of Higher Education*, *22*(2), 404–422.

Schaeper, H. (1995). Zur Arbeitssituation von Lehrenden an westdeutschen Universitäten. Ergebnisse einer empirischen Untersuchung in fünf ausgewählten Disziplinen [On the work situation of lecturers at West German universities. Results of an empirical «study in five selected disciplines]. In J. Enders & U. Teichler (Eds.), „*Der Hochschullehrerberuf"*. *Aktuelle Studien und ihre hochschulpolitische Diskussion*. Luchterhand.

Schmidt, U., Schmidt, F., & Becker, N. (2021). Perspektiven Lehrender und Studierender auf die Digitalisierung von Lehren und Lernen. Ergebnisse einer empirischen Studie an der Johannes Gutenberg-Universität Mainz [Perspectives of teachers and students on the digitization of teaching and learning. Results of an empirical study at the Johannes Gutenberg University Mainz]. *Qualität in der Wissenschaft. Zeitschrift für Qualitätsentwicklung in Forschung, Studium und Administration*, *15*(2), 36–48.

Siegall, M., & McDonald, T. (2004). Person-organization value congruence, burnout and diversion of resources. *Personnel Review*, *33*(3), 291–301.

Tang, M., et al. (2020). A systematic review and meta-analysis on basic psychological need satisfaction, motivation, and well-being in later life: Contributions of self-determination theory. *PsyCh Journal*, *9*(1), 5–33. doi:10.1002/pchj.293

Teven, J. J. (2007). Teacher temperament: Correlates with teacher caring, burnout, and organizational outcomes. *Communication Education*, *56*(3), 382–400.

Tytherleigh, M. Y., Webb, C., Cooper, C. L., & Ricketts, C. (2005). Occupational stress in UK higher education institutions: A comparative study of all staff categories. *Higher Education Research & Development*, *24*(1), 41–61.

Van Emmerik, I. J. H. (2002). Gender differences in the effects of coping assistance on the reduction of burnout in academic staff. *Work and Stress, 16*(3), 251–263.

Vera, M., Salanova, M., & Martín, B. (2010). University faculty and work-related well-being: The importance of the triple work profile. *Electronic Journal of Research in Educational Psychology, 8*(2), 581–602.

Walters, S., Grover, K. S., Turner, R. C., & Alexander, J. C. (2017). Faculty perceptions related to teaching online: A starting point for designing faculty development initiatives. *Turkish Online Journal of Distance Education 18*(4), 4–19. http://search.ebscohost.com.pxz.iubh.de:8080/login.aspx?direct=true&db=eric&AN=EJ1161813&site=eds-live&scope=site

Watts, J., & Robertson, N. (2011). Burnout in university teaching staff: A systematic literature review. *Educational Research, 53*(1), 33–50.

Winefield, A. H., Gillespie, N., Stough, C., Dua, J., Hapuarachchi, J., & Boyd, C. (2003). Occupational stress in Australian university staff: Results from a national survey. *International Journal of Stress Management, 10*(1), 51.

Wingo, N. P., Peters, G. B., Ivankova, N. V., & Gurley, D. K. (2016). Benefits and challenges of teaching nursing online: Exploring perspectives of different stakeholders. *The Journal of Nursing Education, 55*(8), 433–440.

Wörfel, F., Guyb, B., Lohmann, K., & Kleiber, D. (2015). Validierung der deutschen Kurzversion des Maslach-Burnout-Inventars für Studierende (MBI-SS KV) [Validation of the German short version of the Maslach Burnout Inventory for students]. *Zeitschrift für Gesundheitspsychologie, 23*(4), 191–196.

Zaynab S., Hall, N. C., & Saroyan, A. (2018). Antecedents, correlates and consequences of faculty burnout. *Educational Research, 60*(2), 131–156. doi:10.1080/00131881.2018.1461573

Zhang, Q., & Zhu, W. (2008). Exploring emotion in teaching: Emotional labor, burnout, and satisfaction in Chinese higher education. *Communication Education, 57*(1), 105–122.

Zhong, J., You, J., Gan, Y., Zhang, Y., Changqin, L., & Wang, H. (2009). Job stress, burnout, depression symptoms, and physical health among Chinese university teachers. *Psychological Reports, 105*(3), 1248–1254.

CHAPTER 2

Digital Competences of Students

How They Are Assessed and What They Can Contribute to Study Success

René Krempkow and Pascale Stephanie Petri

Abstract

Students are often assumed to be "digital natives", i.e., to be competent in the use of digital technologies. However, observations in the teaching context show that students do not (or cannot) necessarily transfer skills acquired in their leisure time to the study context. To provide concepts for developing appropriate teaching/learning quality and for the efficient use of corresponding technologies, a database is required to document students' digital competences. We therefore refer to the European Reference Framework DigComp2.1 as a conceptual basis as well as selected results from surveys of several large universities in Germany. These conceptualise a new self-report questionnaire to assess digital competences. In this chapter, we first address the question how precisely digital competences can be assessed? Second, we stress the significance of digital competences in the first year of higher education under pandemic conditions. While it has been proven that self-efficacy is a predictor of study success, satisfaction and dropout intentions, this chapter attempts to examine the extent to which digital competences mediate this relationship when students experience their first year in higher education only in a virtual environment. For this purpose, we conducted a longitudinal study spanning the first year in higher education. Ultimately, a recording of digital competences serves as the basis for quality-enhancing concepts for higher education teaching to coordinate the sensible use of digital teaching/learning technologies with existing competences or to promote the acquisition of missing competences.

Keywords

digital competences – quality development of teaching & learning – study success – dropout intention – online learning

1   Why Do We Need to Assess Digital Competences?

In recent years, even before the Corona pandemic, there have been repeated complaints from universities about the lack of students' competences. For example, the President of the German Rectors' Conference, Peter-André Alt, reported in 2019: "in terms of text comprehension and writing skills, there was critical feedback from the universities". Reading and writing longer texts are hard for students; there has apparently been a significant decrease in skill level over the past five years, he said. Some critics, such as the German psychiatrist Spitzer (2012), view reading and attention disorders in connection with a "digital dementia" promoted by increasing digitalisation of everyday life, which affects cognitive and social skills.

Furthermore, in an empirical study about the digitalisation of higher education institutions (HEIs) in Germany, even before the Corona pandemic, more than 85% of the German HEIs named teaching digital competences as a crucial part of their digitalisation concept (EFI, 2019; Gilch et al., 2020). Leiber (see further in this book) also characterises the digital transformation in HEI as of limited success so far. Nevertheless, the assessment of digital competences (DCs) has so far only been used sparsely at German-speaking HEIs (cf. UNESCO, 2018; HFD, 2019; Gilch et al., 2020). This is probably due to the fact that until recently no high-quality measurement tool was available for HEIs in German-speaking countries. Another difficulty is that DCs are "a multi-faceted moving target" (Ferrari, 2012, p. 3). In this chapter, we therefore first present a definition of and an assessment tool for DC among students as well as findings based on data from several large universities. The latter are the prerequisite for making reliable statements about the extent of DC among students, which in turn is the basis for planning and implementing study skills support concepts for DC. Second, we present initial attempts to assess the predictive validity of DC in order to gain insights into the complex process leading to study success or dropout intentions including the potential role that DC plays in this.

2   Conceptualisation of Digital Competences

For the conceptualisation, what constitutes DC are, must first be clarified. In the absence of a generally valid or generally accepted definition, this clarification is based on the existing concepts.[1] For an initial classification, the Future Skills paper of the Stifterverband (2018), a joint initiative started by companies and foundations focused on consulting, networking and promoting improvements in the fields of education, science and innovation in Germany, seems particularly helpful: the Stifterverband differentiated between non-digital and digital key competences and distinguishes these from digital specialist competences. In general DC is understood to mean "skills that enable people to find their way in a digitalised environment and to actively participate in it" (ibid., p. 5).

In a similar context, the Aktionsrat Bildung (2018) [Action Committee on Education, an expert committee of independent educational scientists, which was formed in 2005 on the initiative of the Bavarian Business Association] calls for "digital sovereignty"; this means "being able to handle digital media under one's own complete control" as an "essential prerequisite for social participation", thus linking DC to democratic functioning. With regard to the competences mentioned by the Stifterverband, the Hochschulrahmengesetz [HRG, the German Higher Education Framework Act] is an additional central, legal basis. The HRG requires students to be "enabled to act responsibly in a free, democratic and social constitutional state" (§7), which necessitates appropriate skills. Theoretically, this could be discussed via the European Qualifications Framework (EQF), and the German Qualifications Framework for Higher Education Graduates (DQRH), via the requirements for the accreditation of degree programmes down to the requirements for the inclusion of the competences in module descriptions (cf. KMK [Standing Conference of the Ministers of Education and Cultural Affairs in Germany] 2017 and corresponding state ordinances). This would, however, go into too much detail here. Therefore, we refer instead to an argumentation by Huber (2019, p. 154f.): "Key qualifications must (...) always be linked to primary values and reflection on context and consequences: this reflection work, however, must then also be bound to studies; this way, key qualifications would become elements of education" (author's translation). Webler (2018, p. 1f.), however, stated for the implementation of such claims in Germany's higher education teaching: "The idea is still widespread that for academic teaching it is sufficient to merely introduce students to subject content as correctly as possible in order to enable them not only to complete an academic degree but also to prepare them for professional activities; it is contrary to any relevant state of research".

Admittedly, the aforementioned arguments were formulated more for key competences as a whole. However, in our opinion, they are equally applicable to DC – especially since they partly overlap with non-digital generic competences. It could even be concluded that especially in research-oriented universities, independent work, coping with unforeseen difficulties, analytical ability and critical reflection (cf. also Huber, 2016, 2019) are considered "academic competences" in a special way (Schaper, 2012, p. 29) and are of further significance. Thus, linking the discussions on DC to those on the duties of higher education would by no means result in a distinction between the two of them. Rather, it seems to make sense that encouraging digital competences should be an integrated component. As a conclusion in terms of conceptualisation, the following theoretical assumptions are formulated:

- DC should not be understood solely as technological competence, but in a broader sense as *digital education* – including ethical and social dimensions *as central aspects.*
- DC should promote values of educational humanism, critical thinking and emancipation (cf. in detail Krempkow, 2021).

Although a conceptualisation is a prerequisite for a survey instrument, this is of course not sufficient. Rather, a corresponding operationalisation is needed in order to be able to ask concrete questions. Therefore, the available literature on the topic was reviewed and evaluated, especially with regard to the questions: which literature contains suitable adaptable questions/items, either for use within the framework of a new instrument to be designed or (ideally) to be integrated within the framework of existing instruments of quality management at the Humboldt University of Berlin (HU Berlin)? (And furthermore usable for other HEIs?) As a result, the following situation emerged: because there was no assessment instrument for German-speaking countries, the assessment of DC is based on a questionnaire that was developed and piloted at the Quality Management Unit at HU Berlin based on the European Reference Framework DigComp2.1 (EU, 2017): the DigComp2.1.de questionnaire (Krempkow, 2019, 2021). The instrument comprises a total of 20 items in five dimensions (information and data literacy, communication and collaboration, content creation, data security, problem solving).[2]

According to earlier findings, people may over-estimate their own ability to assess the credibility and reliability of information from the internet (e.g., Ihme & Senkbeil, 2017). At the same time, self-reports reflect the students' (action-guiding) perception and, where they are critical, self-reports can reveal their uncertainties in dealing with digital environments. This means, where they are unsure whether their digital competences are adequate and cannot act "under their own complete control" in the sense of "digital sovereignty" (cf. Aktionsrat Bildung, 2018). Shedding light on these uncertainties would be an important starting point for further assessment concepts and – in terms of DC – the improvement of teaching and studying at universities in Germany and beyond.

3   Validity and Reliability of the Instrument

The DigComp2.1.de questionnaire was used at several HEIs in 2020 and 2021 (Humboldt University of Berlin, University of Freiburg and University of

Data Base Humboldt University of Berlin, Universities of Freiburg & of Cologne

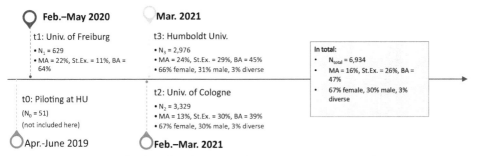

FIGURE 2.1   Overview data base for reliability analyses (Note: MA = Master students,
            St.Ex. = State Exam students, BA = Bachelor students)

Cologne); in total 6,934 cases are now available for the analyses of reliability
(for the distribution of respondents see below) and validity in cross-sectional
studies. The substantial sample from the cross-sectional studies allows us to
evaluate the questionnaire's measurement quality not only for individual HEIs
and across HEIs, but also differentiated by type of degree and study field, as
well as by semester or student's age.[3] Figure 2.1 shows the data base for reliability analyses and some selected characteristics of the sample such as type of
degree.[4] Furthermore we did an additional longitudinal study with about 300
cases (see Section 5 of this chapter).

The analyses of the psychometric quality prove that the DigComp2.1.de
questionnaire is a reliable and valid instrument: it revealed good reliability in
terms of internal consistency for the five dimensions[5] (Cronbach's α = .79–.84,
see Figure 2.2). We found only relatively small differences in the reliability
between subgroups, particularly type of degree and study fields. In addition,
factor analyses were used to examine whether the items can be assigned to
different dimensions and to what extent these correspond to the assignments
postulated in DigComp2.1 framework. This also makes it possible to construct
validity (for an overview see e.g., Krempkow, 2007). The results of factor analyses show that the items in three of five dimensions correspond to the assignments postulated.[6] For two dimensions (security and problem solving), the
majority of the items can be clearly assigned to the postulated dimensions,
but not all of them: this applies to two items, (perception of social responsibility, appropriate use of ICT in order to avoid health problems).[7] This should be
discussed for further development, e.g., towards a possible future DigComp2.2
version of the framework. Interestingly, the answers to the social responsibility were clearly more critical (in the sense of "finding fault with") than others
across universities and subjects. This shows the importance of socio-political
factors as we discussed it for the definition of DC above.

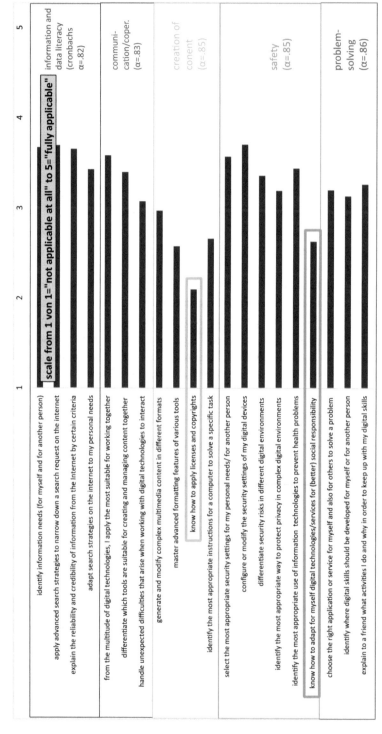

FIGURE 2.2   Digital competences: Overview about results & subscale reliability (N = 6.934)

We decided to check the appropriateness of the self-reports, as some dimensions of DC may not yet be adequately assessable in this modus due to possible tendencies to overestimate one's competences. Accordingly, additional test questions were developed for central aspects (not provided in the EU-DigComp2.1-model) to assess students' knowledge, e.g. for the reliability and credibility of information from the internet. For this purpose, we used open-ended questions so that students actually had to "produce" an answer instead of simply ticking the correct option.

The answers to the open-ended questions were evaluated using a binary coding with "appropriate answer" versus "inappropriate answer". As an example, we present some answers to the statement: "I can explain the reliability and credibility of information from the internet by means of certain criteria" in the following.

Students were instructed with "Please list some criteria below:" [open-ended question, max. 500 characters]:

– "Image of source, accurate source citation, verify information with additional source; bias?"
– "Sources and references, arguing both sides of conclusions from data. Critical questioning".
– Publishers, peer-reviewed, citations, topicality.
– "Search engine e.g. Scholar always provides credible sources, website structure/structure/architecture".

Of the answers, the 1st and 2nd, for example, can relatively clearly be rated as "appropriate", since the citation of verifiable sources in particular is an indisputable criterion for the reliability and credibility of information. In contrast – as mentioned in the 3rd and 4th answer – a search engine such as (Google) Scholar offers by no means exclusively credible or verified sources. The structure of a website, the encryption of the protocol or the location of the website also only provide little information about its content, so that these answers are not rated as "appropriate".

In the first step, the evaluation of the open-ended questions was carried out according to this principle, whereby two persons rated in parallel, independently of each other, in order to be able to check the agreement (or the interrater reliability; cf. Döring & Bortz, 2016). After evaluating data from approximately 1000 respondents and several rounds of voting, good interrater reliability was accomplished (> .70 to .92), so that one could dispense with the (parallel) double evaluation for the subsequent evaluations.

As these results are preliminary, they should be interpreted with caution. But asking the respondents to give examples to prove their actual knowledge or competences, can provide further information. In our study, we compared the percentage of students who rated themselves as "(fully) applies" on the corresponding self-report item with the percentage of "appropriate" answers in the open-ended item. For the item described above 86% gave an "appropriate" answer. This is comparable to the share of 89% of the self-report item that rated their competence herein as (fully) applies.

Nevertheless further research is needed in order to tap into the relation between self-reported versus tested DC.[8] More information on that combined with a larger number of open-ended questions as knowledge test items could help to further examine the validity of the self-report questionnaire.

4   Summary on Measurement Quality of the DigComp2.1 Questionnaire

The present findings show the DigComp2.1.de questionnaire is well suited to be used as an efficient screening instrument across study fields to assess DC at the HU Berlin and beyond.[9] In addition, our analyses provide starting points as to which topics should be further developed in study skills units. Furthermore, the results of the content-analytical evaluation of the open-ended questions on knowledge can help to identify certain typical misunderstandings and knowledge gaps. These, too, can be starting points for further developments and concrete considerations of increased promotion of certain DC s in follow-up measures.

To further tap into the specific importance of DC for study success in the first year HE under pandemic conditions, we present an additional study. The following analyses are based on data from freshmen at different universities in Germany, collected longitudinally over the first year of their studies. The methodological details will be explained in following paragraphs.

5   Predicting Academic Success and Dropout Intentions

In recent years we have witnessed a growing body of knowledge on the prediction of study success in its various operationalisations. In recent years the resulting literature has been aggregated and summarised in meta- (Richardson, 2012; Robbins et al., 2004) and even meta-meta analyses (Schneider & Preckel, 2017).

5.1   *Self-Efficacy as a Predictor of Study Success*
Among the strongest single predictors of study success is a construct called self-efficacy. Defined as the belief in one's own capability to successfully master challenges (Bandura, 1997), it not only proved to be a valid predictor

of success in (higher) education, but also in various other contexts. From the assessment perspective, it is well-known that the more self-efficacy is assessed according to context, the better is the context-specific prediction (Bandura, 1997; Nielsen et al., 2017).

For the (sub-)population of freshmen in higher education, recent findings suggest that self-efficacy is a valid predictor of study success in terms of the grade point average (GPA) as well as study satisfaction (Petri, 2021a). In addition, freshmen self-efficacy was shown to predict dropout intentions. These relations were observed in longitudinal studies spanning the whole first year in higher education under on-site teaching conditions (pre-pandemic).

5.2   *The First Year in Higher Education during Pandemic Times*

Scholars as well as higher education policy makers were interested in the students' study experiences during the pandemic. In 2020 and 2021, several large-scale surveys (Lörz et al., 2020; Marczuk et al., 2021) were conducted among higher education students in Germany. To name but a few, we will outline some key findings in the following.

In a study conducted in the summer term 2020, 68% of the more than 24,000 students surveyed by Lörz et al. (2020) reported that they attended exclusively online courses. More than half of them reported that they missed on-site interactions with peers and faculty members. This was especially true for freshmen. Asked about their satisfaction with the organisation of remote courses, more than one third (40%) reported being (rather) dissatisfied.

In another study using the same large-scale dataset, Marczuk et al. (2021) reported that more than one third (41%) indicated that they were (rather) satisfied with their own academic achievement during the pandemic. Compared to pre-pandemic surveys among students, however, the average satisfaction level was far lower. In addition to several negative aspects of studying during the pandemic, participants of the above mentioned survey also reported positive aspects: what students appreciated in particular was the increased flexibility in their schedules (Marczuk et al., 2021), probably at least to some degree due to asynchronous courses (videos). To sum it up: students reported positive as well as negative aspects concerning their studies during this time.

As most of the learning and teaching scenarios took place online, one might ask if students were prepared for that. In this context, we differentiate between hardware and 'soft skills'. According to Lörz et al. (2020), most of them reported that their hardware equipment as well as their internet access were adequate. However, little is known about whether they felt prepared in terms of their DC. Furthermore, as findings based on data collected during the pandemic are still few and far between, we have little information on differences between study fields.

Intending to shed more light on studying during the pandemic, we conducted a longitudinal study, surveying freshmen repeatedly during their first year in HE under pandemic conditions. This was an additional study conducted independently (further details of the sample will be presented in following sections). Our first two research questions addressed potential differences between study fields:

- Are there differences in freshmen self-efficacy between study fields?
- Are there differences in DC between study fields?

The pandemic has changed conditions within HE. The well-known associations between self-efficacy as a predictor and several outcomes (GPA, study satisfaction, dropout intentions) may no longer hold under the conditions of online teaching and learning for freshmen.

Consequently, building on the findings from pre-pandemic studies, we addressed the additional research questions:

- Do DCs mediate the associations between freshmen self-efficacy and Study satisfaction (model 1), Intention to dropout (model 2), and GPA (model 3)?

6   Method

In this section, we will briefly outline the study design including the instruments used, as well as the final analyses sample.

6.1   *Study Design*

In order to potentially replicate findings from longitudinal studies that were conducted among freshmen during their first year of study before the pandemic (Petri, 2021a), we applied the same study design: we tracked students during their first two semesters and surveyed them three times within nine months. The first point of assessment (t1) was some weeks after they started their higher education studies: within the first weeks of the first semester in November/December 2020. In February/March 2021, at the end of their first semester, we sampled them again (t2) and finally, when they finished their second semester in June/July 2021, we administered the third (t3) and last survey within the study at hand. As well-documented for previous longitudinal studies (Ehlert et al., 2017; Tieben, 2016; Tinto, 1997), our study also suffered from attrition. In concrete terms, we recruited participants studying within their first year at different HEIs in Germany and in different fields of study, using a student mailing list at a mid-sized university and several social networks with specific freshmen groups. At t1, a total of N = 381 students filled in the survey and N = 346 of them gave their email address and the consent to be included in the mailing list that consequently made up the panel for this longitudinal study. Of the N = 346 students invited to take part at t2, N = 252 responded. Finally, we again invited all panellists to participate at the third and last survey, however, only N = 198 of them accepted the invitation and filled in the survey.

6.2 *Instruments*

All the variables relevant for the study at hand were assessed in self-report questionnaires. Table 2.1 displays which instruments were used including

TABLE 2.1   Instruments

Variable (point of assessment)	No. items	Reliability Cronbach's α	Definition, item example, reference
Freshmen self-efficacy (t1)	13	.808 (N = 344)	Belief in one's own capability to overcome challenges characteristic of the first year of study: 'Please rate how confident you are that ... you will be able to organise your schedules on your own' (Petri, 2020)
Digital competences (t1)	21	.912 (N = 341)	Self-reported competence in digital (learning) environment: 'Please rate how competent you are ...in terms of dealing with licences and copyright issues' (Krempkow, 2019, 2021)
Study satisfaction (t2)	9	.528 (N = 238)	Satisfaction in the study context: 'Please give the level of your agreement for the following statements: ...All in all, I am satisfied with my studies' (Hiemisch et al., 2005)
Dropout intentions (t3)	2	– (N = 166)	Intention to drop out of one's studies: 'Please give the level of your agreement to the following statements: ...I plan to leave university permanently without a degree' (Petri 2021b)
Study success (GPA) (t3)	1	– (N = 172)	Current grade point average: 'Please give your current grade point average' (Petri 2021b)

Note: Points of assessment: t1 = beginning of the first semester, t2 = end of the first semester, t3 = end of the second semester. Number of cases slightly differ between variables assessed at the same point of assessment due to missing cases. No reliability coefficient has been calculated if less than 3 items were used.

the respective number of items and the observed reliability (internal consistency) in terms of Cronbach's Alpha. While freshmen self-efficacy and DC were assessed at t1, study satisfaction was assessed at t2 and finally, at t3, we assessed dropout intentions and GPA.

6.3   Sample

At the first point of assessment, N = 346 panellists filled in the survey. 9.8% of them were enrolled in humanities, 7.2% in sports, 17.1% in the social sciences, law and economy, 14.2% in mathematics or the natural sciences, 8.1% in medicine and health sciences, 15.4% in agriculture or nutrition science; 28.1% were enrolled in a field of study that did not fit any of the above-mentioned categories. The information about gender and age is displayed in Table 2.2 for all three points of assessment (t1, t2, and t3 respectively). At the end of first semester (t1), we asked the participants about the organisation of the study programme: Nearly 80% reported that they attended exclusively online courses. In addition, more than half of them (55%) reported that they did not move to their HEI's location at the start of their higher education studies. Therefore, we regard this sample of freshmen as starting under the conditions of digital teaching more or less without on-site courses.

TABLE 2.2   Demographics on the sample for all three points of assessment

Point of assessment (N)	% Female	Age
t1 (N = 346)	79	M = 21.04 years (SD = 3.96)
t2 (N = 252)	81	M = 20.95 years (SD = 3.88)
t3 (N = 198)	83	M = 21.04 years (SD = 3.92)

7   Results

In this section, we describe the bivariate zero-order correlations as well as all the tests that were conducted in terms of pre-analyses. Afterwards, we report the results of the comparison between different study fields in terms of their average freshmen self-efficacy level as well as self-reported level of DC. Finally, the mediation analyses are reported.

7.1   Pre-Analyses

Table 2.3 displays the bivariate zero-order (Pearson) correlations based on the final analyses sample for the mediation analyses (N = 198). These were comparable to those observed based on pre-pandemic data (see Petri, 2021a).

TABLE 2.3   Means, zero-order bivariate correlations

Variable (point of assessment)	M (SD) (theoretical range)	1	2	3	4
1. Freshmen self-efficacy (t1, N = 344)	3.64 (0.46) [1;5]				
2. Digital competences (t1, N = 345)	3.14 (0.64) [1–7]	.39**			
3. Student satisfaction (t2, N = 240)	10.40 (2.24) [3–15]	.42**	.01		
4. Dropout intentions (t3, N = 166)	2.71 (1.45) [1–7]	−.23**	−.06	−.41*	
5. Study success (GPA) (t3, N = 172)	9.88 (3.30) [0–15]	.10	−.16*	.08	−.07

Note: Points of assessment: t1 = beginning of the first semester, t2 = end of the first semester, t3 = end of the second semester; * p < .05, ** p < .01. Number of cases slightly differ between variables assessed at the same point of assessment due to case-wise missings. Correlations based on the final sample used for the mediation models, N = 198.

Mediation models are methodologically based on linear regressions. For the latter, there are prerequisites that have to be met in order to apply these analyses. In concrete terms, the following three requirements should be fulfilled (Bortz & Schuster, 2010): i) linearity (linear relation between predictor(s) and criterion), ii) normality as well as iii) homoscedasticity of the residuals.

From a theoretical point of view and based on previous findings (Richardson, 2012; Robbins et al., 2004; Schneider & Preckel, 2017), we consider the first one as fulfilled because higher levels of freshmen self-efficacy could well be associated with higher levels of study satisfaction as well as higher GPA, but with lower levels of dropout intentions. In addition, the visual inspections of Figure 2.3 (standardised predictor on the x-axis and the criterion variables on the respective y-axis) underpin this.

The normality of the respective residual distribution can be tested: The Kolmogorov-Smirnov test revealed significance for the residuals in the second and third model ($Z_{satisfaction}$ = 0.81, p = .527; $Z_{dropout}$ = 2.93, p < .001; Z_{GPA} = .1.72, p = .005). Consequently, for these models we cannot assume normally distributed residuals.

Summing up the pre-analyses, we can say that not all prerequisites[10] are met for all the three models.[11]

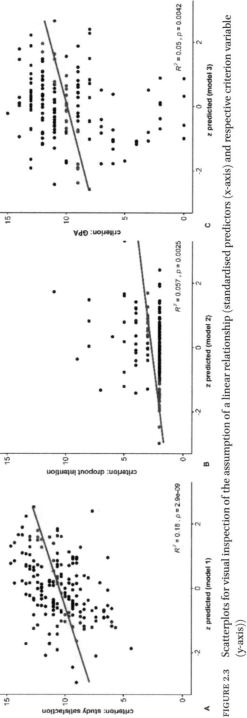

FIGURE 2.3 Scatterplots for visual inspection of the assumption of a linear relationship (standardised predictors (x-axis) and respective criterion variable (y-axis))

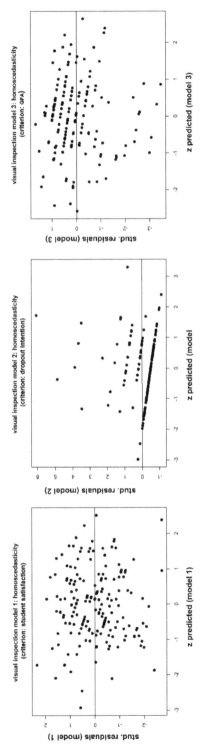

FIGURE 2.4   Scatterplots of the standardised predictors (x-axis) and the standardised residuals (y-axis)

7.2   *Mean Differences between Study Fields*

The first and second research questions addressed potential mean differences between study fields. For the respective analyses, we used the sample of $N = 346$ from t1.

7.2.1   Freshmen Self-Efficacy

The ANOVA (seven fields of study, dependent variable: mean score in freshmen self-efficacy) revealed that there were no significant differences between study fields in the level of freshmen self-efficacy: $F(6) = 0.090$, $p = .997$. Table 2.4 shows the mean, median and standard deviations for each study field.

7.2.2   Digital Competences

The second analysis was a MANOVA – seven fields of study, dependent variables: five mean scores for the above-mentioned dimensions of DC – revealed significance: $F(30, 1670) = 1.709$, $p = .01$. In more detail, study fields differ significantly in their average self-reported competences concerning data security ($F(6) = 2.552$, $p = .020$) and problem solving ($F(6) = 2.798$, $p = .011$). As Table 2.4 shows in concrete terms, students enrolled in the field of sports rated their competences in terms of both dimensions as comparatively low, while students enrolled in the social sciences, law and economics rated their competences in terms of data security as relatively high. Furthermore, when it comes to the dimension problem solving, students enrolled in mathematics and the natural sciences rated their competences as relatively high.

In sum, we observed significant study field-specific differences in the average level of self-reported DC, and these differ across the five dimensions of digital competences assessed here.

TABLE 2.4   Freshmen self-efficacy per study field: means, standard deviations and medians (N = 346)

Study field	1	2	3	4	5	6	7
M	3.64	3.67	3.67	3.63	3.63	3.63	3.62
Median	3.62	3.69	3.65	3.69	3.58	3.69	3.62
SD	0.44	0.46	0.43	0.52	0.42	0.51	0.46

Note: 1 = humanities; 2 = sports; 3 = social sciences, law and economy;
4 = mathematics and the natural sciences; 5 = medicine and health sciences;
6 = agriculture and nutrition science; 7 = others.

TABLE 2.5   Digital competences – Dimensions data security and problem solving per study
field: means, standard deviations and medians (N = 346)

Study field	1	2	3	4	5	6	7
Data security							
M	3.03	2.90	3.50	3.36	3.39	3.19	3.12
Median	3.07	3.00	3.43	3.29	3.36	3.29	3.14
SD	0.87	0.84	0.73	0.74	0.90	0.81	0.83
Problem solving							
M	3.01	2.88	3.33	3.48	3.22	3.24	3.02
Median	3.00	3.00	3.25	3.50	3.25	3.50	3.00
SD	0.90	0.85	0.79	0.83	0.81	0.85	0.86

Note: 1 = humanities; 2 = sports; 3 = social sciences, law and economy; 4 = mathematics and
the natural sciences; 5 = medicine and health sciences; 6 = agriculture and nutrition science;
7 = others.

7.3   *Mediation Analyses*
Figure 2.5 shows the respective mediation models with standardised path
coefficients.

7.3.1   Model 1
The model in total revealed significance ($F(2, 236) = 23.03, p < .001$) and 19% of
the variance on the criterion of study satisfaction could be explained by the two
predictors, freshmen self-efficacy and DC. To explain the model path by path:
as expected, higher levels of freshmen self-efficacy were associated with higher
levels of study satisfaction (path c' and the total effect path c; three months
later). In addition, higher levels of freshmen self-efficacy were associated with
higher levels of self-reported DC (path a). What was surprising, however, was
the fact that we observed a negative standardised path (b) from the (potential)
mediator DC to the criterion of study satisfaction: higher levels of self-reported
DC were associated with lower study satisfaction. This observation will be discussed in more detail in below. Furthermore, the indirect path a*b revealed significance, with its confidence interval not including 0 (CI: −0.1352; −0.0244).

7.3.2   Model 2
The model in total revealed significance ($F(2, 155) = 3.93, p = .022$), but 'only'
6% of the variance in the criterion dropout intention could be explained by

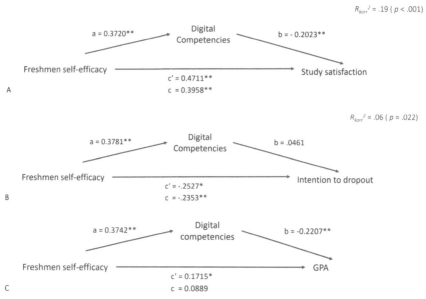

$R_{korr}^2 = .19 \ (p < .001)$

a = 0.3720**   Digital Competencies   b = - 0.2023**

Freshmen self-efficacy   Study satisfaction
                              c' = 0.4711**
A   c = 0.3958**

$R_{korr}^2 = .06 \ (p = .022)$

a = 0.3781**   Digital Competencies   b = .0461

Freshmen self-efficacy   Intention to dropout
                              c' = -.2527*
B   c = -.2353**

a = 0.3742**   Digital competencies   b = -0.2207**

Freshmen self-efficacy   GPA
                              c' = 0.1715*
C   c = 0.0889

FIGURE 2.5   Mediation models (standardised path coefficients, based on N_{t1} = 252 and
             N_{t3} = 198; *p <. 05; **p < .01)

the two predictors, freshmen self-efficacy and DC. To explain the model path
by path: as expected, higher levels of freshmen self-efficacy were associated
with lower levels of dropout intentions (path c' and the total effect c; seven
months later). Furthermore, higher levels of freshmen self-efficacy were positively associated with higher levels of self-reported DC (path a). The standardised path (b) from the (potential) mediator DC to the criterion dropout
intentions did not reveal any significance. The same is true for the indirect
path a*b whose confidence interval included 0 (CI: −0.0498; 0.0900).

7.3.3   Model 3

The model in total did reveal significance (F (2, 161) = 5.34, p = .006), and 'only'
5% of the variance in the criterion GPA could be explained by the two predictors of freshmen self-efficacy and DC. To explain the model path by path: as
expected, higher levels of freshmen self-efficacy were associated with higher
levels of GPA (path c' and the total effect c; seven months later). Moreover,
higher levels of freshmen self-efficacy were significantly associated with higher
levels of self-reported DC (path a). The standardised path (b) from the (potential) mediator DC to the criterion GPA was – again – negative, and significant.
In addition, the indirect path a*b did reveal significance (CI: −0.1574; −0.0260).

In sum, all three models revealed significance in total. However, the amount
of explained variance was largest in model 1 (22% of the variance in study

satisfaction). Especially in model 1 and model 3, only the indirect path (a*b) revealed significance. Hence, only in terms of the criteria study satisfaction and GPA is the indirect path via DC of relevance. To put it in a nutshell, we can say that DCs do not serve as mediators between self-efficacy and drop-out intentions. However, they seem to play a meaningful role in the relation between the well-known predictor self-efficacy and the criteria of study satisfaction and GPA.

8   Discussion

8.1   *Summary of the Empirical Findings*

The present findings show that the DigComp2.1.de questionnaire is well suited to be used as an efficient screening instrument across study fields to assess DC: the observed level of internal consistency (Cronbach's α) was (very) good in different samples. Furthermore, the significant, positive association with GPA after the first year of study can be seen as an indicator for its predictive validity.

The fact that DCs also have a mediating function in the interplay between self-efficacy in the first year in higher education and study satisfaction as well as GPA underpins their importance.

Moreover, as both our studies show, the average level of self-reported DC in terms of the assessed five dimensions varies across fields of study. We observed the overall highest levels of self-reported DC in terms of data security in the fields of social sciences, law and economy. In contrast, the highest levels in terms of problem solving were observed among students in the fields of natural sciences and mathematics. Study skill programmes in different study fields should hence be tailored accordingly to the needs of the respective students.

As the mediation models and in particular model 1 show: DC might serve as a mediator between the well-known predictor "freshmen-self-efficacy" and the criterion of study satisfaction as well as GPA. The surprising observation that self-reported digital competences at t1 were negatively associated with study satisfaction at t2 could have several reasons. One possible explanation is that students who might have overestimated their actual DC at t1 (they rated them as comparably high) might have experienced several setbacks during the first semester and learnt that they are not as competent as they thought they were. Hence, their overall student satisfaction at t2 was correspondingly low. As we did not assess DC twice, we cannot prove that empirically. However, a subsequent qualitative study would be an option to explore the relation of these two variables in more detail by means of interviews.

8.2   *Strengths and Limitations*

To the best of our knowledge, we are among the first authors to provide such assessment of DC, longitudinal and detailed data from freshmen starting during the pandemic. On the one hand, our studies have some limitations: the well-known problem of panel attrition (Ehlert et al., 2017; Tieben, 2016; Tinto, 1997). This means that we have to keep in mind that possible selective attrition (i.e., non-random) could come with a bias for our results. Therefore, the results should be regarded with a certain level of caution. On the other hand, longitudinal data are key for detecting effects over time. Hence, the data set at hand is surely of some value and can at least be indicative in terms of informing future research where to tap into more detail.

8.3   *Implication for Practice*

The questionnaire presented here is a "ready-to-use" solution for HEIs that intend not only to promote DC in students but also to assess in which dimensions of digital competences they rate themselves comparatively low, taking account of their different fields of study. In addition, our analyses based on nation-wide samples provide starting points as to which dimensions of DC should be further promoted in study skills units relevant to all study fields and what should be focused on, if necessary, on a study field specific basis. In particular at the item level: the application of copyrights and licences, as well as the adaptation of digital technologies for better perception of social responsibility and inclusion.

8.4   *Outlook for Further Research*

For the assessment perspective, the next step would be to examine the relation between self-reported competence levels and knowledge tests. The first step has already been taken in so far as five open-ended questions provide first insights into hands-on competences of students.

As a desideratum, every aspect mentioned in the self-reported questionnaire should have an equivalent in a knowledge test on DC in order to compare self-report and test performance more comprehensively.

In addition, further and extended longitudinal studies could help to explore not only whether study skills interventions can indeed promote and foster students' DC (pre-post-evaluation studies). They could also provide insights into long term effects of different levels of DC and skills. For example, building on the systematic analysis provided by Stifterverband (2018), DCs are key for several stages within an individual's career path. Information is still sparse on how far the required and the actual level of student competence differ at various stages (e.g., first year in higher education versus transition into labour market). Therefore, a comprehensive research strategy including the examination of different stages in career paths and different sub-populations should be the starting point to continue our research on 'Digital Competences of Students – how they are assessed and what they can contribute to study success'.

Notes

1 For the general concept of competence, reference is made here to the comprehensive discussion in the expert report on competence orientation, which refers to Weinert's understanding of competence (cf. in detail Schaper, 2012, p. 14f.).

2 In addition to self-report questions based on DigComp2.1, supplementary knowledge test questions were integrated into the questionnaire that also address the latter aspects (cf. Krempkow et al., forthcoming).

3 Furthermore, the evaluation of knowledge test questions with open response format is carried out content-analytically in order to identify misunderstandings and knowledge gaps. In this way, we hope to contribute to the definition and operationalisation of quality criteria in teaching in terms of DC, and to corresponding assessments for quality development in HE (Krempkow et al. [forthcoming]).

4 The response rate of around 13% corresponds to that of similar surveys (cf. contributions in Schmidt & Krempkow, 2021). There were only minor deviations in the respondents by faculty and by institute compared to the basic population.

5 Furthermore a significant correlation ($r = .374$, $p < .001$) with generic competencies according to EQF/DQFH (cf. Plasa et al., 2019) can be regarded as an initial evidence of convergent validity.

6 The data were very well suited for factor analyses with a KMO value of .96. The proportion of variance explained by the five factors is 69% which is relatively high.

7 Both of which are empirically assigned more to the dimension of problem solving (and not to the dimension of security as in the original DigComp2.1 framework).

8 As the reported results are preliminary, they do have some limitations. Most critical is the fact that only a share of max. 64% of students responded to the self-report items, also answered the open-ended question. We discuss it in another publication (cf. Krempkow et al., 2022).

9 Unless it was developed as a specific instrument for a German-speaking university, it exists as an English translation of the instrument (for foreign students). We made it both usable for other HEI, because it was financed by taxes.

10 Finally, homoscedasticity can on the one hand be examined visually in Figure 4. On the other hand, we tested if homoscedasticity is present using the studentised Breusch-Pagan test. The test did reveal significance for model 1 (BP (2) = 8.54, p = .014), but not for the second model (BP (2) = 3.35, p = 0.187) and third model (BP (2) = 2.64, p = 0.267). As the test has the H0 that homoscedasticity is at hand, we consequently have to reject an assumption of homoscedasticity for model 1 (criterion: student satisfaction).

11 Therefore, we follow established recommendations (Baltes-Götz, 2019; Hayes & Cai, 2007), using ordinary least squares estimators and heteroskedasticity-consistent standard errors (HC 3) for estimating the regression coefficients as they are known to be robust.

References

Baltes-Götz, B. (2019). *Lineare Regressionsanalyse mit SPSS* [*Linear regression with SPSS*]. Zentrum für Informations-, Medien- und Kommunikationstechnologie (ZIMK), Universität Trier.

Bandura, A. (1997). *Self-efficacy: The exercise of control.* W. H. Freeman.

Bortz, J., & Schuster, C. (2010). *Statistik für Human- und Sozialwissenschaftler* [*Statistics for the humanities and social sciences*]. Springer. https://doi.org/10.1007/978-3-642-12770-0

Döring, N., & Bortz, J. (2016). *Forschungsmethoden und Evaluation* [*Research methods and evaluation*]. Springer.

EFI. (2019). *Gutachten zu Forschung, Innovation und technologischer Leistungsfähigkeit Deutschlands 2019* [*Report 2019 on research, innovation and technological performance in Germany*]. Expertenkommission Forschung und Innovation.

Ehlert, M., Peter, F., Finger, C., Rusconi, A., Solga, H., Spieß, C. K., & Zambre, V. (2017). *The Berliner-Studienberechtigten-panel (best up) – Methodological and data report.* Deutsches Institut für Wirtschaftsforschung.

EU. (2017). *DigComp2.1 The digital competence framework for citizens.* Science for Policy report by the Joint Research Centre (JRC). Office of the European Union.

Ferrari, A. (2012). *Digital competence in practice: An analysis of frameworks.* JRC Techn. Reports 68116. https://doi.org/10.2791/82116

Gilch, H., Beise, A. S., Krempkow, R., Müller, M., Stratmann, F., & Wannemacher, K. (2020). Digitale Kompetenzen in der Hochschulstrategie – Quo vadis? Ergebnisse einer bundesweiten Schwerpunktstudie zur Digitalisierung an Hochschulen [Digital competences in higher education strategy – Quo vadis? Results of a nation-wide study on digitalisation in HEI]. In R. A. Fürst (Ed.), *Digitale Bildung und Künstliche Intelligenz in Deutschland. Nachhaltige Wettbewerbsfähigkeit und Zukunftsagenda* [*Digital education and artificial intelligence in Germany – Sustainable competitive capacity and future agenda*] (pp. 443–456). Springer.

Hayes, A. F., & Cai, L. (2007). Using heteroskedasticity-consistent standard error estimators in OLS regression: An introduction and software implementation. *Behavior Research Methods, 39*(4), 709–722. https://doi.org/10.3758/bf03192961

Hiemisch, A., Westermann, R., & Michael, A. (2005). Die Abhängigkeit der Zufriedenheit mit dem Medizinstudium von Studienzielen und ihrer Realisierbarkeit [How satisfaction during medicine studies depends on study goals and their feasibility]. *Zeitschrift für Psychologie*, 97–108. https://doi.org/10.1026/0044-3409.213.2.97

Hochschulforum Digitalisierung and German Academic Exchange Service. (2019, December 9–10). *International strategy conference strategies beyond borders – Transforming higher education in a digital age.* Allianz-Forum.

Huber, L. (2016). Studium Generale oder Schlüsselqualifikationen? Ein Orientierungsversuch im Feld der Hochschulbildung [Studium generale or key competences. An attempt at orientation in the fields of higher education]. In U. Konnertz & S. Mühleisen (Eds.), *Bildung und Schlüsselqualifikationen. Zur Rolle der Schlüsselqualifikationen an den Universitäten [Education and key qualifications. On the role of key qualifications at universities]* (pp. 101–122). Peter Lang.

Huber, L. (2019). Bildung durch Wissenschaft als Qualität des Studiums [Education through science as quality in higher education]. *Das Hochschulwesen, 67*(6), 154–159.

Ihme, J. M., & Senkbeil, M. (2017). Warum können Jugendliche ihre eigenen computerbezogenen Kompetenzen nicht realistisch einschätzen? [Why adolescents cannot realistically assess their own computer-related skills?] *Zeitschrift für Entwicklungspsychologie und Pädagogische Psychologie, 49*(1), 24–37. https://doi.org/10.1026/0049-8637/a000164

KMK. (2017). *Qualifikationsrahmen für deutsche Hochschulabschlüsse [German qualifications framework for higher education graduates]*. Kultusministerkonferenz.

Krempkow, R. (2007). *Leistungsbewertung, Leistungsanreize und die Qualität der Hochschullehre. Konzepte, Kriterien und ihre Akzeptanz. Kompetenzen [Performance measurement, incentives and the quality of HE teaching. Concepts, criteria and their acceptance]*. Universitätsverlag Webler.

Krempkow, R. (2019). Fächerübergreifende und digitale Kompetenzen für die Qualitätsentwicklung der Lehre erfassen – ein Projekt der HU Berlin [Assessing generic and digital competences for teaching quality development – A project at HU Berlin]. *Qualität in der Wissenschaft, 13*(2), 64–65.

Krempkow, R. (2021). Wie digital kompetent sind Studierende? Ein Konzept und Erhebungsinstrument zur Erfassung digitaler fächerübergreifender Kompetenzen [How digitally competent are students? A concept and an assessment tool for cross-disciplinary relevant digital competences]. *Qualität in der Wissenschaft, 15*(1), 22–29.

Krempkow, R., Gäde, M., Hönsch, A., & Boschert, C. (2022). Digitale Kompetenzen von Studierenden auf dem Prüfstand. Analysen zur Zuverlässigkeit der Erfassung digitaler Kompetenzen [Digital competences under the microscope. Analyses of the reliability of the assessment of digital competences]. *Qualität in der Wissenschaft, 16*(1), 20–28.

Lörz, M., Marczuk, A., Zimmer, L., Multrus, F., & Buchholz, S. (2020). *Studieren unter Corona-Bedingungen: Studierende bewerten das erste Digitalsemester [Studying under Corona conditions: Students evaluate the first digital semester]*. Deutsches Zentrum für Hochschul- und Wissenschaftsforschung (DZHW).

Marczuk, A., Multrus, F., & Lörz, M. (2021). *Die Studiensituation in der Corona-Pandemie: Auswirkungen der Digitalisierung auf die Lern- und Kontaktsituation von*

Studierenden [*Study conditions during the Corona pandemic: Effects of digitalisation on the learning and social contact among students*]. https://www.die-studierendenbefragung.de/fileadmin/user_upload/publikationen/dzhw_brief_01_2021.pdf

Nielsen, T., Makransky, G., Vang, M. L., & Dammeyer, J. (2017). How specific is specific self-efficacy? A construct validity study using Rasch measurement models. *Studies in Educational Evaluation, 53*, 87–97. https://doi.org/10.1016/j.stueduc.2017.04.003

Petri, P. S. (2020). *Skala zur Erfassung der Studieneinstiegsselbstwirksamkeit (SESW-Skala)* [*Freshmen self-efficacy scale*]. Zusammenstellung sozialwissenschaftlicher Items und Skalen (ZIS). https://doi.org/10.6102/zis274

Petri, P. S. (2021a). *Neue Erkenntnisse zu Studienerfolg und Studienabbruch. Einblicke in die Studieneingangsphase* [*New findings on study success and dropout. Insights into the first year in higher education*] (1st ed.). Universitätsverlag Webler.

Petri, P. S. (2021b). Study success – A multilayer concept put under the microscope. *Zeitschrift für Hochschulentwicklung, 16*(4), 59–78. https://doi.org/10.3217/zfhe-16-04/04

Plasa, T., Kmiotek-Meier, E., Ebert, A., & Schmatz, R. (2019). Generische Kompetenzen von Hochschulabsolventinnen und -absolventen [Generic competences of higher education graduates]. *Qualität in der Wissenschaft (QiW), 13*(2), 48–56.

Richardson, M., Abraham, C., & Bond, R. (2012). Psychological correlates of university students' academic performance: A systematic review and meta-analysis. *Psychological Bulletin, 138*(2), 353–387. https://doi.org/10.1037/a0026838

Robbins, S. B., Lauver, K., Le, H., Davis, D., Langley, R., & Carlstrom, A. (2004): Do psychosocial and study skill factors predict college outcomes? A meta-analysis. *Psychological Bulletin, 130*(2), 261–288. https://doi.org/10.1037/0033-2909.130.2.261

Schaper, N. (2012). *Fachgutachten zur Kompetenzorientierung in Studium und Lehre für die HRK (Ed.)* [Expert opinion on competence orientation in learning and teaching for the rectors conference].

Schneider, M., & Preckel, F. (2017). Variables associated with achievement in higher education: A systematic review of meta-analyses. *Psychological Bulletin, 143*(6), 565–600. https://doi.org/10.1037/bul0000098

Stifterverband. (2018). *Future Skills: Welche Kompetenzen in Deutschland fehlen* [*Future skills: Which competences are missing in Germany*]. Discussion Paper. www.stifterverband.org/download/file/fid/6360

Tieben, N. (2016). *LEAD-Expertise – Studienverlauf, Verbleib und Berufsstatus von Studienabbrecherinnen und Studienabbrechern. Ergänzende Informationen zum Datenreport zum Berufsbildungsbericht 2016* [*LEAD-expertise – Course of studies, retention and employment status of higher education dropouts. Additional information on the data report for the Berufsbildungsbericht 2016*]. Bundesinstitut für Berufsbildung. www.fachportal-paedagogik.de/literatur/vollanzeige.html?FId=1100886

Tinto, V. (1997). Classrooms as communities: Exploring the educational character of
    student persistence. *The Journal of Higher Education, 68*(6), 599. https://doi.org/
    10.2307/2959965

United Nations Educational, Scientific and Cultural Organisation (UNESCO). (2018). *A
    global framework of reference on digital literacy skills for indicator 4.4.2.* Information
    Paper No. 51, UIS/2018/ICT/IP/51.

Webler, W.-D. (2018). Einführung des geschäftsführenden Herausgebers [Editorial by
    the Editor-in-Chief]. *Das Hochschulwesen, 66*(1/2), 1–2.

CHAPTER 3

Digital Transformation in Higher Education Learning and Teaching

The Quality Digital Literacy We Need

Theodor Leiber

Abstract

This chapter attempts to provide answers to the question of why Digital Transformation (DT) in higher education institutions has not been wholly successful. It also looks at how this situation can be overcome through the application of an integrative concept of quality literacy in DT composed of competencies in quality strategies, practice and culture. A SWOT analysis of organisational and individual competencies required for DT in higher education learning and teaching is presented along with preliminary results of an Erasmus+ project on fostering digital competencies of educators and students. These studies help identify organisational, pedagogical and ethical weaknesses, as well as opportunities and challenges in DT. The chapter provides recommendations on how universities can make DT a successful reality and identify DT competencies required by stakeholders.

Keywords

digitalisation – digital literacy – digital transformation – higher education – learning and teaching – quality literacy

1 Introduction

Digital Transformation (DT), also known as Fourth Industrial Revolution (4IR), Industry 4.0, or the Hybrid Age, has been a topic of increasing importance over the last two decades. In general, DT encapsulates the cultural, workforce and technological shifts caused by the ongoing changes throughout the diverse digital landscape of contemporary economically developed societies. The underlying digitalisation amounts to using digital technologies to change business and process models thereby providing new revenues and value-producing opportunities. DT, then, refers to changing and developing organisational processes and individual competencies to improve operational performance and beneficial usage of digital technologies in significant and strategic ways. In this sense, digitalisation permeates every aspect of our lives, a process that has become increasingly visible since the late 1990s, along with the development and interdependence of information and communication technology (ICT), nanotechnology, biotechnology and neurotechnology. These technologies interact with humans, gathering more knowledge about humans, and are increasingly learning to behave like humans. These fundamental societal change processes are realised and implemented, for example, through brain implants, social media, Big Data, and Artificial Intelligence (AI) systems (Royakkers et al., 2018). Therefore, an ambitious understanding of DT amounts to "the transformation of all sectors of our economy, government and society based on the large-scale adoption of existing and emerging digital technologies" (Randall et al., 2018, p. 4).

Since DT should be conceived as a complex, continuous, and substantial transitional process involving all relevant and affected stakeholders a workable definition for DT in higher education institutions (HEIs) is as follows:

– It intrudes and pervades all processes, spaces, formats and objectives of teaching, learning, research, Third Mission, and administration.
– It comprises the design and implementation of new infrastructures.
– It incorporates the increasing use of digital media and technologies for L&T, research, support services, administration.
– It includes the need of students and staff to develop new digital skills for their current and future activities and tasks (cf. Rampelt et al., 2019).

Such DT is generally not straightforward in the context of institutional, organisational and personal transformation, and it requires both material and human resources. Thus, any implementation of digital technologies and tools should be based on a systematic end/means analysis, for example, a strategic SWOT (Strengths – Weaknesses – Opportunities – Threats) analysis (Leiber et al., 2018) of the organisational and individual competencies required for DT in order to identify recommendations for action. This is particularly appropriate for multiple-hybrid social organisations such as HEIs which are embedded into a complicated network of political steering, organisational self-governance, institutional and individual autonomies, and diverse subject fields.

2   Leading Questions and Methodology

The main goal of the chapter is to unfold a SWOT analysis of digital literacy in higher education learning and teaching (L&T)[1] with emphasis on DT issues to answer the following questions:

– What are the strengths, weaknesses, opportunities, and threats of DT in HEIs' L&T?
– What are the most important tasks and activities for HEIs to make DT a successful reality in L&T?
– Which DT competencies are required for stakeholders such as teachers, students, quality managers and leadership?

The chapter suggests that the answers to these questions should emerge from the SWOT analysis of integrative quality literacy in DT that is analytically composed of competencies in DT strategies, DT practice and DT culture.

By means of a SWOT analysis, various factors – strengths, weaknesses, opportunities, threats – are identified that influence the objective in focus, in the present case DT in higher education L&T. The strengths and weaknesses are, by definition, primarily factors that are internal to the process or structure in question (here: DT in higher education L&T), the threats and opportunities are primarily external factors (Figure 3.1). The core utility of a SWOT analysis is to support mitigating weaknesses, seizing opportunities, and counteracting threats using analysed strengths or, if these do not suffice, by additional means and tools that need to be identified. Accordingly, a SWOT analysis can be a relevant step of strategic planning and facilitate suggesting recommendations for decision and action. Specifically, a SWOT analysis may also help to clarify competing strategies and show options relating to decisional dilemmas.

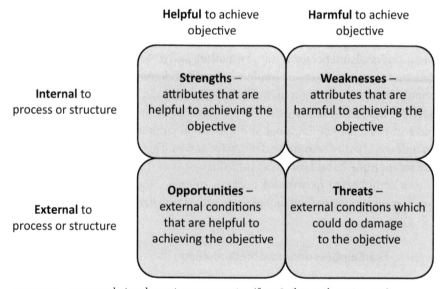

FIGURE 3.1   SWOT analysis, schematic representation (from Leiber et al., 2018, p. 353)

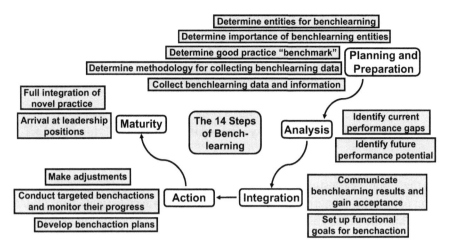

FIGURE 3.2   The 14 steps of benchlearning processes (from Leiber, 2020, p. 4)

In this sense, a SWOT analysis is also an appropriate analytic method to implement the second main phase of a bench learning process; Analysis, to identify performance gaps and development potential (see Figure 3.2). Accordingly, published reports, case studies and literature overviews about DT and AI in higher education in various countries were used to collect bench learning data and information (see, e.g., Bates et al., 2020; Bond et al., 2018; Cope et al., 2021; EFI, 2019; Gilch et al., 2019; Grossek et al., 2020; HFD, 2016; Maltese, 2018; Marks et al., 2020; Renz & Hilbig, 2020; Royakkers et al., 2018; Vicente et al., 2020; Zawacki-Richter et al., 2020). The source selection is situational and based on search items such as digital transformation, digitalisation, digitisation, learning and teaching, higher education, and artificial intelligence in publication titles and abstracts. The investigation therefore does neither make any statement about the frequency of these terms and their related SWOTs in the analysed literature sources nor does it claim statistical representativeness. Instead it draws its conceptual reliability from the qualitative content analysis of the involved core terms. Based on these sources, the most widespread and important SWOTs of DT and AI in higher education L&T were identified, analysed and categorised according to the chosen areas of quality literacy (Tables 3.1–3.3). These SWOTs inform recommendations for corresponding quality literacies in DT of higher education L&T (Section 3.4, Tables 3.4 and 3.5) for HEIs.

In summary, the chapter is conceptual research based on qualitative content analysis and critical reflection of the ongoing discourse on the topic of DT in higher education L&T including a SWOT analysis (Section 3). In addition, the work builds on preliminary results of an Erasmus+ Strategic Partnership

(EDUDIG, 2021) that focuses on developing diagnostic and enhancement tools for (self-)education of educators and students regarding their digitalisation competencies (Section 4). The chapter closes with conclusions (Section 5) and some remarks on the study's limitations and further perspectives (Section 6).

3   SWOT Analysis of Quality Literacy in DT of Higher Education L&T

3.1   *SWOT Analysis of Competencies in DT Strategy*
In the applied case studies and literature on DT in higher education no mention of specific strengths was found referring to strategy competencies (Table 3.1). This can be seen as a symptom of DT in higher education still being in its infancy at many institutions. Therefore, strengths in DT strategy, for the most part, must be developed at many places.

Widespread weaknesses in DT strategy reported in the literature are less specific to DT and AI in higher education but seem to be "classics" of organisational development in complex multiple-hybrid social organisations, particularly if these consist of organisational units and individuals endowed with high degrees of freedom of decision and action. Typically, such weaknesses are a lack of leadership support; a lack of rational and transparent strategies and organisational resistance to change (Table 3.1; cf. Stouten et al., 2018). These weaknesses relate to gaps between stakeholders' assessment of high importance of DT, AI and learning analytics, and a rather low developmental state of DT in (public) HEIs (Gilch et al., 2019), and DT being no (strategic) priority in many institutions.

Opportunities around strategy competencies in DT are: develop comprehensive strategies for DT in HEIs as learning organisations (e.g., watch competitors; define a DT-related profile; develop a DT-related roadmap; support DT-related bench learning and identification of good practices) and develop strategies for the new roles of stakeholders emerging from DT (e.g., teachers as learning coaches and advisors; students as self-directed learners; use of teacher-robots). Such strategies would replace DT investment decisions that are based on contingent availabilities of institutional expertise and digital technologies and tools. These approaches would replace Day-to-day micro-politics of groups and bodies, and situative, if not arbitrary intra-organisational negotiations of stakeholders that are typical for loosely coupled multiple-hybrid organisations. In this sense, universities seem to act relatively "carefree" and clueless[2] in terms of process analysis compared to those commercial enterprises that deal systematically with DT in order not to let transformation processes get stuck in the 'valley of death' (Butter et al., 2020, p. 49). Non-revolutionary suggestions

TABLE 3.1   SWOT analysis of competencies in DT strategy in higher education

Strengths	Weaknesses (mainly involved stakeholders)
– – [no entry]	1. Lack of leadership support (leadership; all stakeholders)
	2. Lack of clear vision & institutional strategies (leadership; all stakeholders)
	3. Organisational resistance to change (potentially all stakeholders)

Opportunities	Threats
1. Develop a comprehensive institutional strategy (leadership; all stakeholders)	1. Monopolising of control over (hidden) algorithms by dominant manufacturers or tech-lords (potentially all stakeholders)
2. Develop strategies for the new roles of stakeholders (leadership; all stakeholders)	2. Cybercrime & related security threats (potentially all stakeholders)

on how this can be achieved relate, for example, to combining expertise, sharing equipment, integrating networks, educating together, and combining markets to minimise the individual risks of transformation (Butter et al., 2020).

Some threats to DT strategy in higher education are related to monopolising of digitalisation tools and activities and cybercrime (Table 3.1). HEIs have already become data providers, for example, for training algorithms of a relatively small number of private companies which dominate and sometimes monopolise the digitalisation and AI software market (Zuboff, 2019). Accordingly, higher education may be already seen as or become a "competitive market dominated by major international universities partnering with digital giants" (Barzman et al., 2021, p. 72). HEIs, particularly public institutions, have therefore a responsibility to develop realistic strategies for a balance of power between private profit maxims of 'big tech' companies and their marketisation strategies on the one hand and data and privacy protection and protection of education as a public good related to human rights of self-determined way of life and education on the other hand.

Further threats arise in the context of cybercrime, for example, internet-connected devices can be subject to hacking or Distributed Denial of Service (DDoS) attacks thereby breaking into or paralysing websites or digitalised systems or gain access to sensitive information. A further security issue and major social problem is identity fraud, that is "the intentional obtaining, appropriating, owning or creating of false identifiers, thereby committing or intending to commit unlawful conduct" (Royakkers et al., 2018, p. 134).

3.2   *SWOT Analysis of Competencies in DT Practice*

The main strength of competencies in DT practice reported in case studies and the literature is that DT and AI literacy are available in some HEIs through the expertise of institution members who are computer scientists and IT and data experts (Table 3.2).

A weakness observed by various investigators is a lack of digital literacy of teachers as well as students,[3] leading to an emphasis of assimilative uses of digital technologies (e.g., learning management systems; online library services; lecture recordings) instead of more constructive and creative uses (e.g., multimedia learning software; virtual and hybrid seminars; virtual labs; simulations or learning games; online exams and tests). Antagonistically, those assimilative uses keep a focus on teacher-centred education processes instead of student-centred L&T (Bond et al., 2018; Marcelo & Yot-Dominguez, 2019). It can be assumed that deficient digital literacy can appear in combination with and may be in part caused by individual resistance to change which itself may be caused by a lack of competencies and skills in DT.[4] Analysis suggests that educators' resistance to DT can originate from their low attention to the potential of AI. Instead, they often seem to focus on assumed threats such as (sometimes overemphasized) ethical issues of data privacy and the scenarios of teachers being replaced by artificial teach-bots. That is why there are authors who call on educational researchers to be more constructive and more participatory in relation to DT opportunities (Bates et al., 2020, p. 6f.; also cf. Zawacki-Richter et al., 2020).

Another "classic" weakness of competencies in DT practice is the lack of acceptance for the implementation and application of DT technologies including learning analytics and AI (e.g., electronic whiteboards; e-portfolios; flipped classrooms; Digitalised Personal Learning Networks (DPLN); Virtual Learning Environment; Augmented, Virtual and Mixed Reality; AI-based L&T solutions). Reasons or motivations for this reluctance that cannot be dismissed out of hand are reported both in the literature and anecdotally: for many stakeholders, the success of learning analytics is not sufficiently convincing yet (Ifenthaler & Yau, 2019; Renz et al., 2020; Viberg et al., 2018). The effectivity and efficiency

TABLE 3.2   SWOT analysis of competencies in DT practice in higher education

Strengths	Weaknesses (mainly involved stakeholders)
1. DT & AI literacy of computer scientists, IT & data experts, informatics, & other STEM professions	1. Lack of DT literacy of stakeholders (teachers; students)
	2. Lack of acceptance for DT, AI, & learning analytics (teachers, students)
	3. Insufficient knowledge & consideration of L&T theories (L&T practitioners: teachers, DT experts)

Opportunities	Threats
1. Implementation of personalised learning & early-warning systems for at-risk students (students)	1. Amplification of the digital divide between the well-equipped & the not so well-equipped (all stakeholders)
2. Emergence of new professional fields for educators (teachers)	2. Endanger data privacy & academic freedom (all stakeholders)
3. Enrichment of pedagogic methods (teachers)	3. Cybercrime & related security threats (all stakeholders)
4. Facilitation of communication & interaction between stakeholders (teachers; students)	4. Replacement of human teachers by teacher-robots (teachers)
5. Improvement of handling massive enrolment numbers of students (students; administration)	5. Alarming increase in consumption of energy & rare metals (all stakeholders)
6. Enabling inter- & transdisciplinary communication & collaboration (all stakeholders)	
7. Contribution to the ecological transition (all stakeholders)	
8. Save money by replacing human teachers by teacher-robots (leadership; teachers)	

of discursive formats is limited in digitalised teaching. It can be difficult to maintain attention in online contexts because of, for example, boredom, sense of isolation, lack of time to follow the different subjects, lack of self-organising capabilities and self-directed learning (Liang et al., 2020; Mishra et al., 2020). Digitalised assessments are in their infancy. There is a lack of data sovereignty of stakeholders regarding data privacy, access, and responsibilities.

A further weakness in DT practice in higher education L&T can make itself felt when digitalised and AI-based L&T processes are designed and implemented without sufficient knowledge and consideration of relevant L&T theories and learning models such as networked learning (Jones, 2015).

As to the opportunities around quality practice competencies in DT practice of higher education L&T the following are identified (Table 3.2): For online learning systems, learning analytics can be successfully used to develop indicators of student success and early-warning systems for at-risk students (Akçapinar et al., 2019; Spörk et al., 2021; Tsai et al., 2020). New professional fields for educators may emerge in becoming learning coaches and advisors and designing digital L&T units. The variety of pedagogic methods gets enriched through digitalised and AI-supported L&T (Daniela, 2019). Digital technologies and tools facilitate communication and interaction between stakeholders, specifically teachers and students, and lead to more efficient handling of massive enrolment numbers of students (e.g., admission; personalised feedback; tests and assessments). DT opens ways for inter- and transdisciplinary communication and collaboration, thus facilitating, for example, open science and citizen science including FAIR (Findable, Accessible, Inter-operable, and Reusable data) principles. DT could contribute to the ecological transition, for example, reducing travel and the consumption of energy and physical resources while increasing collaboration and sharing. Some stakeholders even assume that the replacement of teachers by teacher-robots could save money.

There is no empirical evidence, however, that digitalisation and the use of AI in universities can lead to fundamental cost savings; rather the opposite seems to be the case. Since many university systems are under increasing financial pressure at the same time – for example due to the demographic decline in student numbers, the consequences of the coronavirus pandemic, the expiry of project-oriented national funding programs – (financial) backing of DT by (higher) education politics is even more important in the short and medium term (Hubler, 2020; Goertz & Hense, 2021).

In addition to opportunities, the following five important threats are also named (Table 3.2): DT can amplify the digital divide between well-equipped and not so well-equipped stakeholders and countries and their HEIs (Govindarajan & Srivastava, 2020). DT may endanger data privacy and academic freedom of teaching and research, for example, DT technologies and AI-supported smart digital devices may be persuasive and manipulative and undermine individuals' autonomy. DT allows for new ways of cybercrime and related security threats, for example, HEIs' IT systems can be hacked, and the institutions blackmailed. The possible replacement of human teachers by teacher-robots may lead to frustration, devaluation, and unemployment. The increasing use of digital technologies is accompanied by an alarming increase in consumption of energy and rare metals (World Bank, 2017).

3.3   *swot Analysis of Competencies in DT Culture*

Strengths referring to competencies in DT culture[5] were not identified in the used sources (Table 3.3). Again, this may be seen as symptomatic for DT still being an ongoing early-phase process at many HEIs.

The weaknesses in this area are aroused by insufficient quality culture competencies and academic values related to DT such as poor ethics of digital (performance) data[6] and deficient personality competencies[7] insofar these are relevant for organisational transformation and individual learning in the context of digitalisation.

Opportunities of quality culture competencies of DT in higher education relate to improvements in the shared quality culture competencies and espoused academic values, while any attack on these denotes a threat.

TABLE 3.3   SWOT analysis of competencies in DT culture in higher education

Strengths	Weaknesses (mainly involved stakeholders)
– – [no entry]	1. Lack of shared quality culture competencies & espoused academic values related to DT (all stakeholders)
Opportunities	**Threats**
1. Improvement on shared quality culture competencies & espoused academic values related to DT (all stakeholders)	1. Any attacks on quality culture competencies & academic values related to DT (all stakeholders)

3.4   Recommendations from the SWOT Analyses

Tables 3.4, 3.5 and 3.6 gather the main recommendations for quality literacy in DT of higher education L&T that can be inferred from the above SWOT analyses. These recommendations refer to the main changes, activities and competencies which are required for successful DT.

In the strategy dimension the general and widespread need for most HEIs is to develop institutional policies for DT of L&T on all relevant organisational levels and integrate them in HEIs' strategy documents (e.g., mission statements; structure and development plans). Further recommendations are to improve on the commitment and further education of leadership in DT (e.g., define relevant leadership roles and offer training in DT); establish working communication and coordination channels between leadership and faculties with respect to DT-related issues (e.g., define the roles of leadership, management, and academics); increase financial allocations for sustainable DT implementation that transcends the time-restricted project character of most DT initiatives (see Table 3.4).

In the practice and management dimension (Table 3.5) exemplary issues are to endow the organisation with the required infrastructure; develop and implement systemic, comprehensive, digitalised (performance) data management; manage the sharing of DT resources across organisational units, performance areas and subject fields; support students in optimising their learning progress and learning gain; foster digital skills and qualifications in DT (e.g., by offering further education in DT literacy for internal stakeholders).

Further recommendations are the following (Table 3.5): DT-adequate pedagogies should be implemented (e.g., digitalised blended and hybrid L&T courses; AI tools; blockchain for record keeping of degrees, certificates, and diplomas). A basic recommendation for teachers is ongoing professional development in the use of digitalised educational technology. For example,

TABLE 3.4   Recommendations for quality literacy in DT of higher education L&T – the strategy dimension

Develop DT policies & integrate them in HEIs' strategy documents comprising DT quality management, DT practice, & DT culture
Improve on *commitment & further education of leadership in DT*
Establish working communication & coordination channels between leadership & faculties with respect to DT-related issues
Increase financial allocations for DT projects including their *sustainable implementation*

TABLE 3.5   Recommendations for quality literacy in DT of higher education L&T – the
practice and management dimension

Develop & implement *DT infrastructure* including *L&T spaces* that are fully
equipped from a DT perspective

Develop & implement systemic, comprehensive, *digitalised* (performance) *data
management*

Develop sustainable approaches to *counteract the DT-induced increase in
consumption of energy & rare metals*

Manage the sharing of DT resources across the institution

Offer further education in DT literacy for internal stakeholders[a]

Reinforce cyber security by adopting appropriate safety measures & accreditations
(e.g., secure the digital tools & the institutional intranet against criminal threats)

Provide framework conditions for the validation of acquired DT skills & the *issuance
of certified DT qualifications*

Be critical & active *against* dominant manufacturers & *tech-lords*

Develop, implement & manage DT-adequate pedagogies[a]

Foster professional development of educators in DT[a]

Facilitate learners' DT competencies[a]

Enhance & augment assessment through DT[a]

Support students' learning progress & learning gain through DT (e.g., learning
analytics)[a]

Exploit innovations in mobile technology for communication & collaboration[a]

Leverage cloud technologies for communication & collaboration[a]

Launch AI pilot projects (e.g., AI conversational interfaces for admission process,
online talks with teachers, chat bot to answer queries)[a]

Implement & manage DT-adequate administration services

Collaborate with industry partners specialised in software tools for supporting &
augmenting L&T

Carry out *quality assurance & enhancement evaluations* with respect to DT

---

a   The EDUDIG project specifically focuses on these aspects (see Section 4).

related incentives for teachers should be provided and teacher training units
and workshops should be implemented that facilitate digital L&T competencies (cf. Redecker, 2017; Caena & Redecker, 2019). This applies specifically to
experienced teachers (Englund et al., 2017) and teachers who perceive their
digital skills as not sophisticated enough (Jääskelä et al., 2017; Marcelo &
Yot-Domínguez, 2019). In addition, learners' DT competencies should be facilitated, for example, students supported and motivated to develop their digital

TABLE 3.6   Recommendations for quality literacy in DT of higher education L&T – the
             culture dimension

---

*Share espoused values, expectations, & commitment to quality & continuous quality
improvement* in L&T according to strategic, management & practice competencies[a]
Advocate values of academic freedom & self-governance of L&T[a]
Establish shared understanding of (performance) *data ethics*
Create new team structures consisting of internal & external stakeholders[a]
Strengthen a climate of DT culture by supporting & fostering communication, critical
thinking, collaboration, & creativity[a]

---

a   The EDUDIG project specifically focuses on these aspects (see Section 4).

skills and abilities, including but not restricted to the competencies to con-
figure or adapt the security settings of one's digital devices; to generate and
modify complex multimedia content in various formats; to select the most
appropriate digital technologies for communication and collaboration.[8] Further relevant topics are mentioned in Table 3.5.

Finally, in the quality culture dimension (Table 3.6) the most prominent
recommendations are the following: share espoused values, expectations, and
commitment to quality (enhancement) in L&T according to strategic, management and practical competencies as far as appropriate for stakeholders in
achieving their legitimate goals. Advocate values of academic freedom of L&T
which are ultimately based on the Universal Declaration of Human Rights
(UNGA, 2008) and moral and legal codes in accordance with them. Establish
a shared understanding of (performance) data ethics. Create new team structures ("learning organisation in DT") consisting of internal academic (teaching) staff and administration staff as well as internal and external experts from
L&T (didactics, pedagogy), research in AI and blockchain, DT and software
architecture and user experience. Strengthen a climate of DT culture by supporting and fostering communication, critical thinking, collaboration/partici-
pation, and creativity (the four Cs) across a range of social channels, websites,
and apps.

4   DT Literacy Dimensions Researched in the EDUDIG Project

The recommendations indicated by table note 'a' in Tables 3.5 and 3.6 are
further specified and operationalised in the Erasmus+ project "Enhancing
the Development of Educators' Digital Competencies" (EDUDIG, 2021). The

approach builds on the DigCompEdu Framework (Redecker, 2017; Caena & Redecker, 2019) which attempts to define educators' professional and pedagogic competencies as well as learners' competencies that are organised in the six areas of Professional Engagement, Digital Resources, Teaching and Learning, Assessment, Empowering Learners and Facilitating Learners' Digital Competencies. In the DigCompEdu Framework, each of these six areas outlines several subareas, altogether 22 (Table 3.6). The latter are subdivided into 147 activity competencies for each of which six accumulative levels of progression are defined to assess the respective actor as Newcomer, Explorer, Integrator, Expert, Leader, or Pioneer (Redecker, 2017).

The EDUDIG project has given itself three main tasks: first, further analyse, if necessary, revise, and in any case operationalise the DigCompEdu Framework activity competencies; second, develop an online course for teachers on selected levels of progression; third, establish an e-teaching handbook for self-paced learning towards DT for teachers and students.

Currently, the analysis and operationalisation steps are work in progress. An exemplary case is sub-area 1.1 "Organisational communication" for which the cognitive and action competencies or learning goals for digitally educated educators and learners read:
- To be able to use digital technologies and tools;
- To enhance education-related information flow and (formal and informal) communication with relevant stakeholders including students and teachers throughout the (learning) organisation and beyond;
- To communicate organisational procedures to relevant stakeholders;
- To contribute to developing and improving organisational communication strategies.

These competencies of digitally educated stakeholders are then differentiated according to the above-mentioned six proficiency levels such as, for example, the "expert" level:

I use the tools for professional development, e.g., by participating in online courses, webinars, or consulting digital training materials and video tutorials. I use formal and informal exchanges in professional communities as a source for my professional development.

In the next step, the digital, and where appropriate also non-digital, methodologies and exemplary methods and tools required for the exemplary competency sub-areas 1.1–1.3 (see Table 3.7) are identified which are briefly summarized in Table 3.8. Accordingly, several methodologies and their related exemplary methods and tools are highlighted in Table 3.8. Supplemented by more specific, concrete operationalisations of the methods and tools, this

TABLE 3.7   Educators' and learners' competencies in DT of (higher) education L&T (from
             Redecker, 2017, p. 15)

1	Professional engagement	2	Digital resources	3	Teaching & learning
1.1	Organisational communication	2.1	Selecting	3.1	Teaching
1.2	Professional collaboration	2.2	Creating & modifying	3.2	Guidance
1.3	Reflective practice	2.3	Managing, protecting, sharing	3.3	Collaborative learning
1.4	Digital continuous professional development			3.4	Self-regulated learning
4	**Assessment**	**5**	**Empowering learners**	**6**	**Facilitating learners' digital competencies**
4.1	Assessment strategies	5.1	Differentiation & personalisation	6.1	Information & media literacy
4.2	Analysing evidence	5.2	Accessibility & inclusion	6.2	Communication
4.3	Feedback & planning	5.3	Actively engaging learners	6.3	Content creation
				6.4	Responsible use
				6.5	Problem solving

information will later be organised by the EDUDIG project (EDUDIG, 2021) in a dialogic website that educators and other stakeholders can use to test their education-related digital Professional Engagement competencies and identify options for improvement thus contributing to DT in higher education L&T.

5   Conclusions

The analysis has shown that in higher education DT is still a major topic, not the least because, as studies demonstrate, DT in higher education is not just a technical innovation but rather a transformation of academic, curricular, organisational und structural matters towards digitalisation (HFD, 2016, p. 10) including ethical issues. Consequently, DT (as well as other fundamental organisational

TABLE 3.8   Technologies and tools digitally educated educators should be able to use in the sub-areas 1.1–1.3 of area 1 "Professional Engagement" (sub-area 1.4 omitted due to redundancies with area 1.1)

1.1   Organisational communication (digital; education-related)

Methodologies	*Exemplary methods & tools* (selection)
Team meetings Important element of organisational communication: teams should regularly share ideas, ask for feedback, and freely voice their opinions	Text, audio & video chat (e.g., Discord; Facebook; Google Hangouts; Skype; WhatsApp) Use functions of Campus Management Systems (CMS, e.g., AcademyFive; CampusNet; CAMPUSonline; HISinOne)
Oral, written & video communication (formal & informal; internal & external) Digitalised communication through spoken word, written text & video in real time, mostly over the Internet	Email; Telephone; Text, audio & video chat Use functions of CMS

1.2   Professional collaboration (digital; education-related)

Team collaboration (mostly with other educators on dedicated projects or tasks) One of the most common types of internal collaboration. The members of a team have assigned roles and work toward the same goals, sharing knowledge or information relevant to those goals. Teams often have a leader who oversees the team collaboration.	Digital collaboration tools such as, e.g., Asana; Basecamp; Google Workspace; MS Teams; Slack; Trello; Yammer
Community collaboration (on dedicated projects or tasks) Individuals with a shared interest work together. A typical goal of community collaboration is to learn and share knowledge rather than completing a task or project.	Digital collaboration tools such as, e.g., Asana; Basecamp; Google Workspace; MS Teams; Slack; Trello; Yammer

(cont.)

TABLE 3.8   Technologies and tools digitally educated educators should be able to use in the
sub-areas 1.1–1.3 of area 1 "Professional Engagement" (sub-area 1.4 omitted due to
redundancies with area 1.1) *(cont.)*

1.2   Professional collaboration (digital; education-related)

Network collaboration (on dedicated projects or tasks) Collaboration between more loosely coupled, non-hierarchical groups. Network members can contribute by sharing information or expertise for others to use for their own benefit.	Digital collaboration tools such as, e.g., Asana; Basecamp; Google Workspace; MS Teams; Slack; Trello; Yammer

1.3   Reflective practice

Methodologies	*Exemplary methods* (selection)
Peer learning Educational practice within stakeholder groups (e.g., teachers, students, researchers) to attain educational or learning goals (e.g., peer-to-peer learning; mutual learning among peers; collaborative learning)	Peer observation; Formative evaluations; Stakeholder feedback (e.g., surveys & focus group discussions)
Good practice Practice accepted as superior to alternatives; good practices help to maintain & enhance quality	Benchlearning processes; Formative evaluations; Stakeholder feedback
Experimentation Try digital technologies & software tools while implementing new pedagogical approaches; explore how both ready-at-hand proprietary platforms & open-source tools can support all learners' active engagement & make teachers more proficient	Collaborative Blogs; Crowdmapping; Google Wave; Handbrake; Second Life; Tumblr; Twitter; Wikimedia Commons; Youtube; Zotero
Research Findings (future digital pedagogies) Keep informed about & participate in research on innovative digital pedagogies that support & foster the implementation & application of (new) pedagogical approaches	Formative analytics; Teachback; Place-based learning; Learning with drones; Learning with robots; Citizen inquiry

changes and transformations) in HEIs is not a sure-fire success but is based on complicated negotiation processes that, on the one hand, reflect the academic autonomy and multiple-hybrid organisational nature of HEIs. On the other hand, these negotiations are influenced and frequently compromised by lack of evidence-informedness one cause of which is the complex, time-extended and sometimes faulty processes of transforming evidence for decision-making, policy and practice.[9] In addition, these "political" negotiation processes and debates must grapple with unclear responsibilities and slow opinion-building and decision processes (Cohen et al., 1972) which are co-structured (and sometimes may be dominated) by inter- and intra-institutional power games about resources and reputation. These specific organisational complexities of HEIs and seemingly everlasting stumbling blocks of complex social organisations plus ubiquitous bureaucratic obstacles are the core reasons why DT developments in higher education are of limited success so far and keep the issue still in the focus of quality management, organisational development, and strategy.[10]

While there seems to be no shortage of temporary DT projects in higher education L&T, the strategic and structural advancement of DT is deficient. In summary, main obstacles of DT in higher education reported in the literature are a lack of clear vision and institutional strategies (Orr et al., 2019a, 2019b); insufficient digital literacy of stakeholders; insufficient DT-related pedagogies; limited infrastructure, resources, and technical support; a conservative academic and organisational culture; sometimes overly strict data privacy regulations; doubts about the benefit/cost ratio of digitalisation; technology rejection (see Section 3).

SWOT analyses of DT literacy in higher education L&T have led to recommendations for action, which are listed in Tables 3.4–3.6. Some of these recommendations are being taken up and further pursued in an ongoing Erasmus+ Strategic Partnership (EDUDIG, 2021), as indicated in Section 4.

6   Limitations of the Study and Research Perspectives

As always, the research underlying this chapter has some limitations and open questions for future research: First, it is worthwhile to notice that the field of DT in higher education (as well as elsewhere) is rather dynamic implying that impact studies and systematic longitudinal studies focusing on temporal progress and development would be helpful to better understand the prospects, hindrances, and pitfalls of DT. Second, the exemplary HEIs underlying the reports and research papers on which the present SWOT analyses are based are selective, limited in number and cannot be statistically representative. It is therefore desirable to have further intensive case studies on the status and progress of DT in HEIs, particularly for different countries and higher education systems, different institutional types, and different faculties and subject fields. Third, any SWOT analysis can be improved because it is an analytical tool that stands or falls with the best available conceptual analysis and differentiation of strengths, weaknesses, opportunities, and threats.

Acknowledgment

Since this chapter relates to intermediate results of the Erasmus+ project EDU-DIG (grant no. 2020-1-AT01-KA226-092677), the author would like to thank the European Commission (EC) as well as the project partners for their cooperation and support. However, the EC support for producing this publication does not constitute an endorsement of the contents, which reflect the views only of the author, and neither the EC nor the project's national funding agency OeAD (Austria) can be held responsible for any use which may be made of the information contained therein.

Notes

1 The restriction to L&T is of a pragmatic and not fundamental nature: in L&T, DT is particularly complex and at the same time the (acute) need is particularly high.
2 This is not to deny that there are some digital innovation hubs, for example in German higher education the "University Network Digitalisation" and the "Virtual University of Bavaria". However, the organisation of multi-layered innovation ecosystems for DT with regional, national, and European university partners is only just beginning.
3 For empirical results for students, see, e.g., Krempkow and Petri in this book.
4 A lack of competencies may cause the fear of failure meaning that people won't support a change if they are not confident in their own abilities to adapt to it. Accordingly, they try to avoid failure by resisting the change. This aspect of resistance to change may be accompanied by other aspects such as mistrust and lack of confidence in the change agents, emotional responses to the announced change, poor communication about and unrealistic timelines of the change process.
5 The concept of quality culture is used following Harvey and Stensaker (2008).
6 Among the core values of ethics of digital personal (performance) data are the following: data informedness; data accessibility; data rectification; data erasure; restricted data processing (SQELT-ECPPDM, 2020).
7 Personality competencies can be differentiated into self-competencies (e.g., abilities for self-determination, decision-making, learning) and social competencies (e.g., abilities for teamwork, leadership, communication). For a conceptual framework model of personality competencies that also suggests, as selected examples, related indicators, operationalisable L&T processes and quality assessment procedures, see Leiber (2016, pp. 9ff.).

8   For these and further digital competencies suggested by students' self-assessment, see Krempkow and Petri (2021, p. 9).

9   These and further, more specific factors influencing the transfer and use of research results in decision-making, policy and practice in complex social organisations including HEIs have been identified in general organisational research (e.g., Alkin & King, 2017; Bowen & Zwi, 2005; Contandriopoulos et al., 2010; de Man et al., 2020; Oliver & Boaz, 2019). Among these factors are differences in conceptual understanding, scientific uncertainty, strategic or unintended misunderstandings, timing, confusion, the mechanisms behind the academic-practitioner or theorist-practitioner gap, relative advantage, compatibility with values and past experiences; cost, flexibility, reversibility, and revisability to name a few. Accordingly, 'it is difficult for evidence to remain intact through the process given the policy context, decision-making factors, and the need to adapt' (Bowen & Zwi, 2005, p. 603). Therefore, from an optimistic perspective, 'effective knowledge transfer is not a "one off" event, rather it is a powerful and continuous process in which knowledge accumulates and influences thinking over time' (Bowen & Zwi, 2005, p. 603). Needless to add this process can also sometimes end with complete ignorance of the scientific evidence previously provided.

10 It is true that effects of the Corona pandemic accelerated digitalisation in HEIs, but it is uncertain whether these changes will be enduring. Rather, it is again contested already at some places to which extent digitalisation of L&T should be maintained in an assumed post-pandemic era.

References

Akçapınar, G., Altun, A., & Aşkar, P. (2019). Using learning analytics to develop early-warning system for at-risk students. *International Journal of Educational Technology in Higher Education*, *16*(1), 1–20.

Alkin, M. C., & King, J. A. (2017). Definitions of evaluation use and misuse, evaluation influence, and factors affecting use. *American Journal of Evaluation*, *38*(3), 434–450.

Barzman, M., Gerphagnon, M., Aubin-Houzelstein, G., Baron, G.-L., Bénart, A., Bouchet, F., Dibie, J., Gibrat, J.-F., Hodson, S., Lhoste, E., Martin, C., Moulier-Boutang, Y., Perrot, S., Phung, F., Pichot, C., Siné, M., Venin, T., & Mora, O. (2021). Exploring digital transformation in higher education and research via scenarios. *Journal of Future Studies*, *25*(3), 65–78.

Bates, T., Cobo, C., Mariño, O., & Wheeler, S. (2020). Can artificial intelligence transform higher education? *International Journal of Educational Technology in Higher Education*, *17*(1), 1–12.

Bond, M., Marin, V.I., Dolch, C., Bedenlier, S., & Zawacki-Richter, O. (2018). Digital transformation in German higher education: Student and teacher perceptions and usage of digital media. *International Journal of Educational Technology in Higher Education*, *15*, 48–67.

Bowen, S., & Zwi, A. B. (2005). Pathways to "evidence-informed" policy and practice: A framework for action. *PLoS Medicine, 2*(7), e166, 600–605. https://doi.org/10.1371/journal.pmed.0020166.g001

Butter, M., Gijsberg, G., Goetheer, A., & Karanikolova, K. (2020). Digital innovation hubs and their position in the European, national and regional innovation ecosystems. In D. Feldner (Ed.), *Redesigning organizations: Concepts for the connected society* (pp. 45–60). Springer.

Caena, F., & Redecker, C. (2019). Aligning teacher competence frameworks to 21st century challenges: The case for the European Digital Competence Framework for Educators (DIGCOMPEDU). *European Journal of Education, 54*(3), 356–369.

Cohen, M. D., March, J. G., & Olsen, J. P. (1972). A garbage can model of organizational choice. *Administrative Science Quarterly, 17*(1), 1–25. https://doi.org/10.2307/2392088

Contandriopoulos, D., Lemire, M., Denis, J.-L., & Tremblay, É. (2010). Knowledge exchange processes in organizations and policy arenas: A narrative systematic review of the literature. *Milbank Quarterly, 88*(4), 444–483.

Cope, B., Kalantzis, M., & Searsmith, D. (2021). Artificial intelligence for education: Knowledge and its assessment in AI-enabled learning ecologies. *Educational Philosophy and Theory, 53*(12), 1229–1245.

Daniela, L. (2019). *Didactics of smart pedagogy. Smart pedagogy for technology enhanced learning.* Springer.

De Man, A. P., Luvison, D., & de Leeuw, T. (2020). A temporal view on the academic-practitioner gap. *Journal of Management Inquiry*, 1–16. https://doi.org/10.1177/1056492620982375

EDUDIG. (2021). *Enhancing the development of educators' digital competencies.* Erasmus+ Strategic Partnership SQELT. Retrieved January 26, 2022, from https://www.evalag.de/edudig/

EFI. (2019). *Report on research, innovation and technological performance in Germany.* EFI (Commission of Experts for Research and Innovation).

Garvin, D. A. (1993). Building a learning organisation. *Harvard Business Review*, July–August. Retrieved January 26, 2022, from https://hbr.org/1993/07/building-a-learning-organization

Gilch, H., Beise, A. S., Krempkow, R., Müller, M., Stratmann, F., & Wannemacher, K. (2019). *Digitalisierung der Hochschulen. Ergebnisse einer Schwerpunktstudie für die Expertenkommission Forschung und Innovation.* Studien zum deutschen Innovationssystem Nr. 14-2019. Expertenkommission Forschung und Innovation. Retrieved January 26, 2022, from http://hdl.handle.net/10419/194284

Goertz, L., & Hense, J. (2021). *Studie zu Veränderungsprozessen in Unterstützungsstrukturen für Lehre an deutschen Hochschulen in der Corona-Krise.* Arbeitspapier Nr. 56. Hochschulforum Digitalisierung.

Govindarajan, V., & Srivastava, A. (2020). What the shift to virtual learning could mean for the future of higher ed. *Harvard Business Review, 31*(1), 3–8.

Grossek, G., Malița, L., & Bunoiu, M. (2020). Higher education institutions towards digital transformation – The WUT case. In A. Curaj, L. Deca, & R. Pricopie (Eds.), *European higher education area: Challenges for a new decade* (pp. 565–581). Springer.

Harvey, L., & Stensaker, B. (2008). Quality culture: Understandings, boundaries and linkages. *European Journal of Education, 43*(4), 427–442.

HFD (Hochschulforum Digitalisierung). (2016). *Discussion paper 20. Thesis on digital teaching and learning in higher education.* Retrieved January 26, 2022, from https://hochschulforumdigitalisierung.de/sites/default/files/dateien/HFD_AP_Nr%2018_Discussion_Paper.pdf

Hubler, S. (2020, October 26). Colleges slash budgets in the pandemic, with "nothing off-limits". *New York Times.* Retrieved January 26, 2022, from https://www.nytimes.com/2020/10/26/us/colleges-coronavirus-budget-cuts.html

Ifenthaler, D., & Yau, J. Y.-K. (2019). Higher education stakeholders' views on learning analytics policy recommendations for supporting study success. *International Journal of Learning Analytics and Artificial Intelligence for Education, 1*(1), 28–42.

Jääskelä, P., Häkkinen, P., & Rasku-Puttonen, H. (2017). Teacher beliefs regarding learning, pedagogy, and the use of technology in higher education. *Journal of Research on Technology in Education, 49*(3–4), 198–211.

Jones, C. (Ed.). (2015). *Networked learning: An educational paradigm for the age of digital networks.* Springer.

Krempkow, R., & Petri, P. S. (2021). *Digital competencies of students – How they are captured and what they can contribute to student success* [Paper presentation]. 43rd Annual Forum of EAIR – The European Higher Education Society, Humboldt University Berlin. https://doi.org/10.13140/RG.2.2.33782.52808

Leiber, T. (2016). Persönlichkeitsentwicklung als elementares Bildungsziel. Methodische Optionen der Umsetzung und Bewertung im Hochschulbereich. die hochschullehre. *Interdisziplinäre Zeitschrift für Studium und Lehre, 2.* Retrieved January 26, 2022, from http://www.hochschullehre.org/wp-content/files/diehochschullehre_2016_leiber.pdf

Leiber, T. (2020). Performance data governance and management in learning and teaching: Basic elements and desiderata in the light of a European case study. In Gesellschaft für Hochschulforschung (GfHf) (Ed.), *Transformation of society, transformation of science.* Documentation of the annual meeting 2019 of the Society for Higher Education Research (GfHf). Retrieved January 26, 2022, from https://www.gfhf2019.de/api-v1/article/!/action/getPdfOfArticle/articleID/3045/productID/34/filename/article-id-3045.pdf

Leiber, T., Stensaker, B., & Harvey, L. (2018). Bridging theory and practice of impact evaluation of quality management in higher education institutions: A SWOT analysis. *European Journal of Higher Education, 8*(3), 351–365.

Liang, S.-W., Chen, R.-N., Liu, L.-L., Li, X.-G., Chen, J.-B., Tang, S.-J., & Zhao, J.-B. (2020). The psychological impact of the COVID-19 epidemic on Guangdong College students: The difference between seeking and not seeking psychological help. *Frontiers in Psychology, 11,* 2231. https://doi.org/10.3389/fpsyg.2020.02231

Maltese, V. (2018). Digital transformation challenges for universities: Ensuring information consistency across digital services. *Cataloging and Classification Quarterly, 56*(7), 592–606.

Marcelo, C., & Yot-Domínguez, C. (2019). From chalk to keyboard in higher education classrooms: Changes and coherence when integrating technological knowledge into pedagogical content knowledge. *Journal of Further and Higher Education, 43*(7), 975–988.

Marks, A., Al-Ali, M., Attasi, R., Abualkishik, A. Z., & Rezgui, Y. (2020). Digital transformation in higher education: A framework for maturity assessment. *International Journal of Advanced Computer Science and Applications, 11*(12), 504–513.

Mishra, L., Gupta, T., & Shree, A. (2020). Online teaching-learning in higher education during lockdown period of COVID-19 pandemic. *International Journal of Educational Research Open, 1*, 100012. https://doi.org/10.1016/j.ijedro.2020.100012

Oliver, K., & Boaz, A. (2019). Transforming evidence for policy and practice: Creating space for new conversations. *Palgrave Communications, 5*, 60. https://doi.org/10.1057/s41599-019-0266-1

Orr, D., Lübcke, M., Schmidt, P., Ebner, M., Wannemacher, K., Ebner, M., & Dohmen, D. (2019a). *AHEAD – Internationales Horizon-Scanning: Trendanalyse zu einer Hochschullandschaft in 2030. Hochschulforum Digitalisierung.* Retrieved January 26, 2022, from https://hochschulforumdigitalisierung.de/sites/default/files/dateien/HFD_AP_Nr_42_AHEAD_WEB.pdf

Orr, D., Weller, M., & Farrow, R. (2019b). How is digitalisation affecting the flexibility and openness of higher education provision? Results of a global survey using a new conceptual model. *Journal of Interactive Media in Education, 5*(1), 1–12.

Rampelt, F., Orr, D., & Knoth, A. (2019). *Bologna digital 2020. White paper on Digitalisation in the European higher education area.* Retrieved January 26, 2022, from https://hochschulforumdigitalisierung.de/sites/dcfault/files/dateien/2019-05_White_Paper_Bologna_Digital_2020_0.pdf

Randall, I., Berlina, A., Teräs, J., & Rinne, T. (2018, January). *Digitalisation as a tool for sustainable Nordic regional development. Preliminary literature and policy review* [Discussion paper]. Nordic thematic group for innovative and resilient regions, Stockholm. Retrieved January 26, 2022, from https://www.nordregio.org/wp-content/uploads/2017/04/Digitalisation_Discussion-Paper_Jan-31.pdf

Redecker, C. (2017). *European framework for the digital competence of educators: DigCompEdu.* Publications Office of the European Union.

Renz, A., & Hilbig, R. (2020). Prerequisites for artificial intelligence in further education: Identification of drivers, barriers, and business models of educational technology companies. *International Journal of Educational Technology in Higher Education, 17*(14), 1–21.

Renz, A., Krishnaraja, S., & Gronau, E. (2020). Demystification of artificial intelligence in education – how much AI is really in the educational technology? *International Journal of Learning Analytics and Artificial Intelligence for Education, 2*(1), 4–30.

Royakkers, L., Timmer, J., Kool, L., & van Est, R. (2018). Societal and ethical issues of digitization. *Ethics and Information Technology, 20*, 127–142.

Spörk, J., Tauböck, S., Ledermüller, K., Krikawa, R., & Wurzer, G. (2021). Analyse von Studierbarkeit mittels Prognose- und Simulationsmodellen. *Zeitschrift für Hochschulentwicklung (ZFHE), 16*(4), 163–182. Retrieved January 26, 2022, from https://zfhe.at/index.php/zfhe/article/view/1555

SQELT-ECPPDM. (2020). *Ethical code of practice for (performance) data management. Sustainable quality enhancement in higher education learning and teaching.* Erasmus+ Strategic Partnership. Retrieved January 26, 2022, from https://www.evalag.de/fileadmin/dateien/pdf/forschung_international/sqelt/Intellectual_outputs/sqelt_ethical_code_of_practice_08_200930_final_sec.pdf

Stouten, J., Rousseau, D. M., & De Cremer, D. (2018). Successful organizational change: Integrating the management practice and scholarly literatures. *Academy of Management Annals, 12*(2), 752–788.

Tsai, S.-C., Chen, C.-H., Shiao, Y.-T., Ciou, J.-S., & Wu, T.-N. (2020). Precision education with statistical learning and deep learning: A case study in Taiwan. *International Journal of Educational Technology in Higher Education, 17*(12), 1–13.

UNGA (United Nations General Assembly). (2008). Universal Declaration of Human Rights: Adopted and proclaimed by UN General Assembly Resolution 217 A (iii) of 10 December 1948 Text. UN Document A/810, p. 71 (1948). *Refugee Survey Quarterly, 27*(3), 149–182.

Viberg, O., Hatakka, M., Bälter, O., & Mavroudi, A. (2018). The current landscape of learning analytics in higher education. *Computers in Human Behavior, 89*, 98–110.

Vicente, P. N., Lucas, M., Carlos, V., & Bem-Haja, P. (2020). Higher education in a material world: Constraints to digital innovation in Portuguese universities and polytechnic institutes. *Education and Information Technologies, 25*, 5815–5833.

World Bank. (2017). *The growing role of minerals and metals for a low carbon future.* World Bank Publications.

Zawacki-Richter, O., Marin, V. I., & Bond, M. (2019). Systematic review of research on artificial intelligence applications in higher education – where are the educators? *International Journal of Educational Technology in Higher Education, 16*(39), 1–27.

Zuboff, S. (2019). *The age of surveillance capitalism: The fight for a human future at the new frontier of power.* Profile Books.

CHAPTER 4

Challenges on the Digitalisation of the Universities in the European Higher Education Area
The Case of Germany

Uwe Cantner, Helge Dauchert, Katharina Hölzle and Christopher Stolz

Abstract

In digital transformation, universities take a pivotal role in relation to the scientific basis of new digital technologies and the provision of digital education in an academic context. A university system, properly equipped with digital-related human and real capital is essential for driving a country's digitalisation agenda. This chapter evidences the challenges faced by Germany in the development of societal digital potential and digital universities. German universities find the development of a digital university difficult as the process of digitalisation requires collective cross-discipline working and cultural change. Research activities need to be reconceived in the context of digitalisation, in terms of better and new data and methods. Respective digital solutions need to be communicated to secure engagement. Through digitalisation, teaching approaches will become less didactic and more personalised. Here again, universities need to pursue their ways of reform. Furthermore, the university administration will face a cultural change from pure budgetary administration to sophisticated strategic management. Several logics are evolving, the research logic and the educational logic, the communication logic in research and teaching, and the administrative and control logic. Higher education systems around the world have gone through large reforms during the past decades – although with different speeds and to varying degrees of success. However, it seems clear that Nordic and Baltic university systems are much further developed and more successful than the German one. The case of Germany is one where the need for improvement, for learning from others, and for a positive stance toward self-reflection and criticism is quite obvious. The COVID-19 crisis and the uncovering of many digital weaknesses in the German university system have proven to be powerful push factors. A number of improvements are already visible, such as in online teaching formats, digital exams, and video-conferencing. Nevertheless, policy makers and university managers are still obliged to take further, more purposeful steps.

DOI:10.1163/9789004520912_005

Keywords

universities – digitalisation – digital technologies – digitalisation gaps – digital skills – digitalisation of research – digitalisation of teaching – digitalisation of administration

1   Introduction

Modern knowledge-based societies derive their economic prosperity and social achievements less from the availability of natural resources than from their ability to generate new ideas and bring them into economic and social application. It is innovations in the form of new technologies, new products and services, new business models, but also new social concepts that are the engine of development in these societies. The activities of research and development as fundamental sources of new ideas, the innovation activities for the implementation and utilisation of these ideas as well as the activities for adoption and diffusion play a central role in this context. In a society and economy, these activities are organised and coordinated via a division of labour between various actors, which is referred to as the research and innovation system.

Actors from the private and the public sector; from the field of science and research; from the education sector with schools, vocational and university education but also further education; from politics, including political support; and from society all make up this research and innovation system.

In research and innovation systems, universities play an important role and take on a number of pivotal tasks. These primarily include research into fundamentally new scientific findings and the development of basic solutions for a wide range of relevant scientific and social, including economic, problems and questions. Of equal importance, the task of universities is to offer and carry out the academic training of young people who with the knowledge and the skills they have acquired can work in broad areas of the economy and society and can contribute to further development. In this sense, universities are part of the education system that is responsible for ensuring that a society and its members are well educated, i.e., that they have the appropriate knowledge and skills to implement and apply it, so-called human capital.

The availability of sufficient human capital and at a considerably high level is a basic requirement for the successful functioning of the research and innovation system. On the supply side of the economy, it is a decisive factor in the research and development of new technologies, new products, and new services. On the demand side, human capital enables users to apply new technologies competently and to consume new products and services appropriately.

Now and then, radical technological innovations come up with far-reaching consequences for further development. They not only offer completely new development potentials for societies and economies, but they also confront them and their research and innovation systems with special and quite demanding challenges. A current case in point is digital technologies and with them the so-called digitisation or digital transformation of society and economy. Digital technologies are unlocking substantial opportunities for the industrial and service sectors, as well as private and public sectors. Furthermore, they are expected to help societies around the world solve the grand societal challenges of today, i.e., to address, among others, climate change, demographic change, impoverishment, and social inequality. However, the introduction of digital technologies is accompanied by major challenges because with digitalisation, significant parts of existing technologies will no longer be relevant and will be replaced by new, digitally enhanced ones. New types of jobs and work opportunities will displace previous ones, and conversions to new ways of life and behaviours will become necessary. During this process, the suitability of existing knowledge and skills to accomplish the digital turn is called into question because only if society and the economy have human capital available which can properly deal with the challenges of digital technologies will the digital transformation succeed.

The degree of mastery of the challenges posed by digital change, the intensity of digitalisation in societies and economies worldwide, the degree of digitalisation of the different sectors, and the breadth and depth by which people are prepared, educated, and able to use digital technologies are rather different across nations. There are numerous reasons for these differences – among them are the competencies and abilities of societies for pushing digitalisation and for coping with it.

This is where universities come into play again. They are located at a neuralgic point in the research and innovation system, namely where knowledge, competencies, and skills related to digitalisation are generated and offered. They are the place where the scientific foundations of digitalisation are laid and where the scientific-academic teaching and training of digital knowledge and digital skills are offered and implemented. In pursuant of these tasks, universities, the education system more broadly, and society as a whole have all faced these challenges of digitalisation.

With these challenges and considerations in mind, this chapter addresses the case of Germany and its universities. We proceed as follows. In the following section we address the challenges that Germany and its research and innovation system are currently facing with respect to radical technological change via selected digital technologies. A comparative view on the German position at the international level is taken. Section 3 offers a brief digression into the challenges radical change imposes on knowledge and skills, into the demand for digital competencies in Germany, and into the requirements for the system of vocational and continuing education and training to support the digital turn. This discussion paves the way for a discussion of the process of digitalisation undertaken by universities. In Section 4, a closer look at German universities and their state of development into a digital university is taken. This chapter closes with a brief outlook of the challenges ahead.

2   Digitalisation as Radical Technological Change and Germany's Gaps

Germany has been facing a number of challenges in the field of digital technologies in recent years. Global economic competition in highly innovative digital technologies has increased, forcing German actors to react in order to remain competitive. To date, these reactions have been rather weak and Germany's international position in various digital technological fields is under pressure. A few examples from prior analyses of the German Commission of Experts for Research and Innovation illustrate this aspect.

The cases selected from digital technology fields (robotics, autonomous systems, artificial intelligence) and applications (digital business models, e-government) are evidence enough for Germany's worrying state of development in the field of digital technologies. By presenting existing digitalisation deficits in other fields of the German research and innovation system, the challenges of digitalisation faced by universities are placed in a larger picture.

2.1   *Robotics*[1]

In their 2016 report, the Commission of Experts has taken an in-depth look at the current status and development of robotics in Germany. Here, robotics is understood as the design, construction, operation, and use of robots. The goal of robotics is to design machines that can help and assist humans. Scientific publications and patents as indicators of R&D activity, from 2000 to 2004 and 2009 to 2013, respectively (see Figure 4.1), are used to understand Germany's position in the field of robotics (industrial robotics and service robotics). While Germany is the leader of patents for industrial robotics, it occupies only a midlevel position in patents for service robotics in an overall country comparison. In terms of publication performance, the USA dominates in both industrial and service robotics.

Looking at patenting activities in the field of industrial robotics over time, however, Germany's strong position is put into perspective. In the period from 2009 to 2013, the number of German patent applications was 12 percent higher

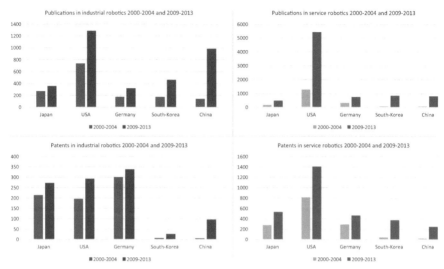

FIGURE 4.1 Publications and patents in industrial robotics and service robotics, 2000–2004 and 2009–2013

than during the period from 2000 to 2004. In comparison, the aggregated patent figures for the reference countries Japan, USA, South Korea, and China increased by 64 percent. The picture is similar for publications. In Germany, the number of publications increased by 86 percent while in the reference countries, publications rose by 134 percent.

In the field of service robotics, the publication and patenting dynamics in Germany are also significantly weaker than in the reference countries: In Japan, the USA, South Korea, and China, the number of publications on service robots increased by 390 percent whereas in Germany it increased by only 143 percent. The number of patents grew in the reference countries by 123 percent, but in Germany it grew only by 61 percent. Overall, Germany's relatively strong position in the patenting of industrial robotics is increasingly under attack from competitor countries (EFI, 2016: B2). This assessment is particularly problematic in light of the fact that forecasts predict that service robotics will outstrip industrial robotics (Sander & Wolfgang, 2014). The greatest potential is expected in the demand for private systems in the home and entertainment, as well as in the medical, agricultural, defence, and logistics sectors (IFR, (2015).

For a long time, government research funding by the Federal Ministry of Education and Research has paid little attention to this development. Larger funding programs were almost exclusively focused on promoting industrial robotics (EFI, 2016: B2).

Against the backdrop of the development outlined above, it will be important for Germany to not focus exclusively on industrial robotics but rather to also exploit the growth potential of service robotics. Other countries such as Japan and South Korea are far ahead here (EFI, 2016: B2).

2.2   *Autonomous Systems*[2]

Autonomous systems solve complex tasks with the help of software and methods of artificial intelligence. They learn on the basis of data and are thus able to act without human intervention even in unknown situations. The use of autonomous systems is still in its infancy in many areas but offers high technological opportunities for innovation. In their 2018 report, the Commission of Experts examined Germany's position regarding research and application of autonomous systems. For this purpose, the Commission of Experts distinguished several subdomains, namely autonomous vehicles, industrial production, smart home, and hostile environments. Germany's international position in these fields can be analysed by looking at international patenting activities, evidenced by transnational patent applications as filed between 2002 and 2016. Figure 4.4 shows the according patents' distribution with respect to the country of invention.[3] The results are shown explicitly for inventors from Germany, the USA, Japan, South Korea, and China. Patents of inventors from other countries are shown in summary form (other countries). The figures show a country's share in total transnational patent applications in the respective field. In the area of application of autonomous vehicles, inventors from Japan (24.3 percent), Germany (23.3 percent), and the USA (20.4 percent) have comparably high shares of the total number of patent families. These results indicate that Germany is a highly significant location for R&D in the application-area of automated driving and that German patent applicants have a competitive patent portfolio. In the area of application of industrial production, inventors from the USA (35.3 percent) and Japan (30.1 percent) occupy the leading positions while inventors from Germany (13.4 percent) hold an intermediate position. Inventors from South Korean (5.3 percent) and China (2,6 percent) have significantly lower patenting activities. Patenting in the area of application of the smart home is dominated by South Korean inventors, who make up 32.4 percent of the identified patent families. They are followed by inventors from the USA (20.1 percent), China (15.1 percent), Germany (10.3 percent) and Japan (9.9 percent). In the area of application of hostile environments, inventors from the USA (34.0 percent) again reveal particularly strong activities. German inventors follow with 18.6 percent. All in all, these data indicate a particularly strong position for Germany in the application field of automated driving and autonomous systems in hostile environments. In the other areas of application, there is no evidence for particularly strong German specialisation.

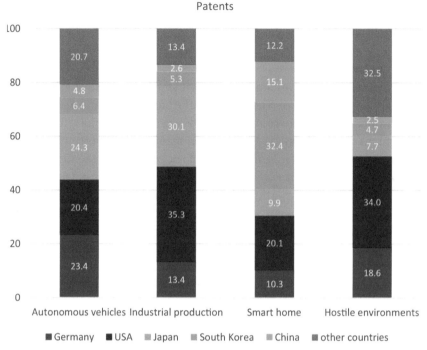

FIGURE 4.2   Germany's share of transnational patents by international comparison for the
              four examined areas of application of autonomous systems, 2002–2016

2.3   *Artificial Intelligence*[4]

The term artificial intelligence (AI) is used to describe procedures, algorithms, and technical solutions that allow complex processes previously carried out by humans to be transferred to machines and software. A generally accepted definition of AI does not yet exist. The field of AI has been experiencing a radical change from symbolic AI to neural AI in recent years. The fulminant development of neural AI was triggered by breakthroughs in improving the precision and speed of image recognition algorithms.

In their 2019 report, the Commission of Experts used scientific publications in symbolic and neural AI to measure the scientific basis of countries herein, taken as an early indicator for future innovative and economic development respectively. Classifying related publications from 1988 to 2018 according to country and AI approach produces interesting differences (see Figure 4.5).[5] China and the USA record the highest numbers of publications. However, Chinese research has primarily concentrated on neural AI, especially in recent years. The United Kingdom, Germany, and France are the leading European counties in terms of the number of publications. While Germany has a comparatively strong position in the field of symbolic AI, it has not yet been able to

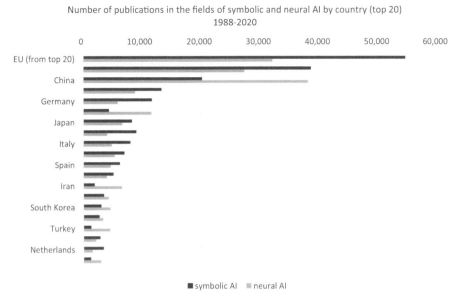

FIGURE 4.3   Number of publications in the fields of symbolic and neural AI by country
(top 20), 1988–2018

establish a comparable position in the field of neural AI. Many other countries, including Iran and India, are better positioned in this respect. One of the reasons for this development is to be found in the funding policy of the German government, which for a long time persisted in almost exclusively promoting symbolic AI.

2.4   Digital Business Models[6]

New digital business models are key drivers of the digital transformation. Accordingly, the economic importance of data-driven service and business models have increased significantly in recent years. It can be captured by the market capitalisation of companies in the internet economy and ICT sector. As the Commission of Experts pointed out in its 2016 and 2017 reports, Germany has not yet been able to build up any comparative advantage in the internet economy and the ICT sector. Both sectors continue to be dominated by US players.

The three most valuable companies in Germany which have a focus in the ICT sector are Siemens AG, SAP AG, and Deutsche Telekom AG (see Figure 4.2), yet their growth dynamics are weak compared to the dynamics of the US, American-based internet companies. German companies in the internet industry with the strongest capital base include Zalando, United Internet, and long-established companies such as Axel Springer. However, even their market

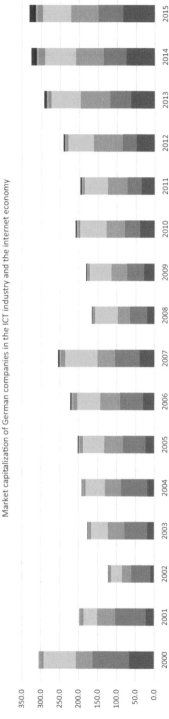

FIGURE 4.4 Market capitalisation of German companies in the ICT industry and the internet economy (from Müller et al., 2016)

capitalisation has grown rather slowly compared to US companies. Overall, Alphabet's market capitalisation alone exceeds that of all German companies in the internet economy and in the ICT sector. The gap between Germany and the US has been sharply increasing.

2.5   E-Government[7]

E-government can increase the quality and scope of government services and ensure greater transparency and reliability. An increased use of e-government also increases the demand for IT solutions and therefore represents both a driver of innovation as well as an innovation per se. By international comparison, Germany is severely lagging behind other nations, leaving important potential for innovation and value creation untapped. The United Nations E-Government Development Index shows that the quality of government-related services in South Korea, Estonia, and the USA is significantly more advanced than in Germany (see Figure 4.3) (UN DESA, 2016). The E-Government Development Index reflects the status of e-government offerings in all UN member states on the basis of a four-stage measurement: The first and second stage include a one-way form of interaction such as the provision of information by public authorities or links to websites of other institutions (stage 1) as well as one-way electronic communication with, among others, downloadable documents (stage 2). Stage 3 services include the possibility of two-way communication and interaction e.g. applying for, issuing, and paying for licenses and certificates. From stage 3 onwards, the requirements of full digitisation are fulfilled, i.e., a transaction can be executed without changing the information-carrying medium. Stage 4 services are defined as fully interconnected services allowing a barrier-free exchange of information and data between authorities and citizens or businesses. As Figure 4.3 shows, German e-government currently is at the level of the pioneering nations – Estonia, Finland, South Korea, and the USA – in simple forms of interaction such as the provision of information by public authorities. However, when it comes to the more advanced services of stage 4, Germany lags considerably behind.

E-government in Germany is fragmented and often not entirely digitised. The situation is further aggravated by the fact that the existing services are not designed to be user-friendly. In order to be user-friendly, an e-government service needs to broadly publicise the service-offers that are available online; it also needs to be clearly structured, easy to operate and transparent. In addition, the electronic information and services should be bundled and offered in one place: in a 'one-stop shop'. As a result of the fragmentary range of services and low level of user-friendliness, e-government is used less intensively by citizens in Germany than in other countries.

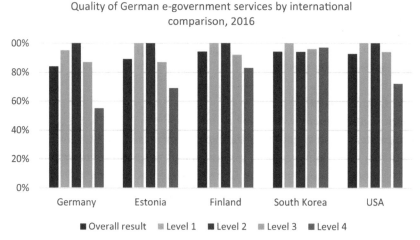

Quality of German e-government services by international comparison, 2016

FIGURE 4.5   Quality levels of German e-government services by international comparison, 2016

The low use of e-government has negative consequences not only for the citizens but also for business and science. The digitisation of public administration creates large amounts of data. Such data can be made available as open government data on online portals and used by companies and civil society actors to develop new services and innovative business models. Open government data also represents an important source of data for science. In Germany, as a result of the insufficiently developed e-government and the inconsistent approach of the administrative bodies, the potential of Open Government Data can only be used to a rudimentary extent.

These three cases of digital technologies and two application fields indicate Germany's problems in internationally keeping pace in the development and adoption of such new and promising technologies. That puts quite a burden on Germany's ability to successfully accomplish the digital transformation in reasonable time. In this context, the availability of digital skills and competencies plays a crucial role, the topic of the following section.

3   Developing and Adopting Digital Technologies Needs Appropriate Skills

There are a couple of possible reasons that can explain why a country is falling behind in developing and adopting digital technologies. From an economic standpoint, switching from an established technology to a new technology usually implies a depreciation of recent investments in the established technology and affiliated investments in systems, processes, and human resources. Depending on how recent and the amount of the investment, it might be reasonable to continue using the established technology, stop any further investments, and switch technologies at a later point in time. However, this can lead to an economic lock-in of the old technology. The implementation and use of a new technology often requires different skills and knowledge compared to the old one. To switch is an effort a company might not be willing to make if the existing knowledge and skills suffice, causing a so-called cognitive lock-in. These arguments are relevant primarily for established companies, as new market actors such as start-ups should be able to switch more easily in this context, as they tend not to be locked-in either economically or cognitively. However, start-ups face other type of problems in the early stages, such as acquiring VC funding for investing in the new technologies or hiring skilled employees trained in the necessary competencies relevant to the new technology. For the latter, they are often outcompeted by the large established players who can pay higher salaries for these high-skill workers.

The lack of skills and competencies is an obstacle when implementing and applying a new technology.[8] In Germany, the acquisition of knowledge, competencies, and skills required for developing, adopting, and using radical new digital technologies is limited. Digital technologies based on artificial intelligence, big data, and cloud computing – and their associated disruptive business models – challenge Germany's previous specialisation advantages. The degree of digitisation and the depth of digitisation, not only in different industries but even in companies in the same industries, will vary greatly and have a differentiating effect on future business models. New digital technologies are leading to more online-based and platform-supported business models and will further change work processes (Klös & Meinhard, 2019). Over time, skills in software and algorithm development or correspondingly qualified specialists have become important prerequisites for productivity growth and innovation. There is a high demand for skilled personnel who can actively shape the digital transformation.

Key digital skills, e.g., all computer, data and IT-related skills, are an important basis for the effective use of digital technologies. In addition, the ability to create software has meanwhile become a requirement in many professions. Simple software applications and even artificial intelligence will relieve workers of routine and physically demanding tasks. At the same time, the use and further development of technologies place new and changed demands on employees (Pfeiffer et al., 2016).

In their study "Digitalisation in the German Labour Market – Analysing Demand for Digital Skills in Job Vacancies" the authors show the rising demand for digital skills in the German labour market between 2014 and 2018 based on an analysis of 26 million online job advertisements (O'Kane et al., 2020). Digital skills range from basic knowledge required for the use of a computer and the application of various software programs to the mastery of highly specialised programming languages. Their results give a clear indication that digitisation is arriving across the board in the world of work. Of all the online job ads studied, the proportion of advertisements requiring at least one digital skill increased from 38.1 percent to 47.5 percent between 2014 and 2018. Distinguishing occupations by how intensively they require digital skills shows that in 2018, nearly 80 percent of online job ads were for occupations for which digital knowledge and skills were a basic requirement. Broken down by qualification level, however, significant differences can be seen: in job ads for highly qualified people, the proportion of occupational activities in which essential digital skills are required was 94 percent while the same proportion was only 62 percent in job ads for jobs with a low qualification requirement profile, for example, for helper jobs in logistics or catering. Differences are also evident between various sectors of the economy. In addition to the information and communications sector, digitisation is already well advanced in financial and insurance services as well as in freelance, scientific, and technical services. This contrasts with the hospitality industry and health and social services, which are comparatively less digitised.

The digital transformation requires employees to acquire additional professional qualifications, as there is not only an increasing demand for digital skills, which are necessary for the design of transformative technologies, but also for so-called essential core skills.[9] These include problem-solving skills, creativity, initiative, adaptability, and perseverance. Young people coming out of the education system must be equipped with both digital and core skills to be well prepared for a successful career in the digitalised working environment. Only if the diverse core skills are sufficiently available in the labour force can the economic and social potentials of new technologies unfold completely, allowing for digitalisation to drive through all parts of the economy. This also strengthens Germany's innovation capacity and competitiveness in the long term. Therefore, the system of vocational and continuing education and training (VET/CET) in Germany needs to keep pace with the changes in the economy and working environment brought about by digitalisation. To this end, VET opportunities must be further developed, and structures must be designed in such a way that core and digital skills are imparted to the workforce in line with demand. All private stakeholders involved, especially companies and people in the labour force, play a key role in the necessary adjustments in VET/CET. However, there is also a need for impulses from public authorities to reinforce the readiness for relevant changes and to establish the necessary conditions.

Therefore, education in and teaching of these skills is warranted. Furthermore, a focus on software development or coding alone is not sufficient – rather, interaction with other skills is necessary. The supply of qualified personnel must be increased through improved digital education across the entire breadth of the education system, i.e., in schools, dual vocational training, continuing education, and not least in universities. Building on this background, the following section takes a closer look at the digital university, a core player not only in the education system but also in the research and innovation system.

4 The Digital University

The relation of universities to digitalisation is manifold. First, universities themselves apply digital technologies, digital knowledge, and digital skills. Tasks in research, teaching, transfer, and administration increasingly build on these skills. Hence, to progress in these tasks, digital and core skills (see above) are mandatory. Second, universities function as facilitators of digital knowledge and digital competencies. Students and young researchers are educated and trained in these skills by their respective universities. Courses on topics such as computer sciences, data sciences, or artificial intelligence but also Entrepreneurship, Ethics, and sustainability provide students with relevant skills. Third, digitalisation can enable structural changes within the universities by digitalising processes in its research, teaching, and administration. Lastly, universities as such are a source of digital ideas, innovative concepts, and technologies such as artificial intelligence, robotics, and autonomous systems.

4.1 *The University as User of Digital Technologies*
The digitalisation of research, teaching, and administration poses significant challenges for universities.[10] In contrast to private companies, there are certain aspects specific to universities that delay the digitalisation process. According to the report of the Imboden Commission, an international expert commission for the evaluation of the excellence initiative, the governance of many German universities is characterised by a lack of efficiency orientation (Internationale Expertenkommission Exzellenzinitative, 2016). In addition, universities overall have been suffering for years from structural underfunding, which makes it challenging to invest in digitalisation when there are more urgent things like leaking roofs to be taken care of.

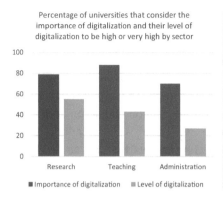
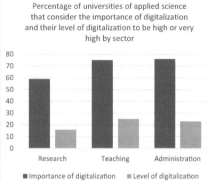

FIGURE 4.6   Difference between importance and level of digitalisation at German
              universities (from Gilch et al., 2019)

Alongside these internal problems, universities face numerous external requirements – such as increasing the number of enrolled students and a growing dependence on third-party funding – which have led to heightened complexity in the governance of universities.[11] One possibility by which universities can respond to the challenges of digitalisation is to develop a digitalisation strategy. This strategy should be based on the university's profile, its target groups, and its development objectives. However, in a survey conducted on behalf of the Commission of Experts for Research and Innovation in 2018, and as shown in Figure 4.6, only 14 percent of the participating universities confirmed that they have a digitalisation strategy in place. A further 41 percent state that they were developing a digitalisation strategy, while 31 percent were planning to do so. The most commonly stated objectives pursued with a digitalisation strategy were improving the quality and efficiency of administration and enhancing the quality of teaching.

4.1.1   Digitalisation of Research[12]
German universities are well placed in terms of the digitalisation of research. Digitalisation of research relates to the increasing application of computer-assisted procedures and the systematic use of digital resources. The state of digitalisation in research, as shown in Figure 4.7, varies considerably between universities and universities of applied sciences. This can be explained mainly by the stronger research focus of universities in comparison with the universities of applied sciences. Research information systems have been fully or partially implemented at almost half of universities. In addition, around 30 percent of universities have implemented research data management systems either in part or in full. Researchers' use of digital data collections is considered to be high or very high by 63 percent of universities. In addition, 45 percent of universities

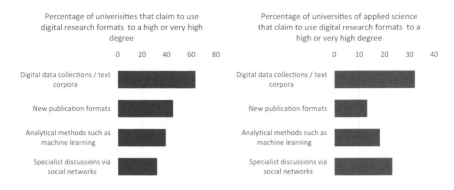

FIGURE 4.7   Use of digital research formats (from Gilch et al., 2019)

state that they use new publication formats often or very often while 39 percent use digital analysis methods to a high or very high degree. In contrast, at universities of applied sciences, less than 20 percent of institutions have implemented research-related IT systems. Digital research formats such as digital data collections and new publication formats are also used less frequently.[13]

Regardless of the type of HE institution, the level of digitalisation in research depends to a large extent on the engagement of individual researchers and research groups. Researchers use a variety of digital tools of their own accord to simulate, model, visualise, collect, and analyze data, as well as to publish research results, without central support by their respective institution. However, this gives rise to wide-ranging requirements for support, training, and other services, for which universities need to develop and provide suitable offers (Gilch et al., (2019). This is particularly pertinent, as support requirements will continue to grow as artificial intelligence and data science become increasingly important (Pongratz, 2017).

4.1.2   Digitalisation of Teaching
With regard to digital teaching formats, there is significant potential for improvement. In terms of teaching, digitalisation denotes the permeation of digital components and learning tools in teaching and learning processes. As a survey conducted on behalf of the Commission of Experts for Research and Innovation shows, universities primarily regard the digitalisation of teaching as a strategic element by which the quality of teaching can be improved. Furthermore, digital learning formats provide a higher degree of flexibility, such as through time-independent and location-independent learning or individualised learning paths (EFI, 2019: B4).

Learning management systems (LMS) are central IT systems to support teaching (Baumgartner et al., 2002; Schmid et al., 2017). In the survey, 85 percent of universities stated that these systems have already been implemented either partially or in full. However, most universities only use their LMS as a structured document storage system. More demanding applications, such as exams and peer grading by course participants, are exceptions to this (Schmid et al., 2017).

In addition, almost 90 percent of the universities have established service centres to support teaching staff in using digital tools and to develop digital teaching content.[14] Compared to the infrastructural framework conditions the use of digital teaching and learning formats continues to lag behind the infrastructural framework conditions. The survey shows (see Figure 4.8) that mobile learning is used frequently by 25 percent of the universities; 19 percent state frequent use of social media. Only 13 percent of the universities use inverted classroom formats to a high or very high degree. The proportion of universities who indicate use of adaptive learning, augmented/virtual reality, and digital game-based learning on a frequent or very frequent basis in their teaching was between six and seven percent.

These results are supported by a 2017 survey that examined digital teaching in universities. However, the survey also shows that most teaching staff consider the technical equipment at universities to be good (Schmid et al., 2017).

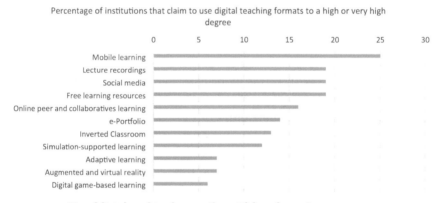

FIGURE 4.8   Use of digital teaching formats (from Gilch et al., 2019)

4.1.3   Digitalisation of Administration

The digitalisation of administration refers to the conversion of administrative workflows into digital processes (EFI, 2019: B4). The results of the survey indicate that study-related IT systems such as campus management systems feature a higher degree of implementation than non-study-related IT systems such as enterprise resource planning systems (see Figure 4.9) (Gilch et al., 2019).

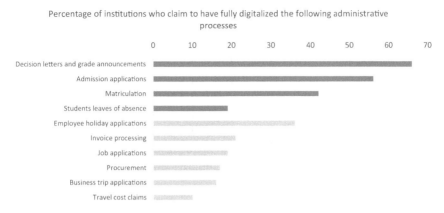

Percentage of institutions who claim to have fully digitalized the following administrative processes

FIGURE 4.9   Degree of digitalisation of university administration (from Gilch et al., 2019)

Study-related administrative processes include inter alia processing admission applications, issuing grade announcements, as well as student enrolment. These processes operate with a high degree of digitalisation across universities. For instance, two-thirds of the universities generate decision letters and grade announcements using fully electronic processes; 56 percent process admission applications in this manner. Furthermore, at 42 percent of the universities, students can use a fully digital process to enrol.

By contrast, the degree to which non-study-related administrative processes – such as processing travel cost claims and procurement requests – have been digitalised is assessed as being markedly lower. So far, less than 20 percent of the universities have fully digitalised these processes. The findings that German universities have some catching up to do, especially in the digitalisation of non-study-related processes, is confirmed by a comparison with the progress made at Swiss universities (Licka & Gautschi, 2017).

The digitalisation of administrative processes at universities is covered by the provisions of the Online Access Act (Onlinezugangsgesetz, OZG), which aims to advance the digitalisation of public administration. The OZG stipulates that by the end of 2022, all administrative services provided by the federal government, the federal states, and local authorities must be accessible online for the respective users via an online administration portal. According to the OZG implementation catalogue, universities must provide all administrative services that relate to a course of study (e.g., enrolment, applying for a leave of absence, and issuing electronic copies of diplomas) in digital form (Stocksmeier & Hunnius, 2018).

To achieve these targets, the digitalisation process and the internal networking of universities' administrative systems will have to accelerate considerably.

In view of these results and observations, it becomes apparent that for digi-talisation to succeed, universities need to develop a digitalisation strategy with clearly defined goals and a suitably coordinated implementation plan. In addi-tion, universities should be supported by politics through the introduction of a lump-sum digitalisation payment, further support for the digitalisation of universities through competitively awarded project funding, and support structures, especially for small universities. If digitalisation leads to increased efficiency and thereby creates additional financial leeway, these should be per-manently available to universities for qualitative improvements in infrastruc-ture, teaching, and research.

4.2   *The University as Locus of Digital Education and Training*

Over the past two decades, a growing importance of computer science at ter-tiary education institutions has been observed. In 2021, more than 130,000 stu-dents enrolled in subjects relating to computer science (Destatis, 2021). This number corresponds to a 25 percent increase compared to 2016.[15] The percent-age of women among the first-year students has been rising gradually but con-tinuously from 20 percent in 2016 to about 23 percent in 2021 (Destatis, 2016, 2021). 50 percent of computer science graduates took their examinations at universities of applied sciences and 50 percent at universities.

Apart from computer science itself, study subjects relating to computer sci-ence also include subjects that were introduced for the purpose of generating interaction between other disciplines with IT content. These subjects include, for example, business informatics, bioinformatics, computational engineering (often also referred to as computer engineering), as well as media informat-ics and medical informatics. More than half of the graduates in 2021 studied computer science without such a focus, and 27 percent specialised in business informatics. Media informatics came a distant third in terms of the number of graduates (making up seven percent).

The relative importance of these subjects can be determined by dividing the number of first-year students in their respective subject by the number of all first-year students. The share of computer science students rose from 3.9 per-cent in 2016 to 4.5 percent in 2021 (Destatis, 2016, 2021). The share of business informatics also grew from 2.1 to 2.3 percent. In 2021, there were almost 31,000 first-year students in computer science, which means that computer science is second rank by subject after business administration (57,500).

Examples of good practice can be found at the universities of Berkeley and Zurich. At the University of California, Berkeley, a course in Foundations of Data Science, which is one of the prerequisites or compulsory courses in many departments, is offered to students of all subjects.[16] It familiarises students inter alia with concepts of statistics and computer-aided calculation. The

University of Zurich has redesigned its study courses in economics so that it now leaves room for a minor subject. The range of minor subjects comprise a selection of IT-related subjects such as computational sciences and computer science for economists.[17]

A recent survey on offerings of digital education and training at German universities delivers a series of interesting results.[18]

As Figure 4.10 shows, universities offer various modules to teach specialised tech competencies. More than 70 percent of the universities provide teaching modules in complex data analysis, AI development and web development and design. A further 67 and 61 percent, respectively, offer networked IT-systems courses as well as smart hardware and robotics development courses to teach technical skills.

These offerings can be classified in separate degree programs, compulsory courses, and elective courses. Figure 4.11 shows that separate degree programs that cover the various dimensions are quite rare, with complex data analysis ranking here first at about 23 percent. In most of the special dimensions, as AI development, networked IT-systems, and robotics development, compulsory courses are dominant. In contrast, Blockchain development and tech-translation courses are frequently offered as elective courses. These results indicate that technical competencies are mainly offered as part of degree programs on rather different topics and in different disciplines. A focus on an explicit study program, on the other hand, is rare so that there is a need to develop these programs more intensely.

Looking more closely to digital competencies, Figure 4.12 illustrates that a considerable share of German universities, at least 60 percent, provide new

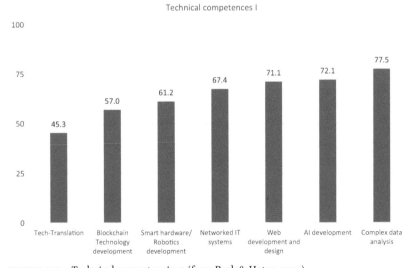

FIGURE 4.10   Technical competencies I (from Burk & Hetze, 2020)

Offerings of specialized tech. competences II, 2018-2020

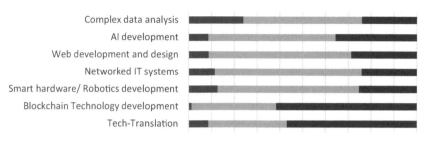

FIGURE 4.11   Technical competencies II (from Burk & Hetze, 2020)

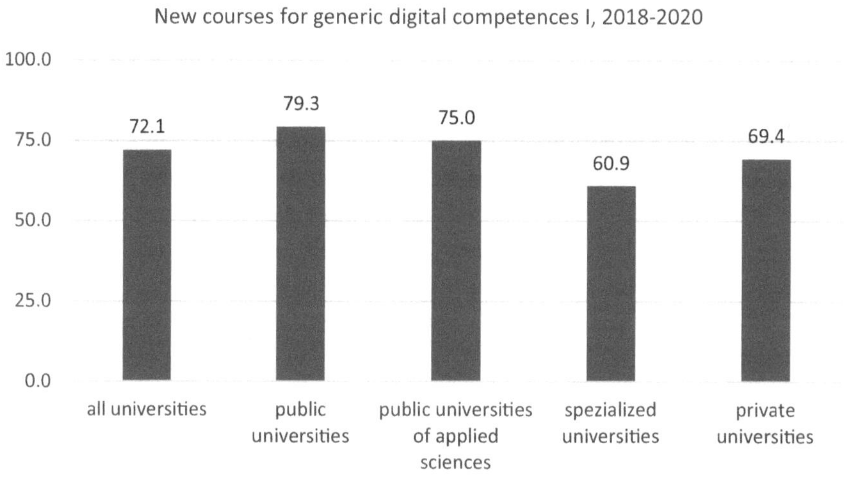

New courses for generic digital competences I, 2018-2020

FIGURE 4.12   Generic digital competencies I (from Burk & Hetze, 2020)

course of digital competencies. There is some variation across university types, with public universities and public universities of applied science being some- what more inclined to go for these formats. Again, these offerings can be clas- sified into compulsory and elective ones and herein into those covering all subject areas and those that apply to at least one course.

5   Challenges Ahead

For the digital transformation, universities take a pivotal role when it comes to creating the scientific basis of new digital technologies and providing digital

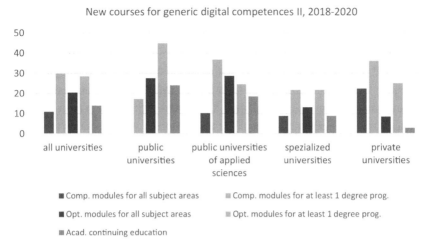

FIGURE 4.13   Generic digital competencies II (from Burk & Hetze, 2020)

education on an academic level. For a country's research and innovation system that strives to successfully push digitalisation, to provide for respective economic and societal potentials, and to take care of widespread digital knowledge and competencies allowing to reap economic and societal benefits, a university system properly equipped with digital related human and real capital is essential and non-substitutable. Countries all over the world show different states of digital development of both, their societies and their universities. In this respect, Germany is currently a case in which the development of both digital technologies and the digital university have considerable room of improvement. When it comes to developing the digital university, universities face increasingly demanding challenges. This process requires to promote various border crossings and respective cultural change. The way research activities are pursued and organised, the type and quantity of data generated and analysed, the kind of interaction and communication, and the methods and instruments applied all need to be considered and upcoming solutions required further pushes and promotion – from within the university system itself but also from the political side, i.e. research and innovation policies with special focus on the university system. Teaching formats will be changing from frontal mass teaching to individualised training and further education. Here again, universities need to pursue their ways of reform – and the COVID-19 crises has been reason enough to find improvements in this dimension; this needs to be accompanied by policy initiatives, i.e. education and training related policies directed toward the university system. Furthermore, university administration is facing a cultural change from pure budgetary administration to sophisticated strategic management. Hence a couple of logics are on the way to be changed, the research logic and the educational logic, the communication logic in research and teaching, and the administrative and control logic.

Additional pressure and challenges arise from university competition within and beyond the digital changes. On the one hand, this implies having to keep pace with global developments, including changes in research and education fields and societal demand. On the other hand, there is the need to reinvent oneself which raises nearly automatically the question of what remains from the freedom of research and teaching. World-wide higher education systems have gone through large reforms during the past decades – although with different speeds and successes. Visions and missions have been set up, underlying strategic and operational plans have been issued, proper key performance indicators developed, and competitive programs for funding installed – again with different breadths and depths as well as different intensities and results among countries. Statistics on that are rare and not fully comprehensive. However, Nordic and Baltic university systems seem to be much further developed and successful than the German one. The case of Germany, although some professionalisation in digital dimension cannot be neglected, is one where the need of improvement, of learning from others, and of a positive stance toward self-reflection and criticism is quite obvious. It is furthermore an exceptional and interesting case as Germany builds on a long and strong history of technology development and urgently needs due to its lack of natural resources and its comparable small size, the development of digital competencies to stay competitive among the nations. The COVID-19 crisis and the uncovering of many digital weaknesses in the German university system have proven to be a powerful push factor. A number of improvements are already noticeable and visible, such as in online teaching formats, digital exams, and video-conferencing. Nevertheless, policy makers and university managers are still obliged to take further proper steps.

Notes

1   In this regard and in the following cf. EFI (2016: B2).
2   Cf. EFI (2018: B3).
3   Calculations of the Commission of Experts based on Pötzl und Natterer (2018) and Youtie et al. (2018).
4   In this regard and in the following cf. EFI (2019: A2).
5   Calculations of the Commission of Experts based on Scopus data. API query with keywords based on Cardon et al. (2018).
6   In this regard and in the following cf. EFI (2016: B3) and EFI (2016: B6-1).
7   In this regard and in the following cf. EFI (2016: B4) and EFI (2017: B 6-2).
8   In this regard and in the following cf. EFI (2018: A4).
9   In this regard and in the following cf. EFI (2021: B2).
10 In this regard and in the following cf. EFI (2019: B4).

11 In this regard and in the following cf. Gilch et al. (2019).
12 Cf. EFI (2019: B4).
13 One-third of researchers at universities of applied sciences use digital collections often or very often. Mean-while, 18 percent of universities of applied sciences claim to use new publication formats often or very often. Only 13 percent of universities of applied sciences consider the level of use of digital analysis methods at their institution to be high or very high. Cf. Gilch et al. (2019).
14 In this regard and in the following cf. Gilch et al. (2019).
15 In 2016 there were 104.750 students enrolled in subjects relating to computer science (Destatis, 2016).
16 See https://data.berkeley.edu/education/courses/data-8 (last accessed on 26 January 2022).
17 See https://www.oec.uzh.ch/de/studies/general/regulations.%20html (last accessed on 26 January 2022).
18 In this regard and in the following, cf. Burk and Hetze (2020).

References

Baumgartner, P., Häfele, H., & Maier-Häfele, K. (2002). *E-Learning Praxishandbuch, Auswahl von Lernplattformen. Marktübersicht, Funktionen, Fachbegriffe.* StudienVerlag.

Burk, M., & Hetze, P. (2020). *Hochschul-Barometer. Lage und Entwicklung der Hochschulen aus Sicht ihrer Leitung, Ausgabe 2020.* Stifterverband für die Deutsche Wissenschaft e.V.

Cardon, D., Cointet, J.-P., & Mazières, A. (2018). La revanche des neurones. *Réseaux, 211*(5), 173–220.

Destatis – Statistisches Bundesamt. (2016). *Studierende an Hochschulen – Fachserie 11 Reihe 4.1 – Wintersemester 2015/2016.* Destatis.

Destatis – Statistisches Bundesamt. (2021). *Studierende an Hochschulen – Fachserie 11 Reihe 4.1 – Wintersemester 2020/2021.* Destatis.

EFI – Expertenkommission Forschung und Innovation. (2016). *Gutachten zu Forschung, Innovation und technologischer Leistungsfähigkeit Deutschlands 2016.* EFI.

EFI – Expertenkommission Forschung und Innovation. (2017). *Gutachten zu Forschung, Innovation und technologischer Leistungsfähigkeit Deutschlands 2017.* EFI.

EFI – Expertenkommission Forschung und Innovation. (2018). *Gutachten zu Forschung, Innovation und technologischer Leistungsfähigkeit Deutschlands 2018.* EFI.

EFI – Expertenkommission Forschung und Innovation. (2019). *Gutachten zu Forschung, Innovation und technologischer Leistungsfähigkeit Deutschlands 2019.* EFI.

EFI – Expertenkommission Forschung und Innovation. (2021). *Gutachten zu Forschung, Innovation und technologischer Leistungsfähigkeit Deutschlands 2021.* EFI.

Gilch, H., Beise, A. S., Krempkow, R., Müller, M., Stratmann, F., & Wannemacher, K. (2019). *Digitalisierung der Hochschulen. Ergebnisse einer Schwerpunktstudie für die Expertenkommission Forschung und Innovation.* Studien zum deutschen Innovationssystem Nr.14-2019. EFI.

IFR – International Federation of Robotics. (2015). *World robotics 2015 – Service robots.* IFR.

Internationale Expertenkommission Exzellenzinitative. (2016). *Internationale Expertenkommission zur Evaluation der Exzellenzinitiative. Endbericht.* IEKE.

Klös, H.-P., & Meinhard, D. B. (2019). *Industrielle Wettbewerbsfähigkeit, Digitalisierung und berufliche Qualifizierung.* IW-Policy Paper.

Licka, P., & Gautschi, P. (2017). *Die digitale Zukunft der Hochschule. Wie sieht sie aus und wie lässt sie sich gestalten?* Berinfor GmbH.

Müller, S., Böhm, M., Krcmar, H., & Welpe, I. (2016). *Machbarkeitsstudie: Geschäftsmodelle in der digitalen Wirtschaft. Studien zum deutschen Innovationssystem.* Nr. 12-2016. EFI.

O'Kane, L., Narasimhan, R., Nania, J., & Taska, B. (2020). *Digitalisation in the German labor market. Analyzing demand for digital skills in job vacancies.* Bertelsmann Stiftung.

Pfeiffer, S., Suphan, A., Zirnig, C., & Kostadinova, D. (2016). *Die digitale Arbeitswelt in Nordrhein-Westfalen heute: Eine deskriptive Untersuchung aus der Sicht der Beschäftigten* [FGW-Impuls Digitalisierung von Arbeit, 1]. Forschungsinstitut für gesellschaftliche Weiterentwicklung e.V. (FGW).

Pongratz, J. (2017). *IT-Architektur für die digitale Hochschule.* Technische Universität München.

Pötzl, M., & Natterer, M. (2018). *Technologietrends in den Bereichen menschenfeindliche Umgebungen, Smart Home, industrielle Produktion und autonome Fahrzeuge.* Studien zum deutschen Innovationssystem. Nr. 17-2018. EFI.

Sander, A., & Wolfgang, M. (2014). *The rise of robotics.* Bcg perspectives.

Schmid, U., Goertz, L., Radomski, S., Thom, S., & Behrens, J. (2017). *Monitor Digitale Bildung. Die Hochschulen im digitalen Zeitalter.* Bertelsmann Stiftung.

Stocksmeier, D., & Hunnius, S. (2018). *OZG-Umsetzungskatalog. Digitale Verwaltungsleistungen im Sinne des Onlinezugangsgesetzes* (1. Auflage). Version 0.98. BMI.

UN DESA – United Nations Department of Economic and Social Affairs. (2016). *UN E-government survey – E-government in support of sustainable development.* UN DESA.

Youtie, J., Porter, A., Shapira, P., Woo, S., & Huang, Y. (2018). *Autonomous systems. A bibliometric and patent analysis.* Studien zum deutschen Innovationssystem. Nr. 14-2018. EFI.

PART 2

Quality

∵

CHAPTER 5

'Positive Mind Monitor'

The Development of a Mental Compass to Enhance Student Wellbeing by Using Data-Feedback

Jessica Nooij, Lieke van Berlo and Lotte J. van Dijk

Abstract

The Avans University of Applied Science is committed to supporting students to acquire the resilience, motivation and persistence needed to engage effectively in complex learning tasks. Approaches to managing stress and responding positively to challenges are also actively developed. These skills are particularly important in times where choices have to be made ever faster and more often, and where uncertainties for students are increasing. To offer support that fits the individual need of a student, the institution developed a data-application that works as a mental compass for students. This tool provides students with insights in their personal needs as well as helping them to understand the causes. It also gives tips on how to deal with those needs and where to find extra support. This chapter documents the process of developing this data-application. Data-feedback techniques are discussed, in particular those that might help students to reflect on their own wellbeing, allow them to actively self-regulate and find help when needed. Thus, we hope to stimulate a process for our students to become more resilient to rapidly changing educational and societal demands and thus enhance their wellbeing.

Keywords

student wellbeing – positive psychology – self-regulation – data-feedback

1   Introduction

In recent years, student wellbeing has become an important and highly discussed topic amongst students, higher education institutions and governmental policy makers in higher education in the Netherlands (Arnsten, 2015). Recent research in the Netherlands has emphasised that student life in general seems to become increasingly challenging and that symptoms and consequences of stress and depression become more common amongst all students (e.g. Dopmeier, 2018, 2021; Dopmeijer, Nuijen, Busch, & Tak, 2021).

Therefore, many higher education institutions want to gain a greater insight in student wellbeing and to make an active contribution to improving student mental health. This motivation is not only focused on preventing problems such as excessive stress, illness, and psychological pressure. Actively improving student wellbeing has shown to be an important aspect in the development of students' social, emotional, and academic competencies (e.g., Noble et al., 2008; Gubbels & Kappe, 2019). Supporting student wellbeing therefore also contributes to study success. In order to improve student wellbeing, it is necessary to first define it and understand the parameters of wellbeing within the general population.

1.1   *Theoretical Background*
A widely shared theoretical idea in relation to the definition of wellbeing is rooted in positive psychology. This approach focuses on positive mental functioning, behaviour that produces growth and is perceived as meaningful and fulfilling (Deci & Ryan, 2008; Ryff, 1989). Jahoda (1958) is widely regarded as the first academic to promote this idea of positive mental health. According to this theory, wellbeing is a continuum with the absence of health (including the prevalence of illness) at one end and complete health at the other. Everyone's health moves along this continuum. Movement is triggered by stress (any kind of negative event or behaviour). The impact that these stressors have on health or wellbeing then depends on the methods (or resources) available to cope with physical, emotional, and social life stressors.

Coping, according to Lazarus et al. (1984, cited in Ganzevoort, 1991), is the ever-changing cognitive and behavioural efforts made to reduce the stressors (internal or external). It involves all behaviours that together are intended to reduce stress. Social support is an important factor that contributes positively to coping by strengthening an individual's resistance and resilience in stressful situations. In addition, social support can directly contribute to wellbeing (Cohen & Syme, 1985, cited in Ganzevoort, 1991).

1.2   *Stress and Coping Amongst Students*
Thus, wellbeing is highly related to perceived stress and the ability to cope adequately with stress. Therefore, these two topics will be discussed from the perspective of student life.

1.2.1   Stress
Entering higher education is a major life transition, which can have a negative impact on wellbeing through heightened levels of stress (Miller, 2016). Stress

results from the challenges associated with higher education, such as, adapting to new roles, challenges and responsibilities. Besides focusing on their study, many students engage in part time work to avoid high study loans, which further contributes to their perceived stress (SER, 2019). High levels of stress, in turn, can have a negative impact on concentration and aspects of memory (e.g., Arnsten, 2015; Diamond et al., 1996; McEwen & Sapolsky, 1995). This can negatively influence study success, thereby heightening stress even further, resulting in a vicious circle due to the perceived consequences of study delay, failure and risks of forced drop-out.

Evidence for high levels of stress among students in the Netherlands comes from various research (e.g., Dopmeier et al., 2013; Dopmeier, 2018, 2021; Gubbels & Kappe, 2019), reporting that high levels of perceived workload, pressure to perform, symptoms of anxiety, depression and burn-out are common amongst all students.

These previous findings were collected prior to the COVID-19 outbreak. More flexible forms of education, with an emphasis on online teaching, were rolled out quickly due to this pandemic, which may have come with a price, knowing that social relationships play an important part in coping with stress.

Indeed, it has become clear in the last year that students, who felt disconnected from their peers because of online teaching and much less offline contact moments, experienced more loneliness, increased mental health problems and higher levels of stress (see report of Caring Universities, Struijs et al., 2020). The first mental health study among students covering the Netherlands as a whole in 2021 confirmed these findings (Dopmeijer, Nuijen, Busch & Tak, 2021).

1.2.2   Coping

According to Huppert (2009, 2014), in order to reduce the burden of stress that students feel nowadays, and the occurrence of mental problems that emerge from this stress, policy needs to deliver a shift in the whole population of students towards positive mental health. Huppert suggests that this can be done by providing students with skills that support positive wellbeing. Such an approach will make students more able to cope with the stressors that they encounter during this period in life. In theory, a very small population shift towards positive mental health might lead to a reduction in the prevalence of common mental problems amongst students, as well as an increase in the percentage of students that thrive in the university environment.

This approach was adopted at Avans University of Applied Sciences. A policy was developed for enhancing student wellbeing. It was aimed at helping students become more resilient to stress by teaching them how to better cope with it. Based on the positive psychological theories, the first step in that learning process is to teach them how to better self-regulate their wellbeing (e.g. Deci & Ryan, 2001; Seligman, 2011). In order to achieve that, we developed a *'positive mind monitor'* for our students. This tool helps students to reflect on their current wellbeing by answering questions about their own perceived wellbeing. These questions are based on multiple underlying aspects of stress and coping. Additionally, the tool provides data-feedback for students with tips on how to work on coping strategies that fit their self-reported, current state of wellbeing. In the next section we describe how we developed this tool.

2   Developing a Positive Mind Monitor

In essence, the idea of the positive mind monitor is as follows. As a student you:
– Measure your current level of resilience;
– Get feedback based on that measurement in the form of advice on topics that you should work on;
– Take a module based on that advice and get more in-depth insight on the current level of resilience on these topics by answering some deepening questions;
– Get information on the topics and information on how to enhance (mental) strength on these topics or where to find more in-depth help/coaching within the university;
– Fill in the mood-tracker as often as possible and learn more about your personal stressors and energizers.

2.1   *Measuring Resilience*

The first step in developing the tool was to decide on the different aspects that measure a student's current level of resilience. That is the amount of stress a student perceives and the strategies they have to cope with it. To decide on the specific aspects of resilience that we integrated in the first version of the tool, we inventoried the suggested aspects by theories of positive psychology and study success. Although there seems to be considerable overlap among all these major theoretical approaches to psychological wellbeing, each scholar has their own preferred list of defining underlying aspects.

In order to determine the bandwidth of our mental compass, we therefore extracted several components that are addressed in almost all those theories in one form or the other. Although we thus aimed at covering what appeared to be the most defining aspects, it is important to note that we did not aim to be complete in the range of underlying aspects that might contribute to a student's resilience. First, because there is still a lot of scientific discussion on the definition and scope of those aspects. Second, because we developed a modular tool, meaning that we first test if the envisioned mechanism works (i.e. stimulating self-regulation of wellbeing by data-feedback) with the use of a few aspects of student's resilience. The amount of aspects can be easily expanded in a later phase, based on the needs of our own student population.

Based on this inventory, we decided to focus on the following aspects of psychological wellbeing in order to strengthen students' resilience to stress during their study. The positive mind monitor aims at giving students insights in their:

– Sense of control and meaning;
– Autonomy in their learning and the choices they make;
– Experience of learning and self-regulation (i.e. feelings of stress or anxiety, mindfulness);
– Motivation (including focus and concentration) and self-esteem;
– Social relationships and sense of belonging;
– Emotional, behavioural and cognitive engagement in their learning success and the collective learning process.

These concepts were translated into questions and scales measuring those aspects. The validated survey contains 50 questions in total. About half of them measure signs of effective coping (e.g. sense of belonging, autonomy, sense of control and meaning) and the other half inventories signs of stress (i.e. negative beliefs, emotions and behaviours). The questions are derived from different validated scales that underlie the theories described above. The derived survey was qualitatively validated in a focus group with students that gave feedback on the comprehensibility and length of the survey. In a quantitative pilot setting, 330 students from Avans University of Applied Science filled in the survey. Through factor analyses and reliability analyses, the structure and reliability of the intended underlying concepts were validated.

2.2   *Reflecting on Mood*

In addition to the resilience measurement in the form of survey questions, the tool also makes it possible for students to reflect on their mood by means of a mood tracker. The mood-tracker is based on the idea that there are two fundamental dimensions of mood (i.e. valence and arousal) (e.g. Fox, Lapate, & Shackman, 2018), that together construct an array of basic moods that students can track in a mood-diary. Students can fill in the mood-tracker as often as they want, but ideally once every day. They can do that by choosing from five smileys depicting their affective mood (how happy are you?) and from five smileys depicting their state of arousal (how agitated are you?). The scores are then translated into one of nine moods (i.e. anxious or angry, troubled, worried, sad, bored, relaxed, content, happy, enthusiastic). If they agree that the constructed mood reflects their actual mood, they can tag reasons that come with the mood from a list of subjects (e.g. study, work, family, friends). Also, they have the chance to make notes. All moods are kept in a diary and students can follow which situations correlate with certain moods.

2.3   Modules and Feedback

The positive mind monitor not only aims at measuring resilience and mood, but also to give students data-based feedback on how they can improve their wellbeing. This by learning which situations and events are perceived as stressful and how they can improve their coping strategies accordingly. To achieve that, we translated the concepts of the resilience measurement into practical modules that are integrated into the tool and aim to stimulate students to actively engage in working on specific topics. To start with, we developed 16 modules that fit into the context of study and life as a student. The topics that are addressed in those modules are:
- Mindfulness;
- Self-esteem;
- Motivation;
- Self-regulation;
- Social relations and integration;
- Study strategies;
- Focus and concentration;
- Performance anxiety;
- Perfectionism;
- Coping as a concept;
- Stressors;
- Defining borders;
- Sleep;
- Lifestyle;
- Health;
- Drug abuse.

The relevance of working on those subjects is advised to a student based on their answers of corresponding questions in the resilience measurement. Thus, every feedback is personally matched to the current state of perceived stress and resilience.

The path through the tool is determined by the student. Students can follow any module that is interesting to them, but ideally they first fill in the resilience survey and then get feedback on which subjects offer them the most chance of growth in wellbeing. Every module has the option for students to get more

FIGURE 5.1
Print screen of the mobile application. On the left side, the tab menu of modules that are advised to be followed are depicted. On the right side, you see the interface of the survey that measures resilience

specific feedback on the topic by answering another short survey on the topic. This way they get more in-depth information on their current state on that topic and can take that into account when following the module with more or less intensity or deciding to make use of extra-curricular course enrolment or coaching on that topic (both offered by the university). As the time that students can spend on those extra-curricular activities is limited, the tool thus helps them to make choices that fit their (current) needs best.

2.4   *Building the Tool*

As mentioned earlier, the positive mind monitor is built in a modular way. Meaning that first the basic functionalities were built and evaluated. From here, other functionalities can be stacked onto the existing tool. For example, the surveys are already implemented, but the mood tracker still needs to be developed and will be implemented with an update of the system in spring 2022. The tool itself also uses building blocks that can be reused when building new functionalities. Making it an application that can keep up with rapid changes in the environment and in research.

The development of the tool is set up as an iterative process. The development of the positive mind monitor started with an idea and a prototype was created as a first solution. This prototype has been tested with real students and the information from the students was analysed and used to improve the tool. The tool is built in such a way that it collects user data, this data is then used as data-input to evaluate the tool and to make constant improvements.

3   Discussion

While the number of applications developed to give feedback based on tracker data is increasing, for example in the form of heartrate trackers or smart sport watches, the use of data-feedback in higher educational learning processes is yet not very common. Nonetheless, the usages of data-feedback for adaptive learning is an upcoming field of knowledge in higher education and research (e.g. Avella et al., 2016; Verbert et al., 2012). The integration of data-feedback in learning is also applied in the positive mind monitor tool.

The primary goal of integrating data-feedback in education is often to improve learning by personalizing and encouraging self-reflection and self-regulation or to use predictive models to prevent negative study outcomes from occurring (e.g. Greller & Drachsler, 2012; Broos et al., 2017). Although the integration of data-feedback into the learning process has great potential in making learning more adaptive to personal needs and thus more effective for the individual, there are also some challenges that need to be taken into account when applying these techniques. Mostly, the discussion of integrating data-feedback as a core aspect in learning evolves around three issues, namely: privacy, data quality, and ethics. These are discussed in the following sections.

3.1   Privacy-by-default and Privacy-by-design

The positive mind monitor is meant to give feedback on something personal, namely how a student thinks and feels about themselves. In order to achieve this, the data need to be of a personal nature. The data we use in the tool is sensitive, as it tells us a lot about a person, and thus we have to make sure that it is solely used for the intended purpose and that the person consents with the way we use it.

Therefore, we applied the principles of privacy-by-default and privacy-by-design to the application. Privacy-by-default means that the strictest privacy settings apply by default, without any manual input necessary from the student. Privacy-by-design states that any processing of personal data is done with data protection and privacy in mind at every step. All decisions we make in building the tool and the data-architecture are tested along those two principles. This means that the data recorded in the tool can only be used to give feedback to the individual student with their own private student login. No other person (e.g. a student coach, teacher or peer) can see the feedback. To see the feedback the student must actively grant access. All access is turned off by default.

The data that we use for general analytics on student wellbeing on an institutional level is anonymous and can only be linked to personal information by using a key-datafile that is kept separate from the recorded data. The use of the key-datafile in order to link personal information to the recorded data works by informed consent only and every consent needs to be registered in the institutions data-processing registry, in accordance with our privacy statement.

3.2   *Data Quality and Ethics*

For the data-feedback to be effective, it is crucial that the data are valid and reliable. Otherwise, errors in feedback might occur and the feedback might even become counterproductive. One of our main goals was to develop a tool of high data-quality. To gain data that is as reliable and valid as possible for our tool, we based the questions and feedback on scientific research and validated the scales methodologically in a pilot amongst the target population. However, as with most data, these data provide only a limited measurement of the student. Therefore, by definition, the data will not provide a complete picture of the student and the feedback contains a certain degree of uncertainty. Therefore, the purpose of the feedback must be carefully considered. How will data-feedback support the student? Will the data-feedback actually provide insight into the factors that are important to student wellbeing? Even though the integration of data-feedback is increasingly being experimented with, little research is available on the impact of specific feedback on student success. It is important to experiment with data-feedback with caution. If not used properly, the information can also backfire.

To make sure that the data-feedback is not the only feedback that our students get on their wellbeing, we integrated the tool into our coaching-trajectory for students. Our teachers and coaches are being trained to interpret and talk about the data-feedback of the positive mind monitor and to make it a topic in their coaching conversations with students. Every student has these conversations at least twice per year, and more often if needed. Students are also actively encouraged to discuss the data-feedback with their study coach as part of the communication strategy and tutorial that comes with the positive mind monitor.

To uphold high data-quality and feedback, we will continue to investigate the way students interact with the tool, evaluate the impact that it has on student success and constantly adapt it in accordance with those insights (see Campbell et al., 2007; Clow 2012, 2013, on the importance of such a cyclic approach in integrating data-feedback into the learning process). In this way, we hope not only to maintain high data-quality, but also to gain more insights in the contribution that such data-feedback can make in teaching students to deal with stress and ever changing demands of modern student life.

4   Conclusion

In this chapter we introduced a novel tool for students to reduce stress and prevent the occurrence of mental problems during their study. The positive mind monitor is based on the theoretical idea of positive mental health and provides students insight in their personal needs as well as helping them to understand the causes. It also gives tips on how to deal with those needs and where to find extra support.

The use of data-feedback in the study context is yet not very common and evidence of the impact on student learning is scant (e.g. Lim, Gašević, Matcha, Ahmad Uzir, & Dawson, 2021). The positive mind monitor is a first step for our university to research the possibilities of data-feedback in helping students learn the skills necessary to enhance their wellbeing. As the monitor is designed to collect data, it is well suited to study how students interact with the application and, based on repeated within-subject measurements, to evaluate the effects of the offered self-regulatory information on wellbeing. The modular design also enables us to keep up with changes in the environment and new insights from data-analytics and research. It helps us to gain better insight in the challenges of implementing data-based technology as an important means for self-regulated learning in higher education, and the organizational structure needed to do so in a responsible way.

The positive mind monitor herewith offers a strong foundation to do necessary empirical research on the impact such an application has on students' coping skills and to investigate if and how the intended effects on resilience and stress reduction can be realized.

References

Arnsten, A. F. (2015). Stress weakens prefrontal networks: Molecular insults to higher cognition. *NatNeurosci, 18*(10), 1376–1385.

Avella, J. T., Nunn, S., Kanai, T., & Kebritchi, M. (2016). Learning analytics methods, benefits, and challenges in higher education: A systematic literature review. *Online Learning, 20*(2).

Campbell, J. P., DeBlois, P. B., & Oblinger, D. (2007). Academic analytics: A new tool for a new era. *EDUCAUSE Review, 42*(4), 40–57.

Clow, D. (2012). The learning analytics cycle: Closing the loop effectively. In *Proceedings of the 2nd international conference on learning analytics and knowledge* (pp. 134–138). ACM.

Clow, D. (2013). An overview of learning analytics. *Teaching in Higher Education, 18*(6), 683–695.

Deci, E. L., & Ryan, R. M. (2008). Hedonia, eudaimonia, and well-being: An introduction. *Journal of Happiness Studies, 9*.

Diamond, D. M., Fleshner, M., Ingersoll, N., & Rose, G. (1996). Psychological stress impairs spatial working memory: Relevance to electrophysiological studies of hippocampal function. *Behavioral Neuroscience, 110*(4), 661–672.

Dopmeijer, J. M. (2018) *Factsheet Onderzoek Studieklimaat, gezondheid en studiesucces 2017* [Report]. https://www.iso.nl/wp-content/uploads/2018/04/Factsheet_Onderzoek_Studieklimaat_april2018.pdf

Dopmeijer, J. M. (2021). *Running on empty: The impact of challenging student life on wellbeing and academic performance.* University of Amsterdam.

Dopmeijer, J. M., Schoorel, B., & Schwartz, D. (2013). *Project #FIVE Studentenonderzoek 2012. Feiten en cijfers over uitval, vertraging, gezondheid en veiligheid* [Report]. Hogeschool Windesheim.

Fox, A. S., Lapate, R. C., Shackman, A. J., & Davidson, R. J. (2018). *The nature of emotion: Fundamental questions.* Oxford University Press.

Ganzevoort, R. R. (1991). Context, coping en zingeving. In T. G. I. M. Andree, P. D. D. Steegman, H. J. Tieleman, & J. Visser (Eds.), *Levensvragen in sociaal-wetenschappelijk perspectief.* Utrecht, U.U.

Greller, W., & Drachsler, H. (2012). Translating learning into numbers: A generic framework for learning analytics. *Educational Technology & Society, 15*(3), 42–57.

Gubbels, N., & Kappe, F. R. (2019). *Studentenwelzijn 2017–2018. Resultaten kwantitatief en kwalitatief onderzoek naar het welzijn van studenten van Hogeschool Inholland.* Lectoraat Studiesucces, Hogeschool Inholland.

Huppert, F. A. (2014). The state of wellbeing science: Concepts, measures, interventions, and policies. In F. A. Huppert & C. L. Cooper (Eds.), *Interventions and policies to enhance wellbeing. Wellbeing: A complete reference guide* (Vol. 6, pp. 1–49). John Wiley & Sons Ltd.

Huppert, F. A., & Ruggieri, K. (2017). Controversies in wellbeing: Confronting and resolving the challenges. In D. Bhugra, K. Bhul, S. Wong, & S. Gillman (Eds.), *Oxford textbook of public mental health.* Oxford University Press, Oxford.

Huppert, F. A., & So, T. T. (2013). Flourishing across Europe: Application of a new conceptual framework for defining well-being. *Social Indicators Research, 110*(3), 837–861.

Jahoda, M. (1958). *Current concepts of positive mental health.* Basic Books.

Lim, L., Gašević, D., Matcha, W., AhmadUzir, N., & Dawso, S. (2021). Impact of learning analytics feedback on self-regulated learning: Triangulating behavioural logs with students' recall. In *LAK21: 11th International Learning Analytics and Knowledge conference (LAK21).* ACM.

McEwen B. S., & Sapolsky, R. M. (1995). Stress and cognitive function. *Current Opinion in Neurobiology, 5*(2), 205–216.

Miller, T. W. (2016). Coping with life transitions. In J. C. Norcross, G. R. VandenBos, D. K. Freedheim, & N. Pole (Eds.), *APA handbook of clinical psychology: Psychopathology and health* (pp. 477–490). American Psychological Association.

Ryff, C. D. (1989). Happiness is everything, or is it? Explorations on the meaning of psychological well-being. *Journal of Personality and social psychology, 57*(6).

Seligman, M. E. P. (2011). *Flourish: A visionary new understanding of happiness and wellbeing.* Free Press.

SER. (2019). *Hoge verwachtingen, kansen en belemmeringen voor jongeren in 2019.*
Sociaal-Economische Raad.

Struijs, S. (2020). *De geestelijke gezondheid van studenten tijdens de COVID-19 pandemie. De eerste voorlopige data uit het Caring Universities consortium.* Rapport Caring
Universities, VU Amsterdam.

Verbert, K., Manouselis, N., Drachsler, H., & Duval, E. (2012). Dataset-driven research to
support learning and knowledge analytics. *Educational Technology & Society, 15*(3),
133–148.

CHAPTER 6

An Evidence-Based Framework for Transforming Higher Education Programs and Processes

Victor M. H. Borden and Seonmi Jin

Abstract

Emerging analytic methods and technologies are transforming approaches to evidence-based practice in higher education institutions. Several critics have noted that these methods, and especially predictive analytics, have serious limitations that are often overlooked and so perpetuate inequities in practice. This chapter provides a framework for designing and implementing evidence-informed transformations within higher education institutions using techniques that have emerged from a focus on equitable, impactful applied research. It was developed as part of an institutional transformation project that seeks to leverage the institutions advanced expertise and technologies for accessing, analysing, and visualizing data from traditional (structured) and emerging (transactional) big data systems.

Keywords

evidence-based practice – applied research – triangulation – learning analytics

1   Introduction

Big data, artificial intelligence (AI), and predictive analytics are among the most significant technologies that promise to provide educators with new approaches to enhance and reform higher education. There is growing acknowledgment that, while they are powerful tools, big data, artificial intelligence, and predictive analytics do not provide "silver bullet" answers to the seemingly intractable issues that face higher education institutions (HEIs) given their nature as complex, multi-mission, institutions that serve objectives that defy simple quantification. While some have characterized higher education resistance to new technologies as a general resistance to change, others note that effective use of such technologies requires significant organizational capacity development that entails more collaborative working relationships among traditionally siloed academic and administrative support programs, optimizing feedback to enable student agency and responsibility in the learning process, an organizational culture of inquiry, and attention to social justice and equity (Zilvinskis & Borden, 2017).

Higher education, like all public- and private-sector industries, is increasingly dependent on technological innovation to sustain, if not enhance organizational effectiveness. Although higher education has been pegged as an industry with relatively high resistance to change (Blin & Munro 2008; Caruth & Caruth, 2013; Chandler, 2013), other accounts demonstrate that the industry has been changing relatively rapidly in recent decades (Marshall, 2011; McRoy & Gibbs, 2009). The reality is that the sector is both resistant to change and responds as needed to change, as noted by Scobey (2018), "It's undeniable that academics and academic institutions can be virtuosos of inaction ... [y]et it is equally true that the past thirty years have been an era of broad, deep, and often unremarked innovation". These sentiments were recently underscored through the sector's rapid response to the COVID-19 worldwide pandemic that required virtually all higher education institutions to quickly reinvent their teaching and support processes to sustain operations.

This chapter provides a framework for designing and implementing evidence-informed transformations within higher education institutions. It was developed as part of an institutional transformation project that seeks to leverage the institutions advanced expertise and technologies for accessing, analysing, and visualizing data from traditional (structured) and emerging (transactional) big data systems. The framework is motivated by several noted limitations of predictive analytics and artificial intelligence and its tenets are synthesized from three inter-related lines of academic and practical literature related to conducting actionable, change-focused research in HEIs specifically, but more generally for large, complex service industries and sectors, like health, government, and non-profit, social and community development organizations. The strands each encompass a range of models that use varying terminology and are referred to in this paper as "actionable research", "research triangulation", and "transdisciplinarity".

The framework presented in this chapter was developed around the practical objectives of a large, public research university in the Midwestern United Status. Like many such institutions, the focus institution has a very large and relatively well-resourced information services infrastructure, with enterprise transactional systems used within processes related to instruction (course management systems; vendor products to promote learning and student collaboration; advanced technology teaching and learning tools and resources);

research (internationally networked library and research information systems; internal research administration and development systems) and service (large customer relation management systems; state-wide data systems tracking citizens from schooling through workforce). In addition to the administrative service organizations that generally support the planning, implementation, assessment and improvement processes of the institution, large research universities also have an abundance of subject matter, technical, and leadership expertise within their faculty ranks as well as within their highly professionalized administrative units.

The framework was labelled the "Insight Engine" to fit within the education technologies (Ed Tech) vernacular of emerging platforms and systems that use big data, machine learning, artificial intelligence, which are now proliferating within higher education institutions. It is intended to help create more permeable bridges between scholarly, pedagogical, research, and technical expertise of the academic staff and the increasing array of operations managed by advanced professional staff in information technologies, institutional research and assessment, instructional design, student counselling and advising that support the educational mission of the institution.

The Insight Engine is built around the concept of triangulation in applied research. More specifically it revolves around connecting traditional institutional research analyses that employ data from structured quantitative sources (student records, surveys, assessment instruments) with analyses that employ transactional learning data or learning analytics (data gleaned from institutional course management systems) and qualitative forms of evidence obtained through interviews, focus groups, non-participant observation and ethnographic research or thick data to assess and improve educational practices and policies.

Whereas most implementations of triangulation models focus on the types of data and methods used, the Insight Engine equally emphasizes the "triangulation of interpretation" through collaboration among scholars, practitioners, and organizational officers concerned with efforts to transform or improve aspects of the university environment and its operations. Within the US context, this necessarily includes those charged with improving the institution's climate for diversity, equity, inclusion, and justice (DEIJ) as institutions acknowledge that students are becoming increasingly diverse across social, economic, and academic dimensions. Involvement by both scholarly and practical experts helps institutional staff better understand and develop plausible explanations (theory) behind phenomena through empirical research, practical experience, and deliberate attention to dismantling structural inequities that have prevented members of historically excluded groups from accessing and succeeding at colleges and universities.

The framework was initially motivated by concepts put forward by O'Neil (2016) and Wang (2016). In her book, Weapons of Math Destruction, O'Neil (2016) notes that the algorithms underlying big data, AI, and predictive analytic applications are encoded forms of human bias that perpetuate the inequities of the past because they are opaque, unregulated, and difficult to contest. Consequently, she suggests that they should be made more transparent, regulated, and contestable. In a similar vein, Wang (2016) chronicles how inattention to the nuances of human experience revealed through ethnographic and other qualitative methodologies led to the downfall of a company. Specifically, the leadership's devotion to predictive analytics and unwillingness to accept findings from ethnographic or "thick data" due to small sample size, prevented the company from seeing that smart phones would make flip phones obsolete. She describes the problem as an overreliance on quantitative analysis of large datasets that requires normalizing them and so stripping them of their human context. Wang proposes that combining big data with thick data solves this problem.

Starting from these motivating concepts, the framework was developed and refined through an analysis of the literature and as pilot projects were developed and implemented as part of a university-wide institutional transformation project funded by a philanthropic organization. Every public and private institution in the state were offered funds, scaled to their size to, "... engage in thoughtful discernment about the future of their institutions and advance strategic planning and implementation efforts to address key challenges and opportunities". As one of the two large public research universities in the state, the philanthropic organization made $5 million USD available to the focus institution for the project.

The Insight Engine was incorporated into the project proposal as an evidence-based infrastructure to advance transformations in three key areas: college readiness – working with secondary school partners to improve college readiness and the transition to college; career readiness – integrating career development into early college advising and first-year classes; and college completion – engaging instructional and professional staff in targeted improvement of key areas of early college curricula (e.g., mathematics requirements for science, engineering and health majors; first-year writing requirements) and key support services (e.g., participants in a state "promise scholarship" program targeted for low-income, first generation, and historically excluded student populations).

2   Literature Review

The framework proposed in this chapter is drawn from three inter-related lines of research that focus on how to make research more useful and usable for organizational and societal change. Different terms have been used to describe these three lines that are here labelled: actionable research; research triangulation; and transdisciplinary research.

2.1   *Actionable Research*

Several models have been proposed to increase the usefulness and impact of research conducted within applied organizational settings. This section describes two models that emerged specifically from research within the higher education sector, followed by two more general perspectives.

Hansen and Borden (2006) trace the historical roots of action research in higher education to the seminal applied research work conducted by Margaret Mead, Kurt Lewin and colleagues during World War II, related to such issues as getting the public to increase use of organ meats when more traditional beef, poultry, and pork products were diverted to feed the troops overseas (Romm, 2014). Although the general idea of making research more actionable remains prevalent, there have been many critiques about its application often related to maintaining suitable levels of rigor in observational (in contrast to experimental) methods, and the loss of rigor that occurs when individuals without formal training are involved in the conduct of research.

St. John and Wilkerson (2006) edited a volume of New Directions in Institutional Research that sought to move away from "paradigmatic research that has vague implications for practice" to "conducting applied studies that can be used to inform faculty and administrators about and engage them in the process of changing their institutions by enabling and encouraging them to experiment with new approaches to their most critical challenges" (p. 1). The chapters of this volume include discussion of the general weak rigor of institutional studies intended to guide critical change decisions (Patton et al., 2006; Braxton et al., 2006) and of structural inequities that are supported by theories and constructs that emerge from research on traditional, dominant culture-students in traditional college settings. The proposed solutions, labelled as "action research" (Hansen & Borden, 2006) and "action inquiry" (St. John et al., 2006; Mousoba, 2006), promote collaborative, rigorous approaches employing well-constructed, workable designs to examine educational processes and practices within their natural contexts. Although triangulation is not specifically a focus of this volume, the chapters describe multi-stage, multi-method examples that include components of triangulation.

Bensimon et al. (2004) take a different approach to impactful applied research in higher education settings. They note that the gap between research and practice is due to the traditional methods of knowledge production and dissemination. They describe as a point of departure the "Practitioner as Researcher" model in which expert researchers model variables that place

people into categories for comparison. They argue that this approach is dehu-
manizing and ultimately leads to criteria evaluation against which membership
within various groups (for example racial/ethnic categories; income categories)
are established and ranked. They further note that the typically quantitative
methods employed in this approach do not provide actionable information for
any specific context and do not pertain to the realities experienced by participants. Building off Reason and Bradbury's (2003) characterization of actionable research as a participatory and democratic process to develop practical
uses, they suggest as an alternative the "Practitioner-as-Researcher" model that
incorporates elements of community, collaborative, and participatory action
research. Within this model, the role of the professional researcher shifts from
designing and executing research to consultant/facilitator for the practitioners
who conduct the research. They liken their approach to St. John et al.'s (2006)
action inquiry model that designs the research more directly around the needs
of the intended users (change decision makers).

Brough and Hawkes (2018) more generally describe five essential ingredients for impactful, applied research, regardless of its area of application: (1)
use of multiple, reliable, and valid measures; (2) sufficient and generalizable
samples; (3) theoretical sophistication; (4) a sufficient basis for causal generali-
zations; and (5) practical implications for the likely users of the research. They
further describe an "intervention research approach" that includes a formal
needs assessment, design and implementation of an intervention, and assessment of the impact of that intervention on performance. Although primarily
focusing on the research process itself and not the practical use or impact of
research, they posit that researchers who pay sufficient attention to the five
key ingredients "will take the correct steps to ensure their research project is
appropriately designed and actually does have some form of external impact"
(p. 12).

Intervention research has been studied within the realm of social work (for
example, Fraser et al., 2009), health applications (for example, Gluud, 2006),
as well as in higher education (Soicher et al., 2020). This approach is also allied
with a more comprehensive approach to actionable research know as implementation science, defined as, "the scientific study of methods to promote the
systematic uptake of research findings into routine clinical practice ..." (ICE-
BeRG, 2006, p. 1). Intervention research focuses on the exploration through
initial research and analysis of an issue or problem that serves as a barrier to
desired outcomes, identifying potential program and process changes that,
according to empirical research, have promise for reducing the problem or
improving performance, and testing the efficacy of that treatment through
experimental or quasi-experimental methods. Penuel et al. (2011) advocate

for "design-based implementation research", to improve educational practices through coordination and collaboration among interdisciplinary teams of researchers and practitioners.

The models and studies noted above are just a small sampling of approaches to applied research that focus on making the results of such research actionable to support organizational improvement. The language and precise nature of the approaches vary according to the disciplinary origins (psychological/ cognitive, economic, sociological, anthropological, etc.) and the applied setting (health, education, public administration, business etc.). The next section of the chapter considers the construct of research triangulation that is common to many of these approaches, followed by a discussion of transdisciplinary research as an approach to problem solving within organizations, institutions, and societies.

2.2   *Triangulation in Applied Research*

Triangulation is a common element of the examples from the literature noted above and other treatments of the topic of applied research related to complex human problems and organizations. The impetus for triangulation is connected to the limitations inherent in any specific research approach that are overcome by using multiple methods and data sources, or as Patton (1999) has noted, "multiple methods of data collection and analysis provide more grist for the research mill" (p. 1192).

The term "triangulation" more commonly appears within the realms of qualitative or mixed methods research and program evaluation research. However, it's roots have been linked to the development of classic quantitative methods. Specifically, Mathison (1988) traces the development of triangulation methods in the social sciences to Campbell and Fiske's (1959) "multitrait-multimethod" approach to validation, which involves the use of multiple, independent assessments of an outcome or trait. As Campbell and Fiske note in their seminal article, such triangulation is a feature of validity research because, "validation is typically convergent, a confirmation by independent measurement procedures" (p. 81). Webb et al. (1966) introduced the label "triangulation" in their classic volume, Unobtrusive Measures. Denzin (1978) subsequently elaborated, describing four types of triangulation: data triangulation (across space, time, and person); investigator triangulation; theory triangulation; and methodological triangulation.

Patton (1999) distinguished similarly between four types of triangulation, with a notable adaptation to data triangulation. Beyond collecting data in different contexts, at different times and from different people as Denzin describes, Patton argues that data triangulation also requires incorporating different forms of data, across both quantitative (behavioural, affective, cognitive) and qualitative (interviews, observations, and documents) forms. Moreover, Patton's treatment of the subject focuses on the credibility and "methodological respectability" of research findings, not just their validity.

Using Denzin's four types as a point of departure, Mathison (1988) first notes that only three of the types – data; method; and investigator – are practical because, as Denzin notes in his original article, theoretical triangulation is problematic if not impossible. Mathison's analysis challenges the assumption that triangulation generally provides clear and consistent findings. Rather, she notes, "triangulation results in convergent, inconsistent, and contradictory evidence that must be rendered sensible by the researcher or evaluator" (p. 13). She describes levels of evidence required to construct plausible explanations of the phenomena being studied, including, "the data at hand ... a holistic understanding of the project itself, its history, the intentions of the developers, the ongoing relationships within the project, and so on. She also notes the contributions to interpretation and sense-making offered by the evaluator, including their methodological and broad subject matter knowledge.

Triangulation processes in interpretation and decision-making require consideration of how participants make sense of and act upon the environment within which applied evaluation research occurs. Higher education institutions are somewhat unique as a sector for this type of sensemaking because many of the participants are formally trained across a broad spectrum of disciplines that vary considerably in their approaches to inquiry and interpretation. On the one hand, this provides a particularly rich resource for interpretive (and even possibly theoretical) triangulation. On the other hand, differences in epistemology, preferences, and experience, often make it difficult to reach consensus.

2.3   Transdisciplinary Research

Transdisciplinary research (TR) has been proposed as an approach to making research useful within situations "when knowledge about a societally relevant problem field is uncertain, when the concrete nature of problems is disputed, and when there is a great deal at stake for those concerned by problems and involved in dealing with them (Pohl & Hadorn, 2007, p. 20). TR was formulated as one pole a spectrum: disciplinary-multidisciplinary-interdisciplinary-transdisciplinary.

Hoffmann-Rein et al. (2007) describe its emergence as an effort to bridge the large gap between the disciplinary cultures of academic knowledge production in the academy and the use of that knowledge to address complex real-world problems.

Multidisciplinary research is a form of triangulation since it involves using multiple methodologies and data sources and types. Interdisciplinary research takes this a step further with participants integrating their methods, tools, and findings. Another term, "convergence research" was coined for when the research produces "a comprehensive synthetic framework for tackling scientific and societal challenges that exist at the interfaces of multiple fields" (National Research Council, 2014, p. 1). As the pole of this spectrum, transdisciplinary research, "integrates the natural, social and health sciences in a humanities context, and transcends their traditional boundaries" (Choi & Pak, 2007 p. 351). Choi and Pak characterize the differences along the spectrum using the common terms additive (multidisciplinary), interactive (interdisciplinary), and holistic (transdisciplinary).

Transdisciplinary research and the disciplinary to transdisciplinary spectrum provide scaffolding for the triangulation of interpretation processes required to make effective use of evidence within a complex organizational setting. Within the highly discipline-structured world of academia, it is useful to create frameworks that accept the contributions of disciplinary research while promoting insights derived through integration and synthesis. This allows for more in-depth understanding of issues within their specific context.

3   The Insight Engine Framework

As noted earlier, the Insight Engine (IE) was developed as part of a practical institutional transformation project. The project's steering group was comprised of the three executive vice presidents and their senior associates from within a large, public, multi-campus university. The steering group set several broad parameters for the project, specifically that it addresses issues related to the core undergraduate teaching and learning mission; take advantage of the institution's advanced information and analytic capacities and resources, and help the institution transform key policies and practices to better serve the state and its citizens in the emerging social and economic climate. The detailed project plans were developed through a series of discussions among the managers and directors of key university systems and services, as well as the professional staff and faculty involved in institutional research and assessment across the campuses of the institution.

The project was planned in the months immediately prior to the COVID-19 worldwide pandemic when expectations of declining demographics and increased diversity among the college-age cohort, along with increased competition from alternative providers, were seen as the most pressing challenges. With the pandemic's outbreak during development, the need for accelerating transformation was further underscored.

Figure 6.1 portrays the original representation of the Insight Engine from the project proposal, showing the triangulation of emerging analytic and AI

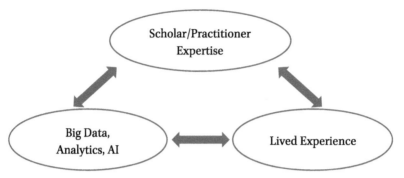

FIGURE 6.1   Initial Insight Engine Framework

technologies (big data) with ethnographic research on the lived experience (thick or rich data), designed, interpreted, and acted on by teams of scholarly and practical experts.

Figure 6.2 presents a more elaborate depiction of triangulation within the Insight Engine Framework. Specifically, the figure identifies three formal types of triangulation most identified as necessary for impactful research: triangulation of data sources, methods, and interpreters. Within the current project, interpreters include investigators or other subject matter and methodology experts, practitioners, and the "voices" of the individuals who are the targets of the research as well as institutional leadership for diversity, equity, and inclusion efforts. Because the project requires communication with individuals across a range of organizational roles, including for example, disciplinary faculty, administrative leadership, academic advisors, and career service staff, as well as collaborating partners from secondary schools and school districts, shorthand labels are used in a less than precise way to convey the types of different methods, data sources and interpreters involved the project.

In practice the Insight Engine provides scaffolding that can be adapted to each of its applications. This chapter concludes with examples of three project initiatives that demonstrate how the broad framework guided the development and implementation of specific transformation activities.

4   Example Applications

4.1   *Example 1: The Summer Academy for Curricular Analysis and Improvement*

Given limited time constraints, participating teams for the first implementation of this component of the project were solicited from the chief academic officers of each campus of the university. Each of the five regional campus selected

	Component	Description	Insight Engine		
			Expert Panels	Ethnographic Research	Analytics/Analysis
College Readiness	Pipeline Model	Work with HS partners to leverage K12, College, State Workforce data systems to assess and improve college/career readiness			
	K12 Collaborations	Expand K12 Outreach through collaborative partnerships that prepare students for college	K12 Engagement; student development; educational leadership; school improvement	K12 student and staff experience w/focus on career and college readiness	Unizin Data Platform
	K12 Engagement Inventory	Document engagements with K12 Sector using Collaboratory Platform			Learning Analytics
Career Readiness	Career Development	Infuse career development into early late high school/early college advising and guidance	Career counseling and development; career services; career networking; communications and networking platforms	IU student experience as related to career selection, and job pursuit	Traditional analysis of administrative records
	Career Services	Expand use and usefulness of career service technologies and in-person services			Linking data across state systems for longitudinal tracking
College Success	Curricular Analysis and Improvement	Identify and guide strategic instructor/staff curricular improvement teams	Learning and performance analytics, curriculum enhancement, student support design	IU faculty and student experience with curriculum with focus on underserved group differences	Needs, program and outcomes assessment support
	Support Service Improvement	Focus on state promise scholarship recipients (low-income, first generation) at regional campuses			

FIGURE 6.2   The Insight Engine as infrastructure to the overall transformation project

one project and two were identified from the two large campuses of the institution. A steering committee was assembled from among university professional staff with responsibilities for teaching and learning development (including instructional designers and program managers), teaching and learning technologies, and institutional research and assessment operations. The nine teams represented a range of curricular focuses, but mostly included introductory courses that were requirements for popular, work-force relevant majors (business, health, science, and technologies) but had large differences in successful completion rates between dominant culture students and students from historically excluded groups (e.g., racial/ethnic minorities and low-income).

Staff participation was incentivized through summer funding by providing teams with consultants and research support chosen to match team needs. The teams were provided guidance and both research and project development support to first investigate in more detail the nature of the problem or issue they were addressing, and to identify potential improvement strategies. The team support staff conducted literature/practice reviews and implemented a series of analyses and dashboards to help the improvement teams explore their issues and identify possible improvement strategies. The teams presented intervention research action plans at the end of the summer and have been conducting those studies during the ensuing academic year with the results reported to each campus' academic administration leadership (projects were reaching this point as this chapter was written).

Teams were encouraged to employ both quantitative and qualitative methods in their assessments. Assessments included analytical dashboards developed using data from the institution's student systems; within class learning analytics using transactional data derived from the institutions course management system; surveys of student perceptions at the start and end of target classes; and ethnographic methods for better understanding how students experience these classes and programs. Strategies adopted by teams included some very simple policy changes, like allowing students to retake exams, supplemental instruction, and "TILTing" the curriculum (making the objectives and tactics of the classes more transparent to the students). Other teams used comparative analyses to first understand how a particular course or course sequence was taught at each campus, and then to identify differences in approaches as related to differences in outcomes (for example, why some classes had common pass rates for minority and majority students while others had large performance gaps).

Formative feedback from the first year from both participants and the expert consultants involved in the process has led to several changes in design for the second-year implementation of this program. Planned improvements include a series of training modules that provide participants with more structured learning opportunities for engaging in such assessment efforts. With more time available to select project teams for the next iteration, project staff have been conferring with academic leadership groups (e.g., Deans' Councils) on each campus to describe the effort and ask for assistance in identifying areas for prospective improvement for which there are staff interested and available to pursue these investigations and improvements.

4.2   Example 2: Promise Scholar Support

The second example focuses on support services provided to students who participate in the state's "promise scholarship" program. There is significant variation in how state promise scholarship programs operate. The focus state's program enlists financially in need students in middle and high school, providing them with the promise of full public college tuition support if they maintain suitable grades and graduate high school. In recent years, several requirements have been added for maintaining the full scholarship. While in college, the scholars must complete full course loads and also attend two career development activities each year. The two large campuses of the focus institution provide intensive support to these scholars, including both additional financial support (e.g., living costs at one campus; books and computer equipment at both) as well as intensive academic support services (tutoring, advising and coaching). However, the smaller, regional campuses, which have a larger proportion of such scholars (although smaller numbers), have been struggling to provide these students the level of support they need since, despite financial support, these students are often less well prepared for college courses compared to their more affluent peers.

To address these issues, the project proceeded with two lines of inquiry. The first, already completed, is a qualitative assessment of the services offered to regional campus scholars as compared to those offered on the two large campuses. The second, currently in development, is a scholar tracking dashboard that shows the success and failure rates of scholars in relation to their individual, academic program, enrolment, and campus characteristics. These analyses are being conducted by project staff for the campus leadership team that work with the staff on each campus who manage supports for these students (typically one person at each regional campus). The project has reserved a pool of money to act on the findings of this research with the only stipulation being that project staff work with service staff to formatively evaluate the activities that are undertaken to promote fidelity and assess effectiveness.

4.3   Example 3: The Pipeline Analysis

The Pipeline Model identified in Figure 6.2 refers to a project that takes advantage of a state government resource that one of the university's research centres maintains which combines data from that state's public K12, postsecondary, and workforce tracking systems. Because of inadequacies in the K12 portion of that system the project sought to work directly with several K12 partners to improve the source information so as to provide more useful feedback reports to the high school. Under the current system, high school teachers and administrators cannot disaggregate or analyse these outcomes according to their programmatic efforts. Through the collaboration, high school partners can assess whether programs they have developed to improve college readiness and success have been effective.

During initial work on this project, staff discovered a separate research centre at the university that works with K12 partner school districts to improve their data systems using the "Ed-Fi" standard.[1] The project forged a collaboration between these two centres that promises to provide a rich data system for improving the granularity and usefulness of the pipeline model data. Colleagues from these centres are also working with relevant state government agencies to improve the tracking platform for use by all K12, higher education, and economic and workforce development groups.

5   Conclusion

The Insight Engine framework was developed as part of a project funded by a philanthropic organization to improve the capacity for higher education institutions throughout the state to improve access to and outcomes of higher education programs. The approach supported by the framework was intended as a way to effectively use the project funds, but also as an organizational development strategy, to more effectively use the institution's own inherent capacities to address strategically critical areas of improvement.

In closing, we consider how this approach compares to more common institutional research and assessment practices at large universities where, As Elken and Vukasovic (2019) note, terms like "loose coupling" and the "garbage-can model" of decision making are used to describe the often ambiguous, complex, and nonlinear nature of higher education administration and management. Within this environment, the application and investigation of mission critical activities and their outcomes is often fragmented and only as loosely coordinated as the institutions is coupled.

At the time this chapter was written, U.S. postsecondary enrolments had experienced their third consecutive year of decline due to a combination of demographic changes and the proliferation of lower cost, more accessible forms of online instruction and training. The COVID-19 pandemic has accelerated the decline and also narrowed the gap between the perceived higher quality of in-person education as compared to online courses and programs. As countries emerge from this unprecedented world-wide transformation, there will be long-lasting implications for how the higher education sector responds and how specific institutions adapt. Levine and Van Pelt (2021) argue that higher education is at a point of profound transformation that can be likened to what the film and record industry faced within the last 30 years, when technologies completely transformed their industry. For the United States, this disruption is compounded by flat or slightly declining demographic population trends.

The Insight Engine, and more generally the strategic approach to academic research and development described in this chapter, provides a framework for advancing the capacities of a large, public university using by leveraging its own capacities and resources and directing them systematically to objectives that the university community can readily support having the highest quality programs and services attainable using its own considerable capacities and resources.

Note

1   https://www.ed-fi.org/

References

Bensimon, E. M., Polkinghorne, D. E., Bauman, G. L., & Vallejo, E. (2004). Doing research that makes a difference. *The Journal of Higher Education*, 75(1), 104–126.

Blin, F., & Munro, M. (2008). Why hasn't technology disrupted academics' teaching practices? Understanding resistance to change through the lens of activity theory. *Computers & Education*, 50(2), 475–490.

Braxton, J. M., McKinney, J. S., & Reynolds, P. J. (2006). Cataloguing institutional efforts to understand and reduce college student departure. *New Directions for Institutional Research*, 2006, 25–32.

Brough, P., & Hawkes, A. (2018). Designing impactful research. In P. Brough (Ed.), *Advanced research methods for applied psychology: Design, analysis, and reporting* (pp. 7–14). Routledge.

Campbell, D. T., & Fiske, D. W. (1959). Convergent and discriminant validation by the multitrait-multimethod matrix. *Psychological Bulletin, 56*(2), 81.

Carnevale, A. P. (2008). College for all? *Change: The Magazine of Higher Learning, 40*(1), 22–31.

Caruth, G. D., & Caruth, D. L. (2013). Understanding resistance to change: A challenge for universities. *Turkish Online Journal of Distance Education, 14*(2), 12–21.

Chandler, N. (2013). Braced for turbulence: Understanding and managing resistance to change in the higher education sector. *Management, 3*(5), 243–251.

Choi, B. C., & Pak, A. W. (2006). Multidisciplinarity, interdisciplinarity and transdisciplinarity in health research, services, education and policy: 1. Definitions, objectives, and evidence of effectiveness. Clinical and investigative medicine. *Medecine clinique et experimentale, 29*(6), 351–364.

Daniel, B. K. (2016). *Big data and learning analytics in higher education.* Springer.

Denzin, M. K. (1978). *The research act: A theoretical introduction to sociological methods.* McGraw-Hill.

Elken, M., & Vukasovic, M. (2019). The looseness of loose coupling: The use and misuse of "loose coupling" in higher education research. *Theory and Method in Higher Education Research, 5*, 53–71

Fraser, M. W., Richman, J. M., Galinsky, M. J., & Day, S. H. (2009). *Intervention research: Developing social programs.* Oxford University Press.

Gluud, L. L. (2006). Bias in clinical intervention research. *American Journal of Epidemiology, 163*(6), 493–501.

Hansen, M. J., & Borden, V. M. H. (2006). Using action research to support academic program improvement. In E. P. St. John & M. Wilkerson (Eds.), *Reframing persistence research to improve academic success. New Directions for Institutional Research, 130*, 47–62.

Hoffmann-Riem, H., Biber-Klemm, S., Grossenbacher-Mansuy, W., Hadorn, G. H., Joye, D., Pohl, C., Weismann, U., & Zemp, E. (2008). Idea of the handbook. In G. H. Hadorn et al. (Eds.), *Handbook of transdisciplinary research* (Vol. 10, pp. 3–17). Springer.

Hout, M. (2012). Social and economic returns to college education in the United States. *Annual Review of Sociology, 38*, 379–400.

Improved Clinical Effectiveness through Behavioural Research Group (ICEBeRG). (2006). Designing theoretically-informed implementation interventions. *Implementation Science, 1*(1), 4.

Levine, A., & Van Pelt, S. J. (2021). *The great upheaval: Higher education's past, present, and uncertain future.* JHU Press.

Ma, J., Baum, S., Pender, M., & Libassi, C. J. (2019) *Trends in college pricing 2019*. College Board.

Marshall, S. (2010). Change, technology and higher education: Are universities capable of organisational change? *Research in Learning Technology, 18*(3), 179–192.

Mathison, S. (1988). Why triangulate? *Educational Researcher, 17*(2), 13–17.

McRoy, I., & Gibbs, P. (2009). Leading change in higher education. *Educational Management Administration & Leadership, 37*(5), 687–704.

Musoba, G. D. (2006). Using evaluation to close the inquiry loop. In E. P. St. John & M. Wilkerson (Eds.), *Reframing persistence research to improve academic success. New Directions for Institutional Research, 130,* 77–94.

National Research Council. (2014). *Convergence: Facilitating transdisciplinary integration of life sciences, physical sciences, engineering, and beyond*. National Academies Press.

O'Neil, C. (2016). *Weapons of math destruction: How big data increases inequality and threatens democracy*. Broadway Books.

Patton, L. D., Morelon, C., Whitehead, D. M., & Hossler, D. (2006). Campus-based retention initiatives: Does the emperor have clothes? In E. P. St. John & M. Wilkerson (Eds.), *Reframing persistence research to improve academic success. New Directions for Institutional Research, 130,* 9–24.

Patton, M. Q. (1999). Enhancing the quality and credibility of qualitative analysis. *Health Services Research, 34*(5 Pt 2), 1189.

Penuel, W. R., Fishman, B. J., Haugan Cheng, B., & Sabelli, N. (2011). Organizing research and development at the intersection of learning, implementation, and design. *Educational Researcher, 40*(7), 331–337.

Pohl, C., & Hadorn, G. (2007). *Principles for designing transdisciplinary research.* Proposed by the Swiss Academies of Arts and Sciences, oekom, München, 124 pp.

Reason, P., & Bradbury, H. (2001). Introduction: Inquiry and participation in search of a world worthy of human aspiration. In P. Reason & H. Bradbury (Eds.), *Handbook of action research: Participative inquiry and practice* (pp. 1–14). Sage.

Romm, C. (2014). The World War II campaign to bring organ meats to the dinner table. *The Atlantic,* p. 25.

Soicher, R. N., Becker-Blease, K. A., & Bostwick, K. C. (2020). Adapting implementation science for higher education research: the systematic study of implementing evidence-based practices in college classrooms. *Cognitive Research: Principles and Implications, 5*(1), 1–15.

St. John, E. P. S., McKinney, J. S., & Tuttle, T. (2006). Using action inquiry to address critical challenges. In E. P. St. John & M. Wilkerson (Eds.), *Reframing persistence research to improve academic success. New Directions for Institutional Research, 130,* 63–76.

St. John, E. P. S., & Wilkerson, M. (Eds.). (2006). *Reframing persistence research to improve academic success. New Directions for Institutional Research, 130*(84).

Wang, T. (2016). *Why big data needs thick data. Ethnography matters.* https://medium.com/ethnography-matters/why-big-data-needs-thick-data-b4b3e75e3d7

Webb, E. J., Campbell, D. T., Schwartz, R. D., & Sechrest, L. (1999). *Unobtrusive measures* (Vol. 2). Sage Publications.

Zilvinskis, J., & Borden, V. M. H. (2017). Concluding thoughts. In J. Zilvinskis & V. M. H. Borden (Eds.), *Learning analytics in higher education. New Directions for Higher Education, 179*, 103–108.

CHAPTER 7

Professional Development – Creating an Arena for Pedagogical Reflections among Academic Staff

A Hermeneutic Phenomenological Study among Learning Teachers at Nord University, Norway

Elisabeth Suzen, Oddlaug Marie Lindgaard and Gunnar Grepperud

Abstract

The competence of academic staff plays a crucial role in the quality of the learning process and student success. There has been an increasing emphasis on pedagogical competence among university lecturers as a way to ensure the quality of university teaching. Pedagogical competence is intended to be developed through participation in different university courses. In our study, we reviewed learning experiences among 48 university lecturers at Nord University, Norway during a three-month pedagogical course. The lecturers maintained a reflection diary, they logged the practical part of the course and completed digital evaluation at the end of the course. The course was delivered through blended, asynchronous teaching, synchronous lessons and practical parts. Our study focused on the lecturers self-reported learning experiences recorded in the diary, the logs and the evaluation form. Our findings showed that the lecturers felt a positive recognition of their experiences, they appreciated the colleague observation and learning dialogues with colleagues, demanded a more strategic and holistic approach to academic development and reflected on actions with intentions to learn from experiences.

Keywords

professional development – pedagogical competence – academic development – blended learning – reflected practitioner

1 Introduction

In recent decades, enormous changes have occurred within universities worldwide, including a shift in focus to academic development for university lecturers.

DOI:10.1163/9789004520912_008

The quality of the learning process and student success cannot be separated from the role and competency of the teaching staff. The teaching competence of academic staff plays an important role in the delivery of lectures and contributes to improving learning performance (Hakim, 2015). Higher education institutions are entrusted with the responsibility of providing society with highly skilled professionals, citizen and leaders (Sugrue et al., 2017), and efforts to enhance the quality of education have grown considerably in recent decades. This greater focus on the university lecturers' professional development has increased the intensity of the debates and research on quality in higher education (Brooks, 2005; Harvey & Williams, 2010; Westerheijden, 2007). However, there is no one best way forward or simple answer to the question of how to improve quality in higher education. The teacher's role in higher education is changing quickly. To be able to respond to these changes, appropriate teacher professionalization is needed (Bos & Brouwer, 2014). In addition, reflection and related notions such as reflective practice and critical reflection have gained increasing importance across a great variety of academic disciplines (Van Beveren et al., 2018).

In this chapter, we present a study based on pedagogical courses for academic staff at Nord University, arranged both in 2020 and 2021. Our research question is as follows: What measures must be taken or considered to create an arena for pedagogical reflections among academic staff?

2   Quality in Higher Education

Findings from various studies on teaching quality have defined a range of key factors of 'good teaching' in higher education: concern for and availability to students, enthusiasm and interest of teachers, clear organization and goals, feedback on learning, the encouragement of student independence and active learning, an appropriate workload and relevant assessment methods, the provision of a suitably challenging academic environment (Biggs & Tang, 2011; Damşa & de Lange, 2019; Gibbs, 2016). These key factors must also be included in an introduction program for novice lectures at the university. Like Ramsden (1991) claimed, it is impossible to become a good teacher by taking a course in how to lecture; rather, aspiring instructors must think about their entire teaching. They must aim for deep rather than surface learning, holism rather than atomism and context rather than an unreflective collection of facts. This view of learning complies with both a phenomenological philosophy and a pragmatic and constructive understanding.

Ramsden (1991) defined good teaching as

Good teaching encourages high quality student learning. It discourages the superficial approaches to learning represented by 'imitation subjects' and energetically encourages active engagement with subject content. This kind of teaching does not allow students to evade understanding, but neither does it bludgeon them into memorizing; it helps them respectfully towards seeing the world in a different way. (p. 86)

In recent decades, the higher education sector has moved toward requiring all lecturers to have teaching qualifications such as a teaching certificate. Among a variety of initiatives and actions, universities have begun to emphasize professional development in academic staff at universities, all with intention of providing high quality teaching (Harvey & Williams, 2010).

2.1   A course for University Lecturers at Nord University

At Nord University, we ran a 3-month pedagogical course mainly for new and temporary or native university lecturers. Our research was based on this course model and run in 2020 and 2021. The course model consisted of digital seminars (asynchrony and synchrony), individual preparations, pedagogical peer observations and guidance, reflection diaries, group work and discussions. In developing the course, we chose to use blended learning to combine online, face-to-face and self-paced learning. Like Serrano et al. (2019) stated, blending significant elements of the learning environment leads to better learning experiences and outcomes if combined appropriately. Due to limitations and restrictions related to COVID-19, we ran most of the course digitally. Only the peer guidance (pedagogical observations and guidance) part of the course could be conducted face-to-face in the classroom.

This was a short, basic course primarily aimed at new and temporary employees. The intention was to give this group a basis for understanding the framework and prerequisites for teaching in higher education and to give them an arena to discuss and further develop their teaching competencies. The course itself was also a modelling of course completion through which we wanted to 'walk the talk'. The courses were intended to promote the teachers' formation awareness and to further develop their critical reflection. To facilitate these goals, we chose the following four guidelines for the course:

– Participants must be given an opportunity to discuss their teaching experiences with each other. One purpose of the course was to highlight the participants' practice experiences and to make them aware of the more tacit knowledge upon which their own teaching practice can be based.
– Use teaching experiences that are close to them. It was important for us to prepare a course with speakers/presenters who were close to the

participants in working life. Consequently, we largely chose speakers from our own university, meaning that most of presenters were colleagues of the participants. We believed that this closeness would create a greater opportunity for experience sharing, a greater degree of perceived closeness and thereby more opportunities for teaching development and future collegial cooperation.

– Include a practice portion during which the participants receive authentic learning experiences. The participants should plan a lesson, observe each other teaching lessons and give and receive supervision. This practice part was mainly self-governed. Peer observation is not a new tool for academic development (Bell & Thomson, 2018; O'Leary & Savage, 2020), however, the term observation has been used in different ways in theory and research (Warren, 2021). We wanted to clarify that observation is a way of forming a disposition of openness and of having an interest in learning from others (McPherson et al., 2015). This must be reinforced by giving teachers the autonomy to manage the process themselves while we as academic developers provide a framework and space for shared conclusions (Warren, 2021).

– Prepare a learning path for the course along which participants were to experience teaching and to learn through experiencing (Dewey, 1916/1997). As academic developers, we are responsible for leading good practice in teaching and learning and for supporting staff to implement the strategic directions of our university (Gibbs et al., 2000). We modelled practice as an underlying strategy for introducing academic staff to the possibilities and problems of student-centred flexible learning. This practice was modelled through a flexible delivered learning path facilitated for learning. Modelling is a powerful learning tool in any professional discipline (Edwards et al., 2000), and we wanted to adopt it for the course.

The course model was based on a pedagogical understanding rooted in pragmatism and socio-cultural theory, mainly Dewey's experience concept (Dewey, 1910/1997, 1916/1997, 1930/1998). Dewey's pragmatism was based on human qualitative experience, though which considered any existing phenomena to be an event (Dewey, 1934/2005). It was important for us to include this and to ensure that the participants gained learning experience by both reflecting on earlier experiences and by gaining new experiences through which they could support and guide each other.

The scholarship on reflection generally refers to John Dewey, who defined reflection as a mode of thought that is systematic and grounded in scientific inquiry (Dewey, 1910/1997). Dewey's holistic perspective requires certain attitudes such as open-mindedness, whole-heartedness and responsibility from the reflective thinker (Van Beveren et al., 2018). It cannot be reduced to a simple logical and rational problem-solving procedure or a set of techniques for teachers to use (Zeichner & Liston, 2013). The study of reflection was further developed through Donald Schön's (2017) reflection-in-action as a new epistemology of practice that values the knowledge gained through everyday practice and that critiques technical rationality as the dominant epistemology of professional practice. A variety of education scholars have developed new notions of reflection founded on the theories of Dewey and Schön. Our understanding is founded on the practical form of reflection to facilitate professional development and awareness. The reflective practitioner is one of the foundations of professional learning communities (Fullan, 2001). Land (2001) place the reflective practice in the middle of the academic development landscape, identifying it as a political, critical, system and individual-oriented. In this way, academic development can occur through reflective practices on both a personal and interpersonal level. Systematic reflection on a person's own teaching activities can initially be useful for the individual's development. In the next round, systematic reflection can be brought into the pedagogical conversation in a local context such as a professional group or department (Allern, 2011; Prosser, 2008).

Our course content was based on didactical categories for education where didactics are embedded in almost all professional activities related to teaching (Gundem, 2000). We chose five core didactical subjects: educational policy, lesson planning, flipped classroom, peer guidance and formative and summative assessment. For each subject the participants received the following:
– Asynchronous material including videos, articles, papers, presentations, book chapters and directions to review prior to the session;
– Synchronous seminars delivered by colleagues from Nord University or other universities. Academic staff presented their experience as teachers as it related to the specific subject of the seminar. During the presentation, they had discussions with participants.
– Reflection diaries, written by participants to reflect their own thoughts, experience, learning and further ideas for their own teaching. These notes were published on a digital platform, and the participants could comment on each other's notes.

Due to the theoretical fundament, we also outlined the following principles for the course:
– Have a practical approach – in other words, primarily focus on what a teacher can do and place less emphasis on theory;
– Focus on the most common forms of teaching in higher education and show some examples of further development;
– Make teaching competence at Nord University visible;
– Create an arena for reflection and discussion about teaching and learning;

- Provide an example of structure of content and structure for learning using the chosen learning management system (LMS);
- The offer must be online and have a scope equivalent to 40 hours.

The course consisted of five synchronous meetings, several asynchronous parts and peer guidance, adding to a total of 40 hours. The participants gave and received guidance and feedback from colleagues who observed their lectures. The guidance was meant focus on different aspects of planning (learning outcome, content, working methods, interaction, and formative assessment). The academic developers of this course came from Nord University and from The Arctic University of Norway (UiT). Since UiT has been preparing for the national regulations and has experience with and understanding of the intentions of the regulations, it was important for Nord university to initially co-create the course with UiT.

Based on the guidelines and principles for the course and the theoretical framework, we chose to avoid the linear perspective used most often in the context of higher education. Instead, we provided an interactive perspective (Bos & Brouwer, 2014), designing a course for which practicing teaching skills, discussion, and reflection on learning activities were core areas. We also wanted to emphasise reflection and further development among the participants; a large part of the course was used for reflection on teaching and learning activities. Even if the participating lecturers could benefit from simple survival tips on lecturing, we wanted to explore beyond such simple tips and support a deeper learning of and understanding for teaching. Like Ramsden (1991) wrote that:

> we are not talking about a few survival tips on lecturing and assessment presented in a one-day staff development workshop (...) but about a lengthy and demanding progression towards professional competence. (p. 250)

Furthermore, like Dewey (1938/2005) wrote many decades ago,

> Nothing has brought pedagogical theory into greater disrepute than the belief that is identified with handling out to teachers recipes to be followed in teaching. (p. 170)

3   Method

This was a qualitative hermeneutical phenomenological study focusing on university lecturers' self-reported learning experiences when participating in a pedagogical course for academic staff. The participants also wrote reflection diaries from the synchronous portions and logged the practice part of the course; altogether, they produced five different mandatory reflection submissions and a three-part practice log. In addition, the participants were sent a separate questionnaire at the end of the course. The questionnaire included both closed and open-ended questions for the participants in a digital format. The questionnaire focused on their reflections and thoughts regarding the course – its content, structure and the participants' own learning experiences.

The first step in the analysis was to review the reflection notes, the practice logs (memo) and the written answers to open-ended questions. Then, from those sources, significant statements or sentences that best described how the participants experienced the phenomena were extracted (Creswell, 2007, p. 61). The next step was to combine the statements into overriding themes. The statements were used as a basis to form a description of what the participants experienced. We analysed the data through direct interpretation, where we sought patterns in the material. For this part, we used abstraction (to group together similar statements from participants), subsumption (underlying recurrent themes in statements that deserve a separate status), polarisation (differences between the statements), frequency (how often they occur) and function (whether the statement has an underlying meaning) (Smith et al., 2009). In this last level of analysis, we developed a theoretical discussion of the main tendencies in the material in line with interpretative phenomenology (Webster-Wright, 2010).

The course is mainly for novice lecturers, but both novice and experienced university lecturers participated in 2020 and 2021.

The participants were academic staff from four faculties: Faculty of Education and Arts, Faculty of Nursing and Health Science, Faculty of Social Sciences and the Business School.

TABLE 7.1   Years of teaching experience among the participants

Years:	
Less than 1 year	18.5%
1–3 year	21%
4–6 year	10.5%
7–9 year	10.5%
10–15 year	10.5%
More than 15 year	29%

4   Ethics

As researchers, we provided the participants written information about the research and its purpose, about who will have access to their information, the intended use of the results and the consequences for participating in the research project. The participants gave written consent to use their reflection diaries, logs and evaluation forms for research purposes. The research followed the guidelines for research ethics outlined by NESH (The National Committee for Research Ethics in the Social Sciences and the Humanities). To secure anonymity, no names or course classes were mentioned.

To maintain anonymity, confidentiality and COVID-19 regulations, we used a digital questionnaire. We used the web form called *Nettskjema*. This is a solution for collection data developed by The University of Oslo, Norway. The web form does not store any IP addresses, usernames, or other information about the participants, thereby securing anonymity.

5   Findings

The main findings are presented by theme and in combination describe the reflection themes and self-reported learning experiences the lecturers encountered throughout the course. The following five themes emerged from the data.

5.1   *Recognition of Their Teaching Experiences*
The aim of the course was not to teach something radically new but to acknowledge and further develop the participants' competencies as teachers. We wanted to highlight their teaching experiences, put words to them, share them and help them become more aware of their tacit teaching knowledge. The reflection diaries, logs and evaluation forms showed recognition of participants' experiences, including adapting and developing their teacher competencies, was one of the success criteria in the course model.

The participants highlighted the course as a development of their own competence. Some already had considerable lecturing experience, but they nonetheless appreciated the course and reported a learning process with new motivations. One of the participants wrote in the evaluation that

> ... all discussions with you as responsible and other participants gave me new impulses to evaluate my own teaching and see it in a new light.

This is supported by Dewey's reflection on experiences for learning (1910/1997).

The participants reported becoming more aware of their own role as university lecturer and as facilitators of learning. They reported that the course gave them the opportunity to further reflected on learning processes in general and on their own practice specifically. One also stated that this reflection was not just wanted but necessary:

> I felt I reached the goal of further developing myself as a professional university lecturer, mostly because the course force you to reflect, assess and discuss your own practical.

Most participants remarked that sharing experiences in the course group and in smaller groups in break-out rooms were important aspects of their own learning processes. One quote from the reflection diaries stated that

> All the discussions with you course supervisors and the other participants has given me impulses and inspiration to assess and see my lecturing in a new light.

Another noted that

> It's been interesting to listen to experiences from colleagues at the university. I think this has been the most useful part of the course so far in terms of what I can take with me further in my own teaching.

Ramsden (1991) emphasised deeper learning among university lecturers, that allowed teachers to think about their teaching in terms of a changed understanding and holism. This adaption of experiences can occur through reflection (Dewey, 1910/1997). The participants stated that the course gave them the opportunity to reflect upon what they wanted the students to learn and how to facilitate this learning using planning, structure and different types of assessment.

Due to the holistic approach, the participants had different ways experiences of and reflections on the notion of a more holistic view as learners. The participants added some comments regarding their own feelings as employees and appreciated the possibility to learn. To exemplify, one participant wrote the following:

> I felt taken care of as an employee at the university, and that they see me as a teacher.

For us, it was important to meet the participants in their own developing zones (Vygotsky, 1978) in which they had potential to develop further based on prior experiences. Like the Danish existentialist Søren Kierkegaard stated: If one truly wants to succeed in leading a person to a specific position, one need to find his/hers location and start from there (Kierkegaard & Kierkegaard, 1946). For further development, both individually and intuitionally, it is essential that those involved appreciate the experiences of others. This appreciation can affects the motivation for development (Deci & Ryan, 2012). What someone owes to every person is the recognition of and respect for their status as a person capable of acting on the basis of reason (Honneth, 1996). Honneth's (1996) theory of recognition means that recognising people's qualities and ability to contribute to the community will help them value themselves. To create successful pedagogical development among academic staff in higher education, the process must have a light touch, be embedded in a supportive environment and encourage reflection (Curzon & Harding, 2002).

5.2   Collegial Supervision

In addition, the part of the course that focused on the implementation and supervision of a person's own teaching session received good feedback. The following quotes from the evaluation form exemplified this:

> I think it was a good exercise and gave room to think through what you actually do in teaching in a new way. It was also nice to be able to see what others are doing, and how I can use what they do.

> This is something I could have imagined more of daily. It was useful with input from a colleague, at the same time as we also played on each other in the teaching. It gave a dynamic that the students were also involved in.

> Meaningful and educational. I think we should create more such situations, where we try to develop each other's skills.

The reflection phase of peer learning, in particular the verbal debriefing, is an essential part of the learning process (Boud et al., 2014). The many practitioners who have implemented peer learning practices in higher education have demonstrated that the difficult issues must be addressed in peer learning (Boud et al., 2014). For instance, peer learning can significantly aid the development of required knowledge and skills, but the design of the peer learning program must vary among faculties to reflect the local context in which it is conducted (Boud et al., 2014). To ensure that ours accomplished this, we wanted to make space for autonomy to allow participants to make their own adjustments regarding the peer learning sessions. Teachers are rarely given the opportunity to see each other "in action". Furthermore, thinking and talking about teaching can become descriptive and narrow (Warren, 2021). Peer observation can be a valuable tool for addressing this narrow perspective (Warren, 2021). For some participants, it was their first time being observed by a colleague.

> It was new for me to get direct feedback on how the teaching worked in terms of, for example, voice use, tempo and interaction with the students. It was valuable to get such concrete feedback.

This quote is linked to another important experience from the observation: teachers can learn from each other even if they are from different academic fields. Teachers are a unit and have much in common, and factors driving the fragmentation of universities may challenge academic development.

The autonomy part again contributed to more critical thinking and a reflective lifelong learning approach. For novice teachers in particular, the usefulness of conceptions of teaching and learning must be proven in order for them to function in their educational practices and then adjusted to fit their own personal contexts (Bos & Brouwer, 2014). Teachers must be facilitated to build upon their own personal theories within their own specific contexts, and the guidance part of the course was meant to contribute and support this practice. Teachers' self-reported learning experience indicated that the peer learning session specifically – though the entire course more generally – helped participants professionally.

5.3   *Modelling a Learning Path*
We established a course model orientation where we emphasis the course as a modelling to inspire the participants to imitate some of the practices we illustrated to help them learn by experience without intentions of best practice. The learning path for the course (the course's structure in terms of order, participant requirements for the participants, etc.) allowed experiences for reflection, which means functioned as intended. Comments from the participants included:

> I like to have such concrete examples of structure and not just hear 'you should have structure'.

> Smart! I liked the learning path on Canvas!

Preparing for the gatherings involved handling out asynchronous learning material a maximum of two weeks before the synchronic lectures. It was important for us to include this type of blended, asynchronous teaching in the course. We wanted to provide an example of structure of content and structure for learning using the chosen learning management system (LMS). One of our aims was to give the participants experience with ideas like a flipped class-room in order to inspire them to apply these techniques in their own learning activities. The flipped classroom has an initial blended-learning approach because it capitalizes om the flexibility of online learning (Ng, 2021).

There was an ongoing alteration between the participants' lecture role and their role as a student in the course. Several of the participants managed to make this process explicit and reflected on the learning related to it. Nearly all participants emphasised the enriching effect of experiencing what it is like to be a 'student' in the context of the course meeting. Lunenberg, Korthagen, and Swennen (2007) noted the important role of modelling by the teacher educa-tor. The equivalent question of what we wanted our students to know in the case of academic staff was as follows: what do we want our teachers to know about teaching (Ramsden, 1991, p. 220)? For both students and teachers, it is all about the goals of teaching. The goals must be properly defined; a well-defined goal helps the learner understand what is expected of them. Course objectives and assessments of whether they have been achieved are not separated ele-ments but are instead closely related to teaching itself and its planning (Rams-den, 1991).

The asynchronous material gave the learners opportunities to become pre-pared in different ways for the subjects and synchronous lessons. This design of a flipped classroom builds on a particular blend of e-learning and face-to-face teaching. It is a special type of blended learning, whereby the learners are presented with web-based lectures prior to classroom sessions (Thai et al., 2017). One participant of this course wrote that it was

> I liked that I could come prepared to the lessons and be able to decide for myself when to do the preparations myself. To come prepared was also expected, hence flipped classroom was a central topic during the course.

Prior research has indicated that a flipped classroom helps students learn at their own pace; they spend more time in preparatory work and become more involved during classroom activities (Johnson, 2013; Kong, 2014). For example, one participant remarked that

> The way we have been working during the course, I need to be better at doing with my own students.

A key competence for a professional teacher is their ability to reflect upon their own practical experience (Klafki, 1998; Schulman, 2004). One of the participants reported that

> The biggest a-ha experience with this teaching session was the use of the video lecture as flipped classroom. After we had flipped classroom on the course, I decided to test this out. A clear difference from previous lectures was that I experienced that the students were much more "connected" and active from the start of the lecture.

They emphasized the pedagogical development they experienced even those with experience in the pedagogy field. One of the participants from the field of pedagogy wrote in the evaluation that

> The course has been great. Even if I have worked in the field of pedagogy at the university for nearly 30 years, I still got impulses for new ideas and input, so it was great to participate.

Thus, though several participants had backgrounds in teacher education and/or pedagogy as a discipline, they felt they learned more by participating in the course.

5.4   *Learning from Each Other*

In a learning organization, there should be a continuous focus on learning from each other and learning together (Senge, 2014). The participants demanded continuous learning paths and communities in the university, in particular communities of practice. Through pedagogical observations and conversations, they found ways to notice their tacit knowledge and actions, enabling them to shape and reshape their emerging academic identities (Warren, 2021). Understanding academics' beliefs is essential to improving educational practice (Pajares, 1992) to the point where individuals' epistemological beliefs greatly influence their conceptions of teaching and research (Brew, 2003). One of the participants wrote

> Thinking forward, it will be important to build network within our own organization. In addition, I would like to inspire my colleagues to build a culture for sharing by doing so myself. Having a conscious mindset about one's own continuous professional learning process, should be a topic on every Nord employee now and then. Hence the team of colleagues will be important to facilitate such a process.

Stensaker (2018) discussed the notion of academic development as cultural work and linked it to a trend within academic development that calls for a more holistic approach to the field. The different aspects of academic work – research, teaching and administration – must be closely related through a better understanding of practice (Boud & Brew, 2013; Stensaker, 2018). The participants appreciated the parts of the course that focused on the link among politics, teaching and research. They valued the holistic approach to quality in higher education.

Land (2001) presented the reflective practitioner as one orientation to academic development practice. This orientation seeks to foster a culture of self- and peer evaluation and critical reflection among colleagues to help them cope with uncertain and ambivalent organisational environments. Communication with other teachers from different backgrounds contribute to the formation of academic identity (Warren, 2021), and can open up new possibilities for conceptualizing learning and working (McPherson et al., 2015). Reflection is central to the activities of a community of practice and identity are worked on through participation in the community (Wenger, 1998).

5.5   *The Didactical Content*

Based on the self-reported learning experiences of the teachers, the themes for the course appeared to work well. The participants highlighted several topics they particularly liked, but overall, they seemed satisfied with all topics. Quotes and results from the evaluation form included this one

> I found all the topics had content interesting and meaningful, they all had aspects that I appreciate.

The participants were asked to rate their own learning outcomes on the different topics for the sessions in the course, with 1 being very low and 5 being very high (see Table 7.2).

Nearly all participants emphasised the enriching effect of experiencing teaching techniques, of discussing good practices during the course meetings and of participating in peer learning. In the practical part of the course (the peer guidance), the findings indicated that the experimentation with new teaching and learning techniques were a key developmental opportunity. The teachers were stimulated to experiment with all kinds of pedagogical techniques not as a demand but as an explorative method of further development.

Dewey principally focused on thoughts and the meaning of thought for learning, viewing reflection as the type of thinking with learning value itself (Dewey, 1910/1997). Reflecting upon experiences allows people to find

TABLE 7.2   Self-reported learning outcome from various course topic (1 = very low, 5 = very
            high)

Course topic	1	2	3	4	5
Educational policy	0%	21%	37%	29%	13%
Lesson planning	2%	16%	13%	40%	29%
Flipped classroom	5%	10%	25%	39%	21%
Formative and summative assessment	5%	0%	25%	45%	25%

meaning. Furthermore, reflection plays an important role in making sense of experiences (Boud et al., 1993). Our findings supported this understanding of reflection on experiences, where the participants reported a learning value in this activities and processes:

> It was good to write a reflection note to challenge oneself to formulate what one had thought and learned.

In the course, we chose to use presenters mainly from our own university. We thought it would be fruitful to gain inspiration from someone close to the participants in working life. This could also contribute to further academic development as cultural work within the university.

6   Conclusions

In our research, we wanted to investigate how we could create an arena for pedagogical reflections among academic staff. Our findings indicated some factors to consider in academic development based on the experiences of the participants. Our participants expressed a feeling of being seen as university lecturers, an acceptance of and respect for their teaching experiences and an appreciation of the possibility to gain further development and understanding. To facilitate for further development through reflection became an important part of the course. Learning and development are interrelated (Vygotsky, 1978) and take place through reflection on experiences (Dewey, 1916/1997).

The participants requested learning networks and a sharing culture within the university. Academic development calls for a more holistic approach to the field and academic development as cultural work is linked to this (Stensaker,

2018). The participants appreciated colleague leaning, and our findings indicated the fruitfulness in mixing groups of employees, meaning mixing university lectures from different academical fields and different length of experience. The university lecturers who participated in the course had different lengths of experience in university teaching and came from four different faculties. Despite these differences, all reported experiencing the course as a learning support, which helped them develop as professionals and achieve different learning outcomes. In combination, themes, structure and the learning methods used were aspects that supported this development.

The course was modelling a learning path, where there was an ongoing alteration between the participants' lecturer role and their role as a student in the course. Several of the participants managed to make this process explicit and were able to reflect on the learning related to it. Lunenberg, Korthagen, and Swennen (2007) emphasised the important role of modelling by the teacher educator.

The intention in academic development is to raise the quality of the university lectures given, to support more student active learning methods, and to raise the value of lecturing. Our research showed that by providing pedagogical programs and courses, universities can raise the pedagogical awareness and support the professional development among university lecturers. Without training in or knowledge of pedagogy, most academics have no reference point for their practice (Ortlieb et al., 2010). Prior research indicated the need for a more holistic approach to the field (Stensaker, 2018), and our findings supported this. The reflected practitioner is one of the foundations of learning communities, and academical development should evolve an ongoing holistic approach based on recognitions of the employees. Universities should facilitate for a mutual reflection in and over actions, including a common sharing of knowledge and experiences.

References

Allern, M. (2011). Scholarship of Teaching and Learning (SoTL) i Norge: Pedagogiske mapper som bidrag til pedagogisk diskurs. *Uniped, 34*(3), 20–29.
Bell, A., & Thomson, K. (2018). Supporting peer observation of teaching: Collegiality, conversations, and autonomy. *Innovations in Education and Teaching International, 55*(3), 276–284. https://doi.org/10.1080/14703297.2016.1212725
Biggs, J., & Tang, C. (2011). *Teaching for quality learning at university.* McGraw-Hill Education.

Bos, P. v. d., & Brouwer, J. (2014). Learning to teach in higher education: How to link theory and practice. *Teaching in Higher Education, 19*(7), 772–786. https://doi.org/10.1080/13562517.2014.901952

Boud, D., & Brew, A. (2013). Reconceptualising academic work as professional practice: Implications for academic development. *International Journal for Academic Development, 18*(3), 208–221.

Boud, D., Cohen, R., & Sampson, J. (2014). *Peer learning in higher education: Learning from and with each other.* Routledge.

Brew, A. (2003). Teaching and Research: New relationships and their implications for inquiry-based teaching and learning in higher education. *Higher Education Research & Development, 22*(1), 3–18. https://doi.org/10.1080/0729436032000056571

Creswell, J. W. (2007). *Qualitative inquiry and research design* (2nd ed.). Sage Publications.

Curzon, P., & Harding, J. (2002). Spreading the word about pedagogic research: The virtual reading group. In R. MacDonald & J. Wisdom (Eds.), *Academic and educational development: Research, evaluation and changing practice in higher education* (pp. 152–163). Routledge.

Damşa, C., & de Lange, T. (2019). Student-centred learning environments in higher education: From conceptualization to design. *Uniped, 42*(1), 9–26.

Deci, E. L., & Ryan, R. M. (2012). Self-determination theory. In P. A. M. V. Lange, A. W. Kruglanski, & E. T. Higgins (Eds.), *Handbook of theories of social psychology* (pp. 416–436). Sage Publications. https://doi.org/10.4135/9781446249215.n21

Dewey, J. (1997). *How we think.* Dover Publications. (Original work published 1910)

Dewey, J. (1997). *Democracy and education.* Free Press. (Original work published 1916)

Dewey, J. (1998). What I believe. In L. A. Hickman & T. M. Alexander (Eds.), *The essential Dewey. Volume 1. Pragmatism, education, democracy* (pp. 22–28). Indiana University Press. (Original work published 1930)

Dewey, J. (2005). *Art as experience.* Penguin Group. (Original work published 1934)

Dewey, J. (2005). *Erfaring og Opdragelse.* Christian Ejlers' Forlag. (Original work published 1938)

Edwards, H., Webb, G., & Murphy, D. (2000). Modelling practice – Academic development for flexible learning. *International Journal for Academic Development, 5*(2), 149–155.

Fullan, M. (2001). *The new meaning of educational change.* Routledge.

Gibbs, G. (2016). Teacher engagement. *Uniped, 39*(2), 184–187.

Gibbs, G., Habeshaw, T., & Yorke, M. (2000). Institutional learning and teaching strategies in English higher education. *Higher Education, 40*(3), 351–372.

Gundem, B. B. (2000). Understanding European didactics. In M. Ben-Peretz, S. Brown, & B. Moon (Eds.), *Routledge international companion to education* (pp. 235–262). Routledge.

Hakim, A. (2015). Contribution of competence teacher (pedagogical, personality, professional competence and social) on the performance of learning. *The International Journal of Engineering and Science, 4*(2), 1–12.

Harvey, L., & Williams, J. (2010). *Fifteen years of quality in higher education*. Taylor & Francis.

Honneth, A. (1996). *The struggle for recognition: The moral grammar of social conflicts*. MIT Press.

Johnson, G. B. (2013). *Student perceptions of the flipped classroom*. https://open.library.ubc.ca/collections/24/items/1.0073641

Kierkegaard, S. A., & Kierkegaard, S. (1946). *Kierkegaard anthology*. Princeton University Press.

Klafki, W. (1998). Characteristics of critical-constructive didaktik. In B. B. Gundem & S. Hopmann (Eds.), *Didaktik and/or curriculum: An international dialogue*. Peter Lang.

Kong, S. C. (2014). Developing information literacy and critical thinking skills through domain knowledge learning in digital classrooms: An experience of practicing flipped classroom strategy. *Computers & Education, 78*, 160–173. https://doi.org/10.1016/j.compedu.2014.05.009

Land, R. (2001). Agency, context and change in academic development. *The International Journal for Academic Development, 6*(1), 4–20. https://doi.org/10.1080/13601440110033715

Lunenberg, M., Korthagen, F., & Swennen, A. (2007). The teacher educator as a role model. *Teaching and Teacher Education*, 586–601. https://doi.org/10.1016/j.tate.2006.11.001

McPherson, M., Budge, K., & Lemon, N. (2015). New practices in doing academic development: Twitter as an informal learning space. *International Journal for Academic Development, 20*(2), 126–136. https://doi.org/10.1080/1360144X.2015.1029485

Ng, E. M. W. (2021). Reflecting on leading flipped classroom practices in a liberal arts university in Hong Kong. *International Journal for Academic Development, 26*(4), 463–467. https://doi.org/10.1080/1360144X.2021.1895169

O'Leary, M., & Savage, S. (2020). Breathing new life into the observation of teaching and learning in higher education: Moving from the performative to the informative. *Professional Development in Education, 46*(1), 145–159. https://doi.org/10.1080/19415257.2019.1633386

Ortlieb, E. T., Biddix, J. P., & Doepker, G. M. (2010). A collaborative approach to higher education induction. *Active Learning in Higher Education, 11*(2), 109–118. https://doi.org/10.1177/1469787410365655

Pajares, M. F. (1992). Teachers' beliefs and educational research: Cleaning up a messy construct. *Review of Educational Research, 62*(3), 307–332. https://doi.org/10.3102/00346543062003307

Prosser, M. (2008). The scholarship of teaching and learning: What is it? A personal view. *International Journal for the Scholarship of Teaching & Learning, 2*(2).

Ramsden, P. (1991). *Learning to teach in higher education*. Routledge. https://doi.org/10.4324/9780203413937

Schulman, L. S. (2004). Knowledge and teaching. Foundations of the new reform. In S. M. Wilson (Ed.), *The wisdom of practice. Essays on teaching, learning, and learning to teach/Lee S. Schulman* (pp. 217–248). Jossey-Bass.

Schön, D. A. (2017). *The reflective practitioner: How professionals think in action*. Routledge.

Serrano, D. R., Dea-Ayuela, M. A., Gonzalez-Burgos, E., Serrano-Gil, A., & Lalatsa, A. (2019). Technology-enhanced learning in higher education: How to enhance student engagement through blended learning. *European Journal of Education, 54*(2), 273–286. https://doi.org/10.1111/ejed.12330

Smith, J. A., Flowers, P., & Larkin, M. (2009). *Interpretative phenomenological analysis*. Sage Publications.

Stensaker, B. (2018). Academic development as cultural work: Responding to the organizational complexity of modern higher education institutions. *International Journal for Academic Development, 23*(4), 274–285. https://doi.org/10.1080/1360144X.2017.1366322

Sugrue, C., Englund, T., Solbrekke, T., & Fossland, T. (2017). Trends in the practices of academic developers: trajectories of higher education? *Studies in Higher Education, 43*, 1–18. https://doi.org/10.1080/03075079.2017.1326026

Thai, N. T. T., De Wever, B., & Valcke, M. (2017). The impact of a flipped classroom design on learning performance in higher education: Looking for the best "blend" of lectures and guiding questions with feedback. *Computers & Education, 107*, 113–126.

Van Beveren, L., Roets, G., Buysse, A., & Rutten, K. (2018). We all reflect, but why? A systematic review of the purposes of reflection in higher education in social and behavioral sciences. *Educational Research Review, 24*, 1–9.

Vygotsky, L. S. (1978). *Mind in society. The development of higher psychological processes*. Harvard University Press.

Warren, F. (2021). Diffracting peer observation: talking about differences, not looking for perfection. *International Journal for Academic Development*, 1–5. https://doi.org/10.1080/1360144X.2021.1998903

Webster-Wright, A. (2010). *Authentic professional learning* (Vol. 2). Springer.

Wenger, E. (1998). Communities of practice: Learning as a social system. *Systems Thinker, 9*(5), 2–3.

Zeichner, K. M., & Liston, D. P. (2013). *Reflective teaching: An introduction*. Routledge.

CHAPTER 8

Performance Agreements in Denmark, Ontario and the Netherlands

Ben Jongbloed and Harry de Boer

Abstract

Several countries have gained experience with performance agreements in higher education. Performance agreements, negotiated between the government and individual institutions, set out an institution's objectives in terms of future performance in return for a government grant. There can be different reasons for using such performance agreements, which is also evident from the three higher education systems (Denmark, the Netherlands and Ontario, Canada) that we have described, analysed and compared. The descriptions, analyses and comparisons are based on document analysis and a number of expert interviews on the design and functioning of performance agreements. Conclusions and policy recommendations are presented on the advantages and disadvantages of performance agreements.

Keywords

higher education – performance agreements – higher education governance – performance-based funding – international comparison

1   Introduction

Performance-based funding (PBF) for higher education institutions (HEIs) continues to attract a great deal of interest from policymakers, academics and institutional leaders (Burke, 2002; Jongbloed & Vossensteyn, 2001). Since the 1990s that saw the emergence of the new public management (NPM) paradigm in higher education governance (Broucker et al., 2017), funding authorities in many countries as well as the leadership of HEIs have started to introduce performance elements in the mechanisms they use to allocate financial resources to academic departments. They have done so in the belief that PBF will contribute to a higher degree of goal orientation and performance. However, there is still a lack of conclusive evidence that PBF indeed results in reaching its intended goals. The literature (Hillman et al., 2015; Ziskin et al., 2018) remains inconclusive with regard to its effects and there have been persistent concerns about the unintended effects of PBF (Dougherty et al., 2016).

In this chapter, we will focus on performance agreements used at system level. Performance agreements are a particular type of PBF in the sense that these agreements are bilateral contracts negotiated between a funding authority and an individual HEI. In the contract, each HEI agrees on its goals for the coming time period in return for a part of its basic – recurrent – government funding. Performance agreements are a forward-looking approach to steering HEIs. They can be contrasted to backward-looking PBF systems that make use of some form of funding formula that links (part of) the HEIs' recurrent funding to performance indicators reflecting the HEIs' past performance. Compared to formula-based funding approaches, performance agreements in principle provide more freedom for HEIs to set their own strategic goals in the context of the broader national goals set by the government.

Based on the experiences in three countries (Denmark, the Netherlands and Ontario in Canada) we present some evidence on the effects of performance agreements. The three cases selected reflect the wide variety in performance agreement systems that exist around the world (de Boer et al., 2015). Our cases are embedded in three different welfare regimes (Esping-Andersen, 1990): a liberal regime (Ontario), a conservative regime (Netherlands), and a social-democratic welfare regime (Denmark). Therefore, the three cases also allow us to pay attention to differences in the wider institutional context that may determine the design and functioning of the performance agreements.

The questions we address are: What are the main characteristics of the performance agreements in the countries selected? What is (or was) their underlying rationale? Where do they differ and what have been their effects – positive as well as negative?

The structure of the chapter is as follows. In the next section we discuss PBF and performance agreements in general. This is followed by a comparison of the performance agreements as used in the three selected countries. In the final section we present some conclusions on the advantages and disadvantages of performance agreements and we make some policy recommendations.

2   Performance-Based Funding: The Bigger Picture

In order to encourage the performance of the HEIs, funding authorities have started to make use of performance-based approaches to steer their higher education systems (Jongbloed & Vossensteyn, 2016). Performance-based funding (PBF) approaches are part of the NPM-inspired governance reforms that aimed to create an environment of quasi markets in higher education (Herbst, 2007).

Using performance agreements enables funding authorities to tie the HEIs' public funding to the achievement of a set of objectives negotiated between the funding authority and each individual HEI. Each HEI receives a particular portion of its basic (i.e., recurrent) funding according to a contract that includes a commitment to fulfil several objectives for the years ahead. The commitment is specified by means of targets – some quantitative, some qualitative – and the degree of success in delivering on those objectives will impact on the HEI's financial resources at the end of the contract period. The contract also specifies the rules of the game in terms of the evidence that needs to be delivered by the HEI to the funding authorities and the positive or negative financial effects that will be connected to meeting the goals. Performance agreements thus are expected to encourage HEIs to improve their performance and to act strategically – in line with their ambitions, strengths and weaknesses.

In the performance agreements, HEIs elaborate their strategic plans, outlining their vision for the future and the actions they will undertake to reach their objectives. Performance agreements allow institutions to select and negotiate their goals with an eye upon their individual context, strengths and key stakeholders. Therefore, performance agreements allow for a more tailored approach to higher education funding compared to the one-size-fits-all approaches that make use of a uniform formula and a small set of indicators applied to all HEIs in the higher education sector. Because of this, the performance agreements can help to increase mission diversity in the higher education system (Van Vught, 2008), alongside their main goal of increasing performance.

Performance agreements have been implemented – under several names and in various forms – in countries like Austria, Australia, Canada, Croatia, Denmark, Finland, Germany, Hong Kong, Ireland, Japan, the Netherlands, Scotland and a number of states in the USA (de Boer et al., 2015; Jongbloed & Vossensteyn, 2016; Jongbloed et al., 2022).

In Figure 8.1 we classify the different mechanisms that can be employed for the basic (i.e., core) funding of HEIs.

We distinguish between formula-based systems, negotiation-based systems, and systems where the previous year's allocation drives the core funding (Jongbloed et al., 2022). In formula funding, the core funds for HEIs are calculated through one or more formulae, based on a set of predefined parameters and indicators. In negotiated funding systems, the amount of core funding allocated to a HEI is an agreed sum negotiated between national ministries (or the

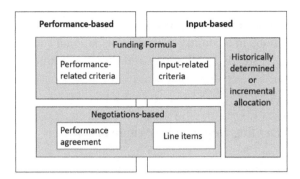

FIGURE 8.1
Funding mechanisms

agency responsible for funding HEIs) and the HEI. The negotiations may be set out in performance agreements (also known as performance contracts or funding agreements). In the historically-based systems, the core funds allocated are based on the previous years' budgets, adjusted according to certain parameters (e.g. average salary increase, inflation) applied to the budget's components (i.e. the line items in the budget, such as salaries, materials or investment budget).

Performance-based funding (PBF) systems are located on the left-hand side of Figure 8.1. They employ a funding formula, a funding agreement, or a combination of the two, and their formula and/or agreement includes performance criteria. A performance-based funding formula awards core funds to the HEI based on performance indicators, for instance, the number of diplomas awarded or the amount of credits accumulated by the HEI's students. In the case of a performance agreement, the funding authority and each individual HEI agree on the goals for the HEI to achieve and/or the activities to be undertaken by the HEI for the year(s) ahead.

Typically, the performance agreement specifies the share of the core funding that is tied to the performance goals. The goals can be described in qualitative terms (e.g., improve equal access of men and women to senior academic positions, improve access for disadvantaged students) but they can also be specified using quantitative indicators (e.g., targets in terms of an increase in the number of female professors or intake of PhD students). The ways and details in which performance agreements are laid out will depend on the rationale for the agreements and the goals that the national authorities have for their higher education system.

Performance agreements usually specify the procedures for assessing the achievement of the goals – the timing and the type of monitoring and evaluation that will take place and the requirements in terms of the data that HEIs may have to submit. The preparation, progress monitoring and the assessment of the agreements can take place in different ways, with some countries arranging discussions between the ministry and the university, and others relying on other mechanisms for exchanging information. Again, this will depend on the particular situation and traditions in a country – its existing national config-uration in terms of governance, steering philosophy and the mix of funding instruments already in place.

3   Performance-Based Funding, Impacts and Welfare Regimes

A natural question to ask is whether performance agreements and other forms of PBF will affect the performance of HEI s. The answer is likely to depend on the design of the performance agreements, including their link to the HEI s' funding – in other words, the funding that is at stake for those HEI s that do and those that do not deliver on the goals included in the agreement.

We expect the design of the performance agreement to depend on the coun-try's broader institutional context – on how its welfare state is shaped. Three types of welfare state regimes were distinguished by Esping-Andersen (1990): liberal, social-democratic and conservative. Employing this welfare regime typology, one may expect countries that can be classified as more liberal wel-fare states (e.g., Anglo-Saxon countries such the US, Canada, the UK) will con-nect more strict accountability procedures and clear rewards/sanctions to their PBF systems. They will rely more on market forces to allocate public funding. In social-democratic welfare regimes (e.g., Denmark, Norway, Sweden, and Finland) there is more steering by the state to make the HEI s focus more on producing outputs for the public good. These regimes will place values like consensus, inclusiveness and collaboration between the stakeholders in higher education higher on their agenda. Conservative welfare regimes (e.g., Austria, France, Germany, Netherlands, Italy, Switzerland, and Belgium) are likely to be situated in-between the previous two welfare regime types. These countries will apply the NPM-based rules in a more modest way, staying closer to the existing structures and established academic hierarchies in higher education.

The broader institutional arrangements of welfare states not only influ-ence the design of PBF systems in higher education (or in other public sector domains), they also will influence the effects that PBF will have on the HEI s and how HEI s perform in terms of education, research and third mission activities. When it comes to the funding of HEI s, these broader institutional arrange-ments include the funding mechanisms through which HEI s receive project funds from research councils, non-profit organisations and business organisa-tions. These non-block grants also include the targeted education funds that HEI s receive from government departments. Such project-based funding, also known as third party funding, in many cases is allocated competitively and awarded for a clearly defined period of time to achieve specific outcomes or to support specific activities. Some countries make relatively more use of competitive project funding than others (e.g., ETER project, 2019) – again, depending on their welfare regime and the associated governance approach in higher education. In addition, and again depending on a country's welfare regime, HEIs receive revenues from tuition fees. In most cases the type and level of the fees are set by national governments, with the more liberal regimes employing high tuition fees and social-democratic ones hardly charging any fees to students. Together with the core public funds and the third-party funds, these private revenues constitute the total revenue base that HEIs make use of to carry out their activities and – ultimately – to accomplish their particular type and level of performance.

Thus, researchers who are interested in the question whether performance agreements or PBF ultimately have had an effect on the performance of HEIs will be confronted with the difficulty of attributing changes in performance to the workings of the PBF system, because they would need to isolate the effects of funding formulas or funding agreements from other factors that co-determine the behaviour and performance of HEIs. This poses many methodological challenges – about the data to be used, the time frames to study, causality to be attributed, and, in particular, a context to be dealt with where everything else is in constant flux (Aagaard & Schneider, 2017). The wider institutional environment and incentive structures around HEIs – say, a country's welfare regime – also affect the effectiveness of PBF or of performance agreements. The available overview studies and meta reviews that synthesize the existing research on the impact of PBF (e.g., Hillman et al., 2015; Kivistö & Kohtamäki, 2016; Ortagus et al., 2020) often have difficulty drawing firm conclusions on the matter, or have found no effect at all.

While there is substantial research on PBF systems used for research funding (e.g., Hicks, 2012; Debackere et al., 2017), much less has been done on the effects of PBF on education. Existing research mainly focuses on the experience of the USA (Hillman & Corral, 2017; Kelchen, 2018), although some work has been done on the Nordic countries (Aagaard, 2015; Kivistö et al., 2017; Mouritzen & Opstrup, 2020) and the Netherlands (Jongbloed et al., 2019). These empirical studies are restricted to specific (country) cases of PBF and limited aspects of performance, making it difficult to generalize their findings.

Notwithstanding the lack of clear evidence, the European Commission in its Modernisation Agendas for higher education (European Commission, 2011, 2017) has suggested EU member states should consider implementing PBF. More recently, the OECD (OECD, 2020) presented some ideas and deliberations about the introduction of these governance instruments to improve the accountability, diversity and efficiency rating in higher education.

To learn about the effects of PBF – or performance agreements in particular – requires detailed studies of how more performance-driven approaches have been experienced by the stakeholders in the higher education system. In the next section we look at three higher education systems – Denmark, Ontario (Canada) and the Netherlands – that have made use of PBF. All three work with performance agreements. Two of the countries (Denmark, the Netherlands) also employ a funding formula that incorporates performance criteria. The three systems are representatives of three different welfare regimes, so studying their performance agreements can contribute to a better understanding of the instrument of performance agreements and how it is embedded in its own national context.

4   Performance Agreements in Denmark, Ontario and the Netherlands

This section presents a comparative analysis of the performance agreement systems that have been implemented in the higher education systems of Denmark, Ontario (Canada) and the Netherlands. Our analysis is based on information collected as part of a larger national evaluation of the development contracts pilot in Norway (Jongbloed & de Boer, 2020). The part of the evaluation that concentrated on Norway was carried out by NIFU (Elken & Borlaug, 2020). For our study, we used insights from desk research (e.g., existing evaluation studies) and a number of interviews that were conducted with national and institutional higher education experts in the countries. The interviews followed an interview protocol that covered the issues shown in Table 8.1.

The table compares the three performance agreement variants. It focuses on ten characteristics, such as the underlying rationale (line 1), the starting year of the agreements (line 2), the duration of the agreements (line 3), the number of goals included in the agreements and the indicators used (lines 4 and 7). How the agreements are employed in the relationship between HEIs and the public authorities is shown through line 6 (goal setting and negotiation procedures), line 8 (monitoring) and line 9 (assessment procedures). An important feature is the link between the agreements and the funding of a HEI, and whether there are any financial rewards or sanctions associated with the degree of goal completion (line 10).

The table illustrates quite a few differences between the three countries. This was also stated in other studies (e.g., de Boer et al., 2010) that presented

TABLE 8.1   Comparison of the performance agreements in three higher education systems

	Denmark	The Netherlands	Ontario
	Strategic Framework Contracts	Performance Agreements	Strategic Mandate Agreements
1 Name of the programme			
Rationale	Strengthen the strategic dialogue between ministry and institution	Strengthen differentiation; improve student success and teaching quality; Alignment of institutional and national strategic goals	Increasing trust and accountability through transparency and improved performance outcomes
2 First contract period	2000–2003	2013–2016	2014–2017
3 Duration of current agreements	4 years	6 years (Quality Agreements)	5 years (third SMA iteration – SMA3)
4 Goals	5–8 broad goals that differ across HEIs and cover their three missions	Three broad goals in 2013 agreements: (1) improve education quality & student success; (2) institutional profiling & programme differentiation; (3) strengthening knowledge transfer & societal engagement. Six broad themes in current (Quality) agreements.	Goals for SMA3: (1) incentivizing positive economic outcomes; (2) alignment with labour market outcomes; (3) incentivizing differentiation and specialization
5 Goal setting & negotiation of agreement	Ambitions set jointly by ministry and institutions. Contracts contain institution's own goals. Renegotiation of goals and indicators possible during contract term.	Institutions set their own ambitions and goals (including quantitative ambitions). For 2013 agreements, an independent Review Committee monitored and evaluated the agreements and HEIs' progress in bilateral discussions. For the current agreements, this is done by the Accreditation Agency (NVAO).	Institution representatives negotiate with ministry on basis of agreed plans and framework (including indicators/metrics) for higher education. Institutions set their (annual) goals for each of the ten metrics. Targets are based on an institution's historical data & established criteria and presented along with a narrative.

(cont.)

TABLE 8.1   Comparison of the performance agreements in three higher education systems (*cont.*)

		Denmark	The Netherlands	Ontario
6	Document size	Concise document (about 14 pages) with uniform lay out/ template.	Up to 50 pages (no template) for 2013 agreements. No template or page limit for 2019-2024 Quality Agreements.	About 20 pages, based on fixed template (including tables and narratives).
7	Indicators in agreement	Indicators determined in negotiations. Goals and indicators are of general and broad nature.	Seven mandatory indicators in 2013 Agreements, focusing on education (student success; quality). Institutions can choose to incorporate additional (non-mandatory) indicators to express further ambitions. No mandatory indicators in current Quality Agreements.	SMA3: 10 mandatory performance metrics (9 system-wide and one institution-specific), plus two 'reporting' metrics.
8	Monitoring of progress on agreements	Yearly dialogue, based on the institution's annual status review and its annual report. Data are provided by the institution on the basis of jointly agreed data sources. Bilateral meetings (stocktaking/progress) can lead to revised action plans.	Each institution reports on progress in its customary annual report. There is a mid-term evaluation (for 2013 agreements, there was a meeting with the Review Committee) to monitor the institution's progress.	SMA3: Performance on each metric monitored and evaluated annually on basis of streamlined reporting process based on annual reports. Some metrics to be activated gradually over 5 year period, allowing for their further refinement. Data for the metrics are predominantly from existing data collections.

(*cont.*)

TABLE 8.1   Comparison of the performance agreements in three higher education systems (*cont.*)

	Denmark	The Netherlands	Ontario
9	Evaluation upon expiry of agreements	Goal achievement assessed upon expiry of the contract, based on assessment by the Danish Agency for Institutions and Education Grants. This assessment is based on a dialogue with the HEI.	For the 2016 agreements, a Review Committee advised the Minister after evaluating each institution's goal achievement. The minister then took final decisions about each HEI's performance budget. The accreditation agency will evaluate the current quality agreements in 2024.	SMA3 to be evaluated by ministry each year on metric-by-metric basis. This will have funding consequences from 2022 onwards. Evaluation takes place against the targets set by the institutions themselves (no inter-institution comparisons). Performance is evaluated using a pass/fail approach, with bands of tolerance and scaling for under-achievement.
10	Link to budget	5% of a HEI's basic educational funds (i.e. the student-independent part of the base funding envelope) is dependent on fulfilment of strategic framework contract. Exact consequence for funding yet to be determined.	For 2013 agreements: 7% of the basic operational education grant for the period 2013-2016 was tied to goal achievement (5% linked to seven mandatory indicators; 2% linked to the institution's plans for profiling and differentiation). Actual consequence depends on assessment by Review Committee and decision of Ministry. The budget related to the 2019 Quality agreements (QA), is about 3% of the total base funds for HEIS. Not achieving goals will not have immediate financial consequences for a HEI as funds will be channelled back to HEI in form of scholarships to help staff improve their pedagogical skills.	From 2022: An institution will receive 100% of the funding for a metric by meeting or exceeding its target. If target is not met, partial funding, commensurate with actual performance, will be received Metric weightings (set by the HEI itself) will impact the share of an institution's notional funding that can be received for successful performance related to a particular metric. At end of SMA3, 60% of the institutions' total operating grant funding will be tied to performance.

examples of performance agreements. Depending on the policy priorities set by governments (line 1), each country will have its own way of implementing and using the performance agreements. While in all three cases the performance agreements are aimed at the objectives of differentiation, encouraging HEIs to be more focused on what they do best, the countries place different degrees of emphasis on objectives such as quality improvement and strengthening accountability.

When comparing performance agreements across countries, it is important to bear in mind the overall governance and welfare regime in which the agreements are embedded. In Denmark, for example, the funding formula is heavily rewarding students' performance, as measured through the number of credits accumulated in a year by an institution's students (Jongbloed et al., 2022). This suggests that, compared to the Netherlands, there may be less of a need for performance agreements to further prioritise degree completions.

The welfare regimes in the Netherlands and Denmark traditionally are characterized by a culture of negotiation and dialogue. The Netherlands already in the mid-1990s had implemented a form of PBF in its funding formula. In Ontario, the development of the Strategic Mandate Agreements and their goals was also affected by changes in the political environment that places a high priority on the economic impact of higher education.

What we also observed is that, over time, the design of the agreements and the financial consequences attached to them underwent changes. In the case of the Netherlands, the table shows that there are marked differences between the performance agreements that were used in the period 2013–2016 and the current iteration of the agreements – known as Quality Agreements. Where the Dutch performance agreements were very much regarded as an indicator-driven NPM manifestation, the quality agreements are much less focused on quantity and aimed at quality and student success. As in other countries, different governments may see reasons to make adjustments to the goals of the agreements and the rules around their practical operation – partly because of their (and the HEIs') experiences with these agreements.

In Denmark, the Strategic Framework Contracts have changed considerably in the past twenty years, partly as a result of government-initiated evaluations (e.g., Danish University and Property Agency, 2009). Explicit efforts were made to strengthen the strategic dialogue between the ministry and institutions in order to jointly determine the course of higher education (see lines 1 and 5 in Table 8.1), but, at the same time, respecting the strategic goals of the individual institutions (line 4). This is a manifestation of the socio-democratic welfare regime that is a characteristic of Denmark.

In the Netherlands, too, the 2013 Performance Agreements focused on the contribution of the HEIs to achieving the goals on the national higher education agenda – such as mission diversity and differentiation in education and research (see lines 1 and 4 in Table 8.1). Yet, at the same time, a high priority was attached to improving education quality and students' degree completion (Review Committee, 2017). In the 2019–2024 Quality Agreements, we detect an even higher priority placed on ensuring that students receive a high-quality education experience. The current Quality Agreements in the Netherlands no longer include ambitions related to research performance, societal engagement, or knowledge transfer, but rather leave those goals to the HEIs themselves and the domains of other policy instruments.

In Ontario, the leading principle of the Strategic Mandate Agreements (SMAs) has been to strengthen accountability and improve performance outcomes (see lines 1 and 4 in Table 8.1). In the current (third round of) SMAs the education ministry in particular stresses the contribution of HEIs to the economy and to the linking of graduates' learning outcomes with labour market needs. This reveals the liberal welfare regime that is very much governing Canadian higher education and that is also manifested in a higher reliance of HEIs on tuition fees and competitive grants – next to the base funding HEIs receive from their provincial government.

The way in which the objectives included in the agreement are set (see lines 4 and 5 in Table 8.1) differs considerably between the three countries. In Denmark, the government and HEIs jointly set the goals, allowing goals to differ from one institution to the other. In the Netherlands, the Rectors' organizations representing the institutions have played an important role in the design of the agreements by first defining the priorities in consultation with the government. This typical feature of a conservative welfare regime led to a sector-wide agreement on seven mandatory indicators that were to be used by the institutions for specifying their ambitions (line 7 in Table 8.1). In Ontario, too, agreements were made on the indicators (metrics) to be included in the SMAs. Similar to the Netherlands, targets are set in a negotiation process in which institutions are taking the lead. In all three countries, however, we have observed a tendency to reduce the number of objectives and indicators included in the agreements in order to avoid target inflation and bureaucratic overload.

Whether institutions are making progress in achieving the goals specified in the agreements (see line 8 in Table 8.1) is reported and reviewed annually in all three countries. In Denmark, the institutions annually provide data on the agreed targets and indicators, and discuss these bilaterally with the ministry. The final assessment on target achievement at the end of the contract period is made by the Danish ministry, which uses a fairly global assessment. In the Netherlands, progress towards goals set in the performance agreements was monitored by an independent Review Committee that met the Executive Board of each HEI at the start, the middle and the end of the agreement period to discuss progress and listen to its 'story behind the numbers'. In Ontario, the monitoring and evaluation of performance is overseen by a special unit in the ministry that makes use of a streamlined process and a limited number of metrics, based on verified data collections (see lines 7 and 8 in Table 8.1).

On the issue of linking the performance agreements to funding (line 10 in Table 8.1), there are some marked differences between the three systems. The Ontario system in its first two rounds of the SMAs did not tie the agreements to the institution's government grant. However, in the third (2020–2025) SMA round there is a more direct link, although the COVID pandemic temporarily put a halt to its implementation. To provide stability and predictability for Ontario's HEIs, the provincial government delayed the activation of the performance funds for two years ensuring that an institution's funding is not linked to its performance until 2022–2023. The funding at stake for HEIs in Ontario is expected to increase to 60% of the basic government grant, but how the implementation delay will affect that ambition remains to be seen.

In Denmark, the share of performance agreement-related funding is comparable to that of the Netherlands. While the share may be regarded as modest, its impact can still be substantial (Jongbloed et al., 2019). Dutch HEIs did take the agreements seriously and evaluations did support the conclusion that the modest link between performance agreements and HEI budgets has contributed to goal achievement in terms of improving student success and programme differentiation in the Netherlands (Evaluatiecommissie Prestatie-bekostiging, 2017).

In earlier versions of the Danish contracts the potential financial penalty was largely symbolic, but in its current version the link is slightly bigger and more explicit – although it is still to be decided how the financial repercussions will be effectuated at the end of the contract period (in 2022). In the Netherlands, as well as in Denmark, however, the naming and shaming of the institution in case of underperformance is seen as more effective than the financial consequences. In other words, while the economic importance of the agreements may be perceived as marginal or even symbolic, the actual impact of the agreements on the HEIs may be much bigger. This observation is in line with earlier research on PBF and in particular on 'how incentives trickle down' from higher hierarchical levels to the 'academic shop floor' when it comes to research performance (Aagaard, 2015).

5   Conclusions

Based on the experiences of the three countries with performance agreements, we now draw some conclusions on their advantages and disadvantages and present some lessons for the design and use of such agreements.

First of all, one needs to make any judgement on performance agreements according to what policymakers actually wish to achieve with this negotiations-based governance arrangement. The government's objectives very much depend on the challenges the higher education system is facing. We have seen that in the Netherlands, these objectives very much relate to student completion rates and education quality. In Denmark and Ontario, there is quite some attention for institutional differentiation – with Ontario stressing the contribution of higher education to the economy (including the labour market). The challenges to be addressed will co-determine the design of performance agreements and the roles they play in steering higher education, that is: the goals included, the emphasis placed on each goal, the choice of indicators and the evidence to be submitted, and the processes around the agreements in terms of dialogue and financial consequences. In our comparison table we showed the different choices made in the three countries.

The different choices are not surprising. Not only because the challenges of the higher education systems differ between countries, but also because of other differences in context. The 'policy mixes' and welfare regimes (Esping-Andersen, 1990) in which the agreements are embedded differ. For Denmark, for example, we could mention that the overall funding system is already focusing on student completions, thus there is less of a need to further stress student performance in the agreements. HEIs in Ontario are to a large extent funded through tuition fees, making them in many ways determined to deliver 'value for money' to students. The design of the performance agreements therefore will depend on these features of the broader governance and funding system. In this respect, the Netherlands and Denmark traditionally are characterized by their culture of negotiation and dialogue, whereas Ontario is more inclined to focus on markets and a more streamlined interaction between ministry and HEIs through metrics.

Policy priorities and governance rationales are subject to change – just like government coalitions and the political climate in general. Political sentiments towards initiatives that resemble steering by numbers or using NPM-like instruments and contracts may change. We have seen an example of this in Ontario, where the issue of the economic relevance of higher education has become more prominent on the (conservative) government's agenda for

higher education. How to translate these political objectives into agreements
and choose the proper indicators for this is not an easy task – and the Ontario
experience shows that it takes a few iterations to 'get the indicators (metrics)
right'. Clearly the SMA exercises in that respect have also been part of a learning process, requiring an open dialogue between ministry and institutions. The
co-construction of the SMA process meant that the sharp edges of a strictly
NPM-oriented steering were to some extent removed.

The consequences of changing (political) sentiments have also been visible in the Netherlands. The increasing aversion particularly of students and
institutions to what they characterise as a 'culture of calculation and quantitative assessment' (under which performance agreements are also subsumed),
ultimately contributed to the minister's decision in 2016 not to continue the
performance agreement instrument in the way it was constructed until then.

The focus on dialogue has helped to create a sense of ownership of the
agreements in the case of Denmark. The room given to the institutions in
setting their own goals has contributed to achieving the government's goals
around institutional profiling and programme differentiation. The mandate
agreements in Ontario also are intended to stimulate the institutions to differentiate themselves, given their strengths and specific opportunities. In the
Netherlands, the wish to create a highly diversified higher education sector
(including differentiation at institutional and programme level) was an important reason for the introduction of the performance agreements in 2016. While
the performance agreements made HEIs pay more attention to their institutional profile, the evidence for increased differentiation was rather weak
(Jongbloed et al., 2019). However, the agreements did result in Dutch HEIs (in
particular, the research universities) making progress on the policy goals of
improving study success and completion rates. The linking of the agreements
to funding has contributed to that outcome, although HEIs were reluctant to
admit this.

In all three countries, goal achievement is linked to funding, but the degree
to which this is the case differs, along with the method of implementation. In
Ontario, the ambition is to increase the amount of funding that is at stake in
the third round of the SMAs but at the same time mechanisms have been put in
place to stabilize the size of institution's annual core funds and above all to prevent it suffering excessive budget shocks due to fluctuations in performance. In
Denmark and the Netherlands, the amount of performance agreement-related
funding is relatively small, but still large enough to make a difference.

From the experiences and assessments in the three countries, we conclude
that performance agreements are a flexible policy tool that has the potential
to contribute to more differentiation and increased performance in the higher

education system. The agreements can work as an interactive trust-based type of coordination in the higher education system – a dialogue-based type of steering – that is less harsh than formula-based NPM approaches. Based on the evidence that was collected in the three countries, we conclude that the agreements have increased transparency and accountability and have encouraged HEIs to focus on agreed aspects of institutional performance such as student success and institutional profiling, although an immediate impact on graduation rates and research productivity has not been proven so far. This is a useful conclusion for policy-makers (national, European, institutional) who are looking for evidence on 'what works' in higher education policy-making – in particular those interested in whether PBF works.

A recent OECD report on resourcing in higher education came to the conclusion that 'negotiated funding has high transaction costs, but offers the chance for the funding agency to reward improved performance and to spell out the directions it wants the institution to focus on' (OECD, 2020, p. 86). However, as stated above, firm conclusions about the effectiveness of performance agreements are hard to reach. Nevertheless, the improved dialogue about 'what matters' in higher education that is encouraged by performance agreements will indirectly contribute to a better functioning of the higher education system. While HEIs that are accustomed to being autonomous may question the necessity of formalizing agreements in a contract and point to the high transaction costs this produces, there are no well-established alternatives to performance agreements that can do the same job of giving direction and translating that in financial resources. In a recent, more extensive study on performance-based funding across EU member states (Jongbloed et al., 2022) we came to the conclusion that dialogue-based steering and funding are on the rise in Europe with several EU Member States making use of a combination of funding formulas and negotiation-based approaches for the funding of HEIs.

The three countries' systems analysed here (and more extensively in Jongbloed & de Boer, 2020) illustrate that in the design of performance agreements a balance has to be found between ministry-imposed performance objectives and institutionally-defined ambitions. This is crucial for preventing tendencies towards uniformity resulting from performance-based systems, in particular if these are linked to funding. At the same time, allowing for institution-specific goals to be included prevents the agreements from reverting to steering tools that will diminish institutional autonomy. Quoting the OECD: 'funding should be delivered in ways that support the autonomy of institutions and that allow leaders to manage efficiently' (OECD, 2020, p. 79). As shown above, to guarantee institutional autonomy, a variety of design options for funding agreements is possible, with designs being driven by the challenges faced by the country.

Blueprints for the design and implementation of performance agreements do not exist, because priorities and contexts will differ from country to country. The agreements allow for flexibility and tailor-made approaches, and this flexibility is precisely one of the major advantages of performance agreements over more uniform approaches. The three countries – representatives from very contrasting welfare regimes – suggest there are different options for constructing the agreements in terms of the choice of goals, indicators, their links to funding, and how to shape the dialogue between higher education funding authorities and the institutions.

6   Finally

From our three-country comparison we have derived some lessons for countries that consider introducing (or revising) performance agreements.
- The first lesson is to leave some room to the HEIs when it comes to the goals included in the performance agreements. Surely, the goals will need to be in line with the broader national goals, but institutions will need some freedom to propose their own goals, as this will allow HEIs to take advantage of their own strengths and opportunities and it will encourage differentiation in the higher education system. With regard to the goals, it is also advisable not to place financial rewards on the achievement of goals that are already incentivized by other policy instruments, such as research grants or targeted subsidies.
- On the choice (and number) of indicators included in performance agreements, one lesson is that it helps to have quantitative evidence on the multiple dimensions of an institution's performance, but evidence on goal achievement can in some cases also be reported in terms of qualitative information (using narratives), thus allowing the HEI to tell 'the story behind the numbers' and contextualise their performance.
- About the connection of the agreements to the base funding, countries have shown that it takes time (i.e., a few iterations of the performance agreements) to develop a well-functioning system. Through consultations and dialogue between ministry and higher education stakeholders a legitimate system can be built. The co-design of a PBF system is crucial.
- PBF systems work best when they are attached to additional money for the sector and avoid 'zero sum games'. Institutions regard it as unfair if they are penalised when their absolute performance improves but if relative to other HEIs that improvement is smaller. From the Dutch and Canadian experiences, it became apparent that care must be taken to ensure that the

performance of an institution is assessed by comparing it either against similar institutions ('comparing apples with apples') or to compare it against the targets it has set for itself and that builds on its own historical performance record.

From the three cases of countries that have implemented performance agreements we conclude that performance agreements can be a policy tool that contributes to a more interactive trust-based type of coordination in the higher education system. The agreements have the potential to increase transparency and performance orientation at the institutional level. Their value very much lies in improving the dialogue between authorities and institutions, thus contributing to a better functioning of the higher education system in general. The HEI s may regard a contract-based approach as intrusive – bureaucratic even – but on the other hand it leaves them with sufficient room to insert their own priorities and deliver their own evidence of performance – thus justifying the public funding they receive from the government.

However, the acceptance and effectiveness of performance agreements very much depends on how agreements are designed, what freedom they leave to the higher education institutions, and how they are integrated within the overall policy context. It will be up to policy researchers to make sure that our knowledge on the design and effectiveness of performance agreements and performance-based funding in general will continue to increase.

References

Aagaard, K. (2015). How incentives trickle down. *Science and Public Policy*, 42(5), 725–737.

Aagaard, K., & Schneider, J. W. (2017). Some considerations about causes and effects in studies of performance-based research funding systems. *Journal of Informetrics*, 11(3), 923–926.

de Boer, H., Jongbloed, B., Benneworth, P., et al. (2015). *Performance-based funding and performance agreements in fourteen higher education systems: Report for the Dutch Ministry of Education, Culture and Science*. CHEPS.

Broucker, B., De Wit, K., & Verhoeven, J.C. (2017). Higher education research: Looking beyond new public management. In M. Tight & J. Huisman (Eds.), *Theory and method in higher education research* (Vol. 3, pp. 21–38). Emerald Publishing Limited.

Burke, J. C. (Ed.). (2002). *Funding public colleges and universities for performance: Popularity, problems, and prospects*. State University of New York Press.

Danish University and Property Agency. (2009). *Danish University evaluation 2009 – Evaluation report*. DUPA.

Debackere, K., et al. (2017). *Performance-based funding of university research.* Publications Office of the European Union.

Dougherty, K. J., Jones, S. M., Lahr, H., Natow, R. S., Pheatt, L., & Reddy, V. (2016). *Performance funding for higher education.* Johns Hopkins University Press.

Elken, M., & Borlaug, S. B. (2020). *Utviklingsavtaler i norsk høyere utdanning: En evaluering av pilotordningen.* NIFU.

Esping-Andersen, G. (1990). *The three worlds of welfare capitalism.* Princeton University Press.

European Commission. (2011). *An agenda for the Modernisation of Europe's higher education systems.* COM(2011) 567 final. EC.

European Commission. (2017). *A renewed EU agenda for higher education.* Commission staff working document. COM(2017) 247 final. EC.

ETER Project. (2019). *How are European Higher education institutions funded? New evidence from ETER microdata.* Analytical Report No. 2/2019. ETER and European Commission.

Evaluatiecommissie Prestatiebekostiging Hoger Onderwijs. (2017). *Van afvinken naar aanvonken.* Ministry of Education.

Herbst, M. (2007). *Financing public universities: The case of performance funding.* Kluwer.

Hicks, D. (2012). Performance-based university research funding systems. *Research Policy, 41*(2), 251–261.

Hillman, N., & Corral, D. (2017). The equity implications of paying for performance in higher education. *American Behavioral Scientist, 61*(14), 1757–1772.

Hillman, N., Tandberg, D., & Fryar, A. (2015). Evaluating the impacts of "new" performance funding in higher education. *Educational Evaluation and Policy Analysis, 37*(4), 501–519.

Jongbloed, B., & Vossensteyn, H. (2001). Keeping up performances: An international survey of performance based funding in higher education. *Journal of Higher Education Policy and Management, 23*(2), 127–145.

Jongbloed, B., de Boer, H., McGrath, C., & de Gayardon, A. (2022). *Study on the state and effectiveness of national funding systems of higher education to support the European Universities Initiative.* DG-EAC (in press).

Jongbloed, B., Kaiser, F., & Westerheijden, D. F. (2019). Improving study success and diversity in Dutch higher education using performance agreements. *Tertiary Education and Management, 26*(3), 329–343.

Jongbloed, B. W. A., & Vossensteyn, J. J. (2016). University funding and student funding: International comparisons. *Oxford Review of Economic Policy, 32*(4), 576–595.

Kelchen, R. (2018). Do performance-based funding policies affect underrepresented student enrolment? *The Journal of Higher Education, 89*(5), 702–727.

Kivistö, J., Pekkola, E., & Lyytinen, A. (2017). The influence of performance-based management on teaching and research performance of Finnish senior academics. *Tertiary Education and Management, 23*(3), 260–275.

Mouritzen, P. E., & Opstrup, N. (2020). *Performance management at universities.* Springer International Publishing.

OECD. (2020). *Resourcing higher education: Challenges, choices and consequences.* Higher Education, OECD Publishing. https://doi.org/10.1787/735e1f44-en

Ortagus, J. C., Kelchen, R., Rosinger, K., & Voorhees, N. (2020). Performance-based funding in American higher education: A systematic synthesis of the intended and unintended consequences. *Educational Evaluation and Policy Analysis, 42*(4), 520–550.

Review Committee. (2017). *Prestatieafspraken: Het vervolgproces na 2016. Advies en zelfevaluatie.* Review Committee.

Van Vught, F. (2008). Mission diversity and reputation in higher education. *Higher Education Policy, 21*(2), 151–174.

Ziskin, M., Rabourn, K. E., & Hossler, D. (2018). Performance-based funding of higher education: Analyses of policy discourse across four case studies. *Journal for Critical Education Policy Studies, 16*(2), 164–215.

CHAPTER 9

Helping Students in the COVID Crisis

Drawing Conclusions Utilising Business Intelligence Data as a Quality Management Tool

Sara-I. Täger, Stephanie Albrecht, Daniel Thiemann and Tilo Wendler

Abstract

In March 2020 the World Health Organization declared the spread of COVID-19 a pandemic. Subsequently, universities had to make many decisions in response to the changing situation. Now, almost two years later, university management as well as quality management departments need information to learn from these experiences and to react to new developments in an informed manner. In this context, Hochschule für Technik und Wirtschaft (HTW) Berlin, a university of applied sciences with almost 14,000 students, used its business intelligence software based on its Campus Management System (CMS) data to gain insights into changes in student dropout rates, exam registrations, and credit point gains.

The findings indicate fewer dropouts at the beginning of the pandemic and lower numbers of exam registrations compared to pre-pandemic semesters, but also that there might be delayed effects that are starting to emerge. HTW Berlin will use the results of its monitoring of study programmes as a quality management tool to discuss future improvements.

Keywords

effects of the pandemic – business intelligence – higher education – quality management – Germany

1   Introduction and Background

After the World Health Organization declared the COVID-19 outbreak a pandemic in March 2020, German universities had to switch exclusively to online teaching for many months, and a wide range of classes continued to be taught online during the 2021 academic year. The shift towards online teaching was sudden and largely unplanned and has therefore been labelled a temporary shift to "emergency remote teaching" (Hodges et al., 2020; Iglesias-Pradas et al., 2021).

Nevertheless, most students in Germany were satisfied with how universities managed the crisis and shifted from in-person to online teaching (Horstmann, 2022; Lörz et al., 2020). However, at the same time, the pandemic has proven challenging for students in Germany, e.g., regarding employment, study-related infrastructure such as learning spaces and libraries, contact with teachers and exchange with fellow students (Horstmann et al., 2022; Lörz et al., 2020, 2021; Marczuk et al., 2021). Learning situations in general worsened for most students. Marczuk et al. (2021) found that a lower percentage of students were satisfied with their knowledge and skills in 2020 compared to a study in 2016. These factors could negatively influence students' future studies (ibid.).

Not all students have been satisfied with how teaching went during the pandemic. For example, 20% of surveyed Master's students in computer sciences, physics and mathematics evaluated the "inspiring and motivating approach of teachers towards students" during online teaching as 4–6 on a scale from 1 (very good) to 6 (very bad) (Horstmann, 2022, p. 18). The type of university might influence such perceptions, with contact and professional exchange with teachers potentially being easier at universities of applied sciences (ibid., p. 7). The structure of tertiary education in Germany differentiates between Universitäten (universities) and universities of applied sciences ((Fach-)Hochschulen or Hochschulen für angewandte Wissenschaften/HAW), i.e., types of universities that award the same Bachelor and Master's degrees but which focus on practical courses of study and practical research. Universities of applied sciences usually have fewer students in total and smaller classes.

Conversely, teaching in study programmes that include regular excursions or lab rotation programmes might have been more negatively affected, as these formats could not be fully replaced by online teaching during the pandemic (Berghoff et al., 2021). Against this background, the conclusion is that continuous support seems necessary in order to establish further online teaching formats (Berghoff et al., 2021, p. 21).

The recent literature thereby indicates that the pandemic might have impacted students' study behaviours in terms of dropout rates, exam registration, credit point gains, exam results and even their long-term prospects for study and graduation. Analysis of such indicators is useful, since it might be necessary to offer support to certain student groups during and after the pandemic. Moreover, even if such indicators are not necessarily negative on the individual level (because a student may find a more suitable career path), they can have negative implications at the institutional level (Neugebauer et al., 2019). Fundamentally, Germany's higher education institutions are funded by the federal regions (the "Bundesländer"). All federal regions have introduced performance-related funding elements to varying extents. In Berlin, parts of state funding are coupled to performance-based indicators (Jaeger, 2008). With the use of performance-related funding structures, declining metrics may negatively affect a university's financial situation.

Against this background, questions concerning potential changes in indicators such as dropout rates, exam registration, credit point gains and exam results formed the starting point for joint analysis of quality management, university management and information technology centre at the Berlin University of Applied Sciences[1] (Hochschule für Technik und Wirtschaft, HTW). HTW Berlin is the largest university of applied sciences in Berlin, with almost 14,000 students in 2021, offering over 70 subjects in the areas of technology, computing, business, culture, and design. Its study programmes are oriented around practical skills that aim to prepare students for their professional working life.

The chapter describes the practical experiences as a larger German technical university of applied sciences, during the pandemic, demonstrating the use of business intelligence software based on its Campus Management System as a quality management tool.

1.1   *HTW Berlin Background and Response to the Pandemic*

In the winter 2020 term the three largest subject areas at HTW Berlin were engineering sciences (approximately 40%), law, economics and social sciences (approximately 30%) and computer sciences (approximately 17%), as shown in Figure 9.1.

Since May 2021, HTW Berlin has been a system re-accredited university, i.e., its quality management system has been shown to be suitable for ensuring that the qualification goals and quality standards of its study programmes are met (German Accreditation Council, n.d.).

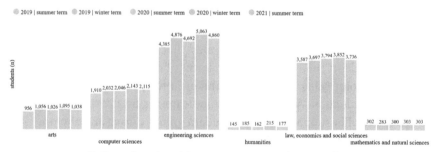

FIGURE 9.1   HTW Berlin students by subject groups, 2019–2021 (numerical)
            (Source: Business intelligence software/Campus Management System, HTW
            Berlin, 29.10.21)

As defined by the university quality management processes, HTW Berlin assigns responsibility for various teaching processes to the relevant stakeholders. This approach includes five levels of responsibility as shown in Figure 9.2. At the beginning of the pandemic, the university management sought to consult all stakeholders on a regular basis, applying the principle of continuous quality improvement or problem solving "on a micro-level" based on the four steps of the "plan, do, study, act" (PDSA) cycle. According to PDSA, continuous quality improvement occurs through iterative application of the "plan, do, study, act" procedural steps (Moen & Norman, 2011). The "plan" phase consists of defining the problem and hypothesising causes, identifying solutions and developing a plan of action. In the second step the plan is applied. The third step involves checking the effectiveness of the actions by reference to their results. The last step helps to finalise the process, either by standardising the solutions if the results are satisfactory or by returning to the first stage to implement opportunities identified for further improvement (Al Ghawiel, 2021; Moen & Norman, 2009, 2011).

European universities' quality management reactions to the COVID-19-pandemic have been described as consisting of two phases (Cirlan & Loukkola, 2021): at first during 2020, responses focused on crisis management with rapid decision-making and were largely linked to the transition to online teaching and university services. In the second phase of European universities starting from autumn 2020, there was a need for information on the experience gained during the first phase to inform more effective planning for the following semester, thereby shifting attention to quality management and improvement (ibid., p. 5).

During the first phase of the pandemic, administrative and managerial colleagues at HTW Berlin and all other universities faced the challenges of making

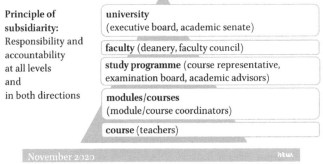

FIGURE 9.2   Subsidiarity principle as a key factor for system re-accreditation
             (Source: HTW Berlin)

and implementing new decisions spontaneously on a daily basis. During the pandemic, universities in Berlin and elsewhere had to react to changes in university regulations at the federal level (Cirlan & Loukkola, 2021). For example, according to the revised Berlin Higher Education Act (Berliner Hochschulgesetz (BerlHG) §126 b 1), exam failures were disregarded during the semesters of summer/winter 2020 and summer/winter 2021 (spanning 1 April 2020 to 31 March 2022), i.e., students were allowed to repeat all exams they failed during this period.

During the process of adjusting to both the pandemic and resulting legal changes, it was not known how new decisions and the revised Higher Education Act would influence students' behaviour with regard to exam registration or participation. For HTW Berlin it became essential to reduce the time lag between problem identification and implementation of adjustments.

HTW Berlin has many years of experience in the use of digital media in university teaching. The eLearning Competence Centre (eLCC) was founded in 2008 to serve as a single point of contact for digital teaching services and learning support and to coordinate e-learning infrastructure projects. For example, eLCC offered teachers, colleagues and student training courses and advice on implementing eLearning; it participated in academic events and fairs. The university's "Academic Services" department now maintains central teaching support services (Moodle, Wiki, Cloud, etc.) and teachers are supported in the technical implementation of digital teaching and learning scenarios.

Since 2019, the university management has also initiated an in-depth strategic examination of digital teaching and learning. Part of that process involved peer-to-peer strategic consultancy by the Higher Education Forum on Digitalisation (April 2019 to March 2020) which provided the university with important advice and recommendations on its further strategic development. A Digitalisation Advisory Board was created, including professorial and student representatives from all departments, to advise the university on the topic of teaching and learning in the digital age. This positive starting position in terms of strategy and (infra)structure was an important basis for HTW Berlin's ability to react rapidly to the urgent need for conversion and sudden up-scaling of digital teaching in response to the COVID pandemic.

Since the pandemic began, HTW Berlin's university management has regularly surveyed all stakeholder groups at short intervals and adjusted the range of support services according to their needs. This was envisioned as a means of installing feedback loops in the sense of short PDSA cycles. This has supported the university management in continuously realigning service provisions with the evolving needs of the target groups.

In summer 2020 HTW Berlin students participated in a nationwide student survey conducted by the German Centre for Higher Education Research and

Science Studies (DZHW) (Lörz et al., 2020), where the university received its own results separately. HTW-specific results confirmed nationwide results by showing high satisfaction with how the university managed the shift from in-person to online teaching. However, the results also showed that some HTW Berlin students thought online teaching formats could be improved (Schäfer, 2021). Most lecturers work only part-time at the university and hold main jobs in related areas of industry. Nevertheless, they were required to manage ad hoc conversion to digital teaching formats and the corresponding adaptation of teaching methods.

In late summer 2020, HTW Berlin surveyed almost 40% (n = 450) of their teaching staff regarding their experiences during the first online semester in 2020 and the (technical) support they required to develop their online teaching (Stifterverband, 2020). Participants were asked to indicate their satisfaction via a five-point Likert-type scale. Most respondents (> 60%) were (very) satisfied with their digital-based teaching in the online summer semester (despite in many cases starting with little experience of digital teaching); and a large majority (75%) was (very) satisfied with the support offered by HTW Berlin (ibid.). Survey responses also showed high demand for the university's information technology centre to provide support via telephone, email and for remote access (ibid.).

In response to teachers' preferences, the university purchased a licence for the Zoom video-conferencing platform in addition to the existing tool that was already in use. In general, teaching staff managed the shift to primarily online teaching only through strong personal commitment and immense time investment (Stifterverband, 2020).

Among other outcomes, the study findings prompted the university management and departments to take further steps. At the beginning of the pandemic, several colleagues were tasked with providing "first aid" during the switch to online teaching.

The university gradually expanded its hands-on support for online teaching and technical support for the Moodle learning platform. Since October 2020 the university has funded a permanent support structure for teaching and learning, the Lecturers' Service Centre ("Lehrenden Service Center", LSC). The LSC shares good teaching practices, offers media and university teaching advice and provides comprehensive technical support and media production for continuing education programmes. This was an important step towards permanently embedding teaching development and digitalisation as an integral part of higher education development at HTW Berlin.

Additionally, the university created guidelines for digital teaching and learning, which redefine the relationship between online and face-to-face teaching and serve as a legal framework for examinations.

Nevertheless, HTW Berlin sees itself as a university with lessons mainly taught face to face (F2F), and due to the many questions and uncertainties concerning online exams, teachers also seem to prefer F2F exams. Parallel to this, a "clearing office" – responsible for the set up and revision of study, training and examination regulations – was created in 2021 with funds from the Berlin Senate project for quality and innovation (Berliner Qualitäts- und Innovationsoffensive, QIO), which teachers can contact for legal requests, e.g., about e-examinations. Also from QIO funds, staff members are employed in all five faculties to support teachers in the technical implementation of courses with Moodle and to function as local "e-learning supporters", i.e., advisors for online teaching.

Additional positions are also being created in the university information technology centre to expand educational technologies. The university therefore systematically links development steps with evaluation and reaction and, accordingly, lives the PDCA cycle.

Moreover, when the counselling department informed the university management about a continuous increase in the number of requests since 2020, the university created a position in April 2021 (at 50% full-time equivalent) to provide additional student counselling support. The university also created an online networking platform (the E-Lounge), where any students lacking contacts or feeling isolated could meet and exchange ideas.[2]

2   BI in Higher Education in Germany

Over the past three decades, higher education institutions (HEI) in Germany engaged in creating infrastructures for quantitative data collection and analysis, and over the last decade German university administrations expanded their use of performance data on teaching and research activities (Hillebrandt, 2020). Interest in monitoring of study programmes, for instance, further increased among German universities following changes to regulations on statistics reporting in 2016 (Eltfeld, 2016). The field seems to be divergent, with some German universities having good practice study-monitoring systems in place (e.g., Hörnstein et al., 2016; Nexus Newsletter, 2016). Implementation of monitoring systems might have been less feasible for universities of applied sciences, which usually have smaller student numbers and fewer administrative resources than other types of universities.

However, for Germany in general, it has been concluded that "number-based data infrastructures are [...] present, growing, and actively promoted in key areas of German higher education governance, but are hardly coupled directly to decisional outcomes" (Hillebrandt, 2020, p. 53).

Business intelligence (BI) software offers one means of integrating CMS data analysis into university decision making. BI software stems from the business domain and is based on the idea of supporting or enabling faster, more accurate and more reliable decision making (Scholtz et al., 2018). The main usage of BI software is to offer management and other stakeholders access to up-to-date information and to quickly depict trends within data and visualise them in a comprehensible way. BI enables the gathering, storing and processing of information. Its usage has strongly increased since the beginning of the 21st century.

BI tools often offer certain data analytics applications. BI usage is usually separated from in-depth approaches of data analytics.

It has been argued that BI reports and dashboards can be usefully applied to higher education (Fowler, 2019); they are used, for instance, for topics such as campus demographics, budgeting, planning, procurement, student enrolment, faculty evaluation, staff assessment, performance appraisal, research output, teaching records (Kamel et al., 2019) and sustainability information (Scholtz et al., 2018).

Common challenges for BI usage are data quality, its complex implementation process and use as well as the support necessary to maintain quality (Scholtz et al., 2018, p. 268), which can also limit BI usage in higher education. As good data quality of the underlying CMS is a precondition for BI reporting and analysis, the BI implementation process should be accompanied by consistent data quality checks.

3   Data Analytics Approach and Hypotheses

3.1   *Data Analytics Approach*
Starting from 2018, HTW Berlin decided to support its qualitative approach by adding more qualitatively-focused key performance indicators and reports, and began creating reports using R Markdown (a file format for producing reports including, for example, graphics within the R statistical computing environment).[3] Based on these reports, goals and objectives of the analyses as well as data operationalisation have been discussed and further developed. To ensure data consistency and greater flexibility, in a second step, the university's information technology department established a data warehouse that stores data from the CMS and provides access to BI software.

Through the BI reports based on the data warehouse, the information technology and quality management departments collaborate closely to produce analyses of the composition of student cohorts, study progression and study achievements, as well as ad hoc evaluations of special topics. These analyses are stored in BI reports and dashboards for licensed users, and the university systematically adds BI reports and dashboards on further topics.

The main user groups targeted by the university's BI-reports are university management and study programme managers. BI licences are provided for all study programme managers (i.e., regular professors who are responsible for a study programme for a certain time), deans, vice-deans and deaneries, the admissions office and other administrative staff. Each semester the quality department regularly offers short online training sessions on the BI reports. In this context, study programmes may obtain additional ad hoc analyses on special topics of their interest. The process is ongoing, necessitating continuous effort to communicate the goals and contents of the BI reports and promote their use.

HTW Berlin uses IBM Cognos Analytics as its BI tool and, while the data exploration tool includes powerful analysis, the documentation is rather limited. IBM SPSS Statistics, a statistical software platform, allows data imports from BI reports to conduct further statistical analysis. The one-way ANOVA (with repeated measures) tests mentioned in the results section below were generated with IBM SPSS Statistics. However, the handling of datasets could be more straightforward, as BI reports had to be reworked to enable data import into SPSS Statistics, where data were restructured again for the analyses.

The data used and presented below derive from the HTW Berlin CMS, which includes data from students' enrolment until they leave the university. These data include, for instance, background information on students, exam registrations and credit point gains. The data cannot say much about social, financial or psychological factors, but can shed light on processes that strongly affect the university, for instance student enrolment, exam registrations and results, credit point gains, dropout and graduation.

The data were converted in an "extract, transform and load" (ETL) process to a data warehouse. During the ETL process, data are normalised into a common framework, where relationships can be established between data points (Fowler, 2019). The data warehouse can be accessed by the BI tool. The figures shown below are taken directly from the Cognos Analytics BI software. They include information on all enrolled students for all of the almost 80 study programmes in six subject groups and for up to nine semesters between summer 2017 and 2021, covering approximately 14,000 students each semester. The HTW Berlin academic year consists of two semesters (1 April–30 Sept and 1 Oct–31 March). Most of the present analyses use data from a data snapshot from 29 October 2021, meaning that all changes made during previous semesters are included. Recent data snapshots from February 2022 have been analysed to grasp all the latest information entered in the CMS for the summer

2021 semester. The university is additionally able to examine daily snapshots of the data (not shown).

3.2   *Hypotheses*

If study conditions worsened during the pandemic, the question is whether this influenced students' behaviour as reflected in dropout rates, exam registration numbers and results. One could argue that student life was more difficult at the beginning of the pandemic, i.e., in the summer and winter 2020 semesters, when various lockdown regulations remained in effect over weeks or months (e.g., working from home, and physical distancing on campus). Universities and teachers were in the process of preparing for the shift to online teaching, and not all new processes had yet been established. Financial problems and psychological distress might have been worse for students during lockdown phases at the beginning of the pandemic (Werner et al., 2021). The first hypothesis, therefore, was that student dropout rates would increase during 2020.

The German concept of *Lernfreiheit* gives students the freedom to plan their study schedule. Thus, students usually decide themselves when to take their exams, while specific exam regulations – such as the number of chances they get to pass – are regulated at the regional level (i.e., by each federated state or *Bundesland*) and at the university level. At HTW Berlin, students have to register themselves for each exam before taking it for the first time. It seems plausible that in the context of the pandemic students might have chosen to postpone their exams and that, due to difficult study conditions, fewer students might have been able to prepare for exams than in previous semesters. Some students might also have reservations about taking exams online. Thus, the second hypothesis was that during 2020 fewer students would register for exams.

The third hypothesis was that those students who registered for exams would achieve lower pass rates due to general inadequacies in their study environments since summer semester 2020. Moreover, less prepared students might have registered for (and sat) an exam anyway, because failed exams did not count in the federal region of Berlin during the three pandemic semesters, defined as summer/winter 2020 and summer 2021.

Hypotheses 1–3 could theoretically affect students in similar ways during any of their study semesters. However, first-semester students might generally be more vulnerable and more frequently affected by worsened study situations, as they lacked prior study and learning experience and had not been able to form personal contacts with teachers and fellow students. Therefore, the fourth hypothesis was that students who attended their first semester in summer or winter semester 2020 might be expected to gain fewer credit points than their first-semester counterparts in the previous semesters.

Moreover, the pandemic might have other effects, such as prolongation of study duration or fewer graduates in future semesters. However, it is not yet possible to observe these potential developments.

4   Results

4.1   *Dropout Rates*

Figure 9.3 depicts percentage changes in dropout rates per semester since 2017 as compared to the previous semester. Dropout numbers include all students who were ex-matriculated from their study programme without graduating (i.e., including changing study programmes at HTW Berlin, transferring to another university or entering the labour market).

Winter and summer semester cohort compositions often differ systematically, i.e., with regard to university entrance certificates because more high-school graduates often enter the university in winter semesters. Because dropout numbers at HTW Berlin have consistently been higher in summer than in winter semesters, the percentage change in dropout rates was positive in summer semesters and negative in winter semesters, the exception being summer semester 2020. In the summer 2020 semester, dropouts showed the first decline (relative to the preceding year) observed since 2018. Contrary to hypothesis 1, dropout rates decreased during the summer and winter 2020 semesters.

When looking at the absolute numbers of student dropout per semester (not shown) a repeated measures ANOVA with a Greenhouse–Geisser correction showed that mean dropout numbers differed significantly between semesters $[F(3.337, 253.609) = 18.152, p < .001]$. Post hoc tests using the Bonferroni correction revealed some significant difference between pairs of semesters: dropout

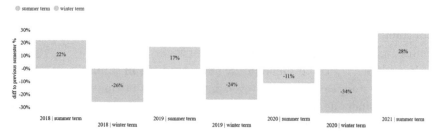

FIGURE 9.3   Differences in dropouts compared to previous semester, 2017–2021 (%)
(Source: HTW Berlin BI visualisation based on CMS data, 27.04.22)

was significantly lower in summer 2020 as compared to summer 2018 ($p < .05$) and significantly lower in winter 2020 than in winter 2018 ($p < .05$). Besides, dropout was significantly greater in summer 2021 as compared to all semesters since winter 2018 ($p < .001$). Thus, the results conflicted the hypothesis of increasing dropout rates in 2020 (hypothesis 1).

The increase in 2021 dropouts in absolute numbers corresponds almost exactly to the decrease seen in summer 2020 (result not shown). This finding might suggest a catch-up effect in the sense that students shifted dropout decisions from summer 2020 to later semesters. Future semesters will show whether dropout numbers stabilise or increase.

It might also be suggested that students decided not to drop out during summer semester 2020 because they chose instead to keep their student status and lacked other (labour market) options, but that they also studied less actively than previously. However, the number of inactive students, i.e., students not receiving credit points, did not increase during 2020 (data not shown).

The statistical significance of changes in dropouts according to subject group was tested separately (using one-way ANOVA) for each semester between the three largest subject groups and between all six university subject groups. This was initially done to check whether certain student groups faced specific challenges during the pandemic; however, the results consistently showed that dropouts did not significantly differ by subject group (not shown). The overall trend of fewer dropouts in summer 2020 and an increase in summer semester 2021 holds for all subject groups (see Figure 9.4).

4.2   *Exam Registrations*

Students have to register for each of their exams at HTW Berlin. Figure 9.5 shows the number of registered exams since summer semester 2017. Repeated measures ANOVA with a Greenhouse–Geisser correction showed that numbers of registered exams differed significantly between semesters [$F(3.774, 279.282) = 7.519$,

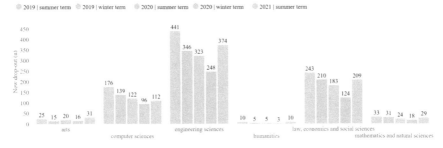

FIGURE 9.4   Dropouts by subject group, 2017–2021 (numerical) (Source: HTW Berlin BI visualisation based on CMS data, 29.10.21)

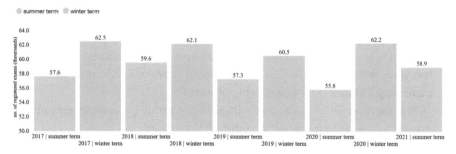

FIGURE 9.5   Exam registrations per semester, 2017–2021 (thousands) (Source: HTW Berlin BI
visualisation based on CMS data, 27.04.22)

$p < .001]$, but post hoc tests using the Bonferroni correction revealed that
there were significant differences mainly between summer and winter semesters. The number of registered exams in summer 2020 semester was significantly lower than in winter semesters of the years 2017, 2018, 2019 and 2020
$(p < .01)$.

Figure 9.6 shows the average number of exam registrations per student and
semester to test whether lower exam registration was influenced by the number of students. Repeated measures ANOVA with a Greenhouse–Geisser correction indicated that the average numbers of registered exams per student
differed significantly between semesters $[F(4.562, 337.575) = 14.962, p < .001]$.
Post hoc tests using the Bonferroni correction revealed no significant differences until summer 2020. The number of registered exams was significantly
lower in summer semester 2020 than in all previous semesters ($p < .001$). The
number of registered exams per student did not differ significantly in winter
semester 2020 from winter semester 2019 but was significantly lower than in
winter 2017 and 2018 semesters ($p < .05$). Also, summer semester 2021 did not
significantly differ from summer semester 2020, but from all other summer

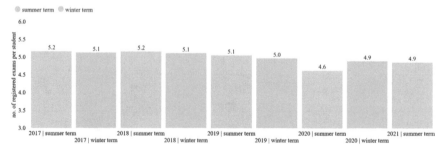

FIGURE 9.6   Number of registered exams per student and semester, 2017–2021 (average
number per student) (Source: HTW Berlin BI visualisation based on CMS data,
27.04.22)

semesters since summer 2017 (p < .001). The results of exam registration numbers per student confirm the hypothesis of lower exam registration in 2020 just for the summer semester 2020.

This suggests that a rebound effect was evident in the winter 2020. After a phase of adjusting to the pandemic in summer 2020, students subsequently registered for their exams as usual after a one-semester delay. Maybe the fact that failed exams were disregarded and that there were lower dropout numbers made some contribution to this finding.

4.3   *Exams Results and Credit-Point Gains*

Figure 9.7 depicts exam results per semester. The main categories were pass, fail, withdrawal and "BerlHG 126" (i.e., failed exams that were disregarded under section §126b BerlHG from 1 April 2020 to 31 March 2022). The status-categories "Exmatric.: 3 failed exams" and "Exmatr.: time-limit" reflect specific cases of failing an exam; they hardly show in the figure due to low case numbers.

Exam results in total were largely unaffected during summer 2020 despite being the first semester with changes in §126b BerlHG in place. Compared to previous semesters, the percentages of exam passes and withdrawals continued at similar levels.

However, the percentage of "BerlHG 126" slightly increased in winter semester 2020, whereas the percentage of withdrawals decreased. This could indicate that, in response to the legal decision that exam failures during those semesters would be disregarded, students sat (and passed or failed) an exam more often rather than withdrawing.

With regard to the hypothesis 3 of lower pass rates during 2020, repeated measures ANOVA with a Greenhouse–Geisser correction showed that the percentage of exams passed differed significantly between semesters [F(3.888, 272.154) = 4.598, p < .05]. Post hoc tests using the Bonferroni correction revealed that the percentage was significantly larger in winter semester 2020 than in all

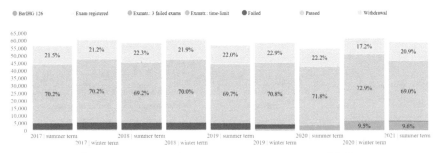

FIGURE 9.7   Performance in registered exams per semester, 2017–2020 (%) (Source: HTW Berlin BI visualisation based on CMS data, 27.04.22)

other semesters since 2018 (p < .05) – more students passed the exam, contradicting hypothesis 3. The exam pass rate was significantly lower in summer 2021 as compared to winter semester 2020 (p < .001), but not significantly different from other semesters. The percentage of exam passes in summer semester 2021 returned to a level similar to semesters before summer 2020.

4.4   First-Semester Students

To analyse whether first-semester students gained fewer credit points during the pandemic (hypothesis 4) compared to their counterparts in previous semesters, inactive students (those gaining 0 credit points) were excluded from the data. The results show that active first-semester students did not gain fewer credit points in the three semesters of the pandemic (see Figure 9.8), contradicting the hypothesis. Repeated measures ANOVA with a Greenhouse–Geisser correction indicated that the average number of credit points did not differ significantly between semesters [$F(5.609, 162.659) = 1.853, p > .05$]. This was not influenced by increased numbers of inactive students or students on leave of absence among first-semester students, since neither increased during the pandemic (results not shown).

5   Conclusions

HTW Berlin has implemented a data warehouse based on its Campus Management System data, which is analysed via Cognos Analytics to provide business intelligence reports in near real-time based on daily snapshots. The university has thereby been able to monitor indicators that might be influenced by the COVID-19 pandemic, such as student dropout rates, exam registration numbers

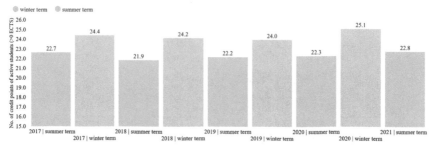

FIGURE 9.8   First-semester students' credit points per student by semester, 2017–2020 (numerical; First-semester students with > 0 credit points) (Source: HTW Berlin BI visualisation based on CMS data, 28.02.22)
Note: Including credits from all types of modules, without approved external credits

and exam results over time. Although the process of implementing the data warehouse and providing meaningful reporting through BI software has been complex and time consuming, the results provide the university management with information necessary for informed decision-making. Moreover, the university provides more than 120 colleagues (management, teachers and administrators) with access to the reports, with the aim of increasing exchange and reflection about the results as well as fostering discussion about follow up-measures at the university.

At a university-wide scale, the first three semesters of the pandemic did not show strongly negative effects on dropout rates, exam registrations or exam results. There was a small decrease in dropouts in the summer and winter 2020 semester and increased dropout rates occurred in summer 2021. These findings might suggest a further 'rebound effect' on the numbers of exam registrations in future semesters.

Furthermore, after registration for exams was lower in the summer semester 2020 the registration was as usual in summer semester 2021. In general, it was a positive result for HTW Berlin that teaching and administrative staff successfully dealt with the number of e-exams taken. Hence, even if exam registration increases in future semesters, the university seems well prepared to accommodate such changes.

In addition, these analyses are a starting point for future work as some BI findings raise questions that call for further in-depth analyses. One finding for future discussion could be the stable credit point gains per first-semester student in the summer and winter 2020 and summer 2021 semesters, despite the changes induced by the pandemic. On one hand, this might simply show that first-semester students, teaching staff and maybe the university in general were better prepared to cope with the consequences of the pandemic in winter 2020, whereas on the other hand there may be other factors responsible for this outcome. The percentage of exam passes showing a slight increase in winter 2020 and returning to its usual level in the summer 2021 semester is also an interesting finding. HTW Berlin will look at data for the following semesters to test further hypotheses.

However, in general this raises the question of how the university wants to proceed in the future, given that predominantly online teaching appears to provide results comparable to in-person teaching. This means, due to these comparably good results during 2020, the question now arises of whether the format of a physical university presence remains relevant at all. If the shift to online examinations is to remain or even expand in future, a minimum prerequisite is to confirm that online and presence-based examinations offer equally high standards.

As some effects of the pandemic might emerge in future semesters, HTW Berlin will make further use of its BI reports; the present analysis was conducted at an aggregate level as a starting point for further analysis. It might be interesting to try to disentangle some of the factors responsible for the overarching trends. For instance, further analysis could look at grades data, monitor changes within single study programmes over time, between type of degree, study durations of students, university entrance certificates and the university entrance certificate/study durations interactions available. Moreover, the results represent a single German university, and so apply only to a specific context that might not be widely applicable. Therefore, it would be interesting to see results from other institutions, to gain a better understanding of the consequences of the pandemic for universities more broadly.

As a next step, HTW Berlin will include more key performance indicators and statistics in its business intelligence software. Future work could include integrating survey data into the data warehouse and work on forecasting analysis.

Notes

1   HTW university management: Prof. Dr. Tilo Wendler (Vice-President for Studies, TeachVice-President for Studies, Teaching & International Affairs) and Stephanie Albrecht (Executive Coordinator to the Vice-President), HTW quality management Department (Dr. Sara-I. Täger) and HTW information technology centre (Daniel Thiemann).
2   For a short description, see: https://events.htw-berlin.de/studium/htw-e-lounge/
3   R is a programming language, see: https://www.r-project.org/

References

Al Ghawiel, S. (2021). *The implementation of the quality process in higher education: A critical approach.* ATINER'S Conference Paper Series, Athens Institute for Education and Research. https://hal.archives-ouvertes.fr/hal-03150508

Berghoff, S., Horstmann, N., Hüsch, M., & Müller, K. (2021). *Studium und Lehre in Zeiten der Corona-Pandemie – Die Sicht von Studierenden und Lehrenden [Studying and teaching in times of the COVID pandemic – Perspective of students and teachers].* CHE Impulse Nr. 3. Centrum für Hochschulentwicklung. https://www.che.de/download/studium-lehre-corona/

Cirlan, E., & Loukkola, T. (2021). *Internal quality assurance in times of Covid-19.* European University Association. https://eua.eu/downloads/publications/internal%20qa.pdf

Eltfeld, E. (2016). Entwicklungen in der amtlichen Statistik. Novellierung des Hochschulstatistikgesetzes [Developments in official statistics: Amendment to statistics law in higher education]. *Zeitschrift für amtliche Statistik Berlin Brandenburg, 2* https://www.statistik-berlin-brandenburg.de/publikationen/aufsaetze/2016/HZ_201602-06.pdf

Fowler, J. (2019). *Business intelligence at the university.* 2019 International Conference on Computational Science and Computational Intelligence (CSCI). IEEE. https://ieeexplore.ieee.org/iel7/9052554/9070327/09070811.pdf

German Accreditation Council. (n.d.). *System accreditation.* Retrieved November 23, 2021, from https://www.akkreditierungsrat.de/index.php/en/accreditation-system/system-accreditation/system-accreditation

Hillebrandt, M. (2020). Keeping one's shiny Mercedes in the garage: Why higher education quantification never really took off in Germany. *Politics and Governance, 8*(2), 48–57. https://doi.org/10.17645/pag.v8i2.2584

Hodges, C., Moore, S., Lockee, B., Trust, T., & Bond, A. (2020). The difference between emergency remote teaching and online learning. *Educause Review.* https://er.educause.edu/articles/2020/3/the-difference-between-emerge

Hörnstein, E., Kreth, H., Blank, C., & Stellmacher, C. (2016). *Studiengang-Monitoring. Studienverlaufsanalysen auf Basis von ECTS-Punkten.* Shaker (Verlag).

Horstmann, N. (2022). *Check – Informatik, Mathematik, Physik – Studienbedingungen an deutschen Hochschulen im zweiten Jahr der Corona-Pandemie* [Computer sciences, mathematics, physics – Study conditions at German universities during the second year of the Covid pandemic]. https://www.che.de/download/masterstudium-corona/?wpdmdl=20197&refresh=61fe6fed52cfb1644064749

Iglesias-Pradas, S., Hernandez-García, A., Chaparro-Pelaez, J., & Prieto, J. L. (2021). Emergency remote teaching and students' academic performance in higher education during the COVID-19 pandemic: A case study. *Computers in Human Behavior, 119*, 106713. https://doi.org/10.1016/j.chb.2021.106713

Jaeger, M. (2008). Wie wirksam sind leistungsorientierte Budgetierungsverfahren in deutschen Hochschulen? [How effective are performance-related funding mechanisms at German universities?] In S. Nickel & F. Ziegele (Eds.), *Bilanz und Perspektiven der leistungsorientierten Mittelverteilung. Analysen zur finanziellen Hochschulsteuerung* (pp. 36–49). CHE Arbeitspapier Nr. 111. https://www.che.de/download/che_ap111_analyse_leistungsorientierte_mittelverteilung-pdf/?wpdmdl=11061&refresh=621deff3998d71646129139

Kamel, S. H., Megahed, I., & Atteya, H. (2019). The impact of creating a business intelligence platform on higher education: The case of the American University in Cairo. In Z. Sun (Ed.), *Managerial perspectives on intelligent big data analytics* (pp. 232–259). IGI Global. https://doi.org/10.4018/978-1-5225-7277-0.ch013

Lörz, M., Marczuk, A., Zimmer, L., Multrus, F., & Buchholz, S. (2020). Studieren unter Corona-Bedingungen: Studierende bewerten das erste Digitalsemester [Studying under Covid conditions: Students evaluate the first digital semester]. *DZHW Brief, 2020*(5). https://doi.org/10.34878/2020.05.dzhw_brief

Lörz, M., Zimmer, L. M., & Koopmann, J. (2021). Herausforderungen und Konsequenzen der Corona-Pandemie für Studierende in Deutschland [Challenges and consequences of the Covid pandemic for students in Germany]. *Psychologie in Erziehung und Unterricht, 2021*(4). http://dx.doi.org/10.2378/peu2021.art28d

Marczuk, A., Multrus, F., & Lörz, M. (2021). Die Studiensituation in der Corona-Pandemie: Auswirkungen der Digitalisierung auf die Lern- und Kontaktsituation von Studierenden [Study situation during the Covid-pandemic: Consequences of digitalisation for learning situations and student contact]. *DZHW Brief, 2021*(1). https://www.die-studierendenbefragung.de/fileadmin/user_upload/publikationen/dzhw_brief_01_2021.pdf

Moen, R., & Norman, C. (2009, September 17). The history of the PDCA cycle. In *Proceedings of the 7th ANQ congress.* https://rauterberg.employee.id.tue.nl

Moen, R. D., & Norman, C. L. (2011). Circling back. *Quality Control and Applied Statistics, 56*, 265–266.

Neugebauer, M., Heublein, U., & Daniel, A. (2019). Studienabbruch in Deutschland: Ausmaß, Ursachen, Folgen, Präventionsmöglichkeiten [Dropout in Germany: Amount, causes, consequences and options for prevention]. *Zeitschrift für Erziehungswissenschaft, 22*, 1025–1046. https://doi.org/10.1007/s11618-019-00904-1

nexus Newsletter. (2016). HAW Hamburg: Kontinuierliche Messung des Studienerfolges über ECTS [HAW Hamburg: Continuous measurement of study success via ECTS]. *nexus Newsletter, 5.* https://www.hrk-nexus.de/hrk-nexus-newsletter/nexus-newsletter-52016/#c16987

Scholtz, B., Calitz, A., & Haupt, R. (2018). A business intelligence framework for sustainability information management in higher education. *International Journal of Sustainability in Higher Education, 19*(2). https://www.emerald.com/insight/content/doi/10.1108/IJSHE-06-2016-0118/full/html

Senatsverwaltung für Bildung, Wissenschaft und Forschung. (2011). Leistungsbasierte Hochschulfinanzierung [Performance-based higher education funding]. Retrieved February 2, 2022, from https://www.berlin.de/sen/wissenschaft/politik/finanzierung/broschure_leistungsbasierte_hochschulfinanzierung_2011.pdf

Stifterverband. (2020). *Befragung der Lehrenden an der HTW Berlin zur Lehre im Online-Sommersemester 2020. Zusammenfassung der Ergebnisse* [Survey of lecturers at HTW Berlin on teaching in summer semester 2020. Summary of results] [Unpublished report]. HTW Berlin.

PART 3

Trust

..

CHAPTER 10

Trust during an Era of COVID-19

An Analysis of British Higher Education

Rosalind Pritchard

Abstract

Trust is a key element in the personal, political and social domains. The chapter will
seek to determine what the effect of the recent pandemic has been on trust within
British higher education (HE), and what the implications may be for HE and for British
society. COVID-19 has caused crisis within higher education and has forced many people into the experience of anxiety and mistrust. Initially the essay defines various types
of trust and suggests how they may apply to higher education. It examines the personal impact of COVID-19 on students and staff, discussing perceptions of online and
face-to-face teaching, value for money and mental health. Consideration is also given
to how the pandemic is affecting efforts to achieve diversity and equality of opportunity. Knowledge has to some extent been rendered unfashionable by political pop-
ulism, but when COVID-19 urgently needed vaccines, science was the hero of the hour.
However, human suffering during the pandemic has highlighted the need to bridge the
divide between the sciences and the humanities, though this is currently somewhat
neglected in the UK. Trust is at a low ebb within the British body politic, and lack of
trust is dysfunctional. This is an issue that will remain important even when "fighting"
COVID-19 becomes less urgent due to medical progress. The example of some other
countries such as Finland provides ideas and inspiration.

Keywords

COVID and UK higher education – trust and UK higher education – British academy
and COVID – Finland and COVID – trust and COVID

•••

The last two years of this pandemic have shown how important the
trust in politics, science and societal discourse is – but also how

fragile it can be. Democracy depends on solidarity and trust, including the trust in facts.

> ANGELA MERKEL (Farewell Speech to the German people on 2 December
> 2021)

∵

1   Crisis and Transformation

It is hard to imagine a greater crisis than COVID-19. With about 266m cases
and 5.26m deaths worldwide,[1] the pandemic has caused a tsunami of shock
and grief, threatening existing certainties and straining trust between citizens and states, both nationally and internationally. COVID-19 has caused the
largest global recession since the Great Depression, and global stock markets
have experienced the worst crash since 1987; more than one third of the global
population has been placed on lockdown.[2] Shops, retail centres and restau-
rants have reduced their hours or closed, some never to reopen. Travel and
tourism have been impacted to the point of destruction for certain companies. There have been shortages of food, pharmaceuticals, household basics
and personal protection equipment; events have been cancelled in sport,
technology, religion, fashion, theatre, cinema, art galleries and libraries with
great, sometimes life-changing, loss of income. Families have been forbidden
to attend the bedside of their moribund relatives and denied physical contact
with those in care homes. Major events such as the Hajj in Saudi Arabia and
Chinese New Year have been cancelled or limited to a fraction of the usual
number of participants.[3] COVID-19 mostly halted face-to-face teaching and led
to a huge increase in online delivery for which the institutions were at first
inexperienced and ill-equipped; 58% of students and 47% of teaching staff
polled by a British study (Office for Students (OfS) 2021) had no experience of
digital teaching and learning before the pandemic. By December 2020, 92% of
students surveyed were learning either fully or mostly online (ibid.). The purpose of the present essay is to discuss how the pandemic has affected trust in
higher education (HE) within British society. It will draw most of its examples
from the United Kingdom, though some reference is made to other countries
as appropriate, notably Finland which is a high-trust country.

2   Concepts and Importance of Trust

Trust is theoretically complex, contested and multi-dimensional. At its most basic level, it involves "reliance on and confidence in the truth, worth, reliability etc. of a person or thing" (Collins Dictionary). Faith is often given as a synonym for trust. Lane (1998) considers that trust contains three elements:
- Trust provides a way to cope with risk or uncertainty in exchange relationships.
- "[T]rust is a belief or an expectation that the vulnerability resulting from the acceptance of risk will not be taken advantage of by the other party in the relationship" (ibid., p. 3).
- There is a degree of interdependence between the trustor and the trustee.

Interpersonal trust is based on familiarity, often derived from membership of the same ethnic, religious or family group (Lane, 1998, p. 14). It is a process that develops over time, and eventually achieves a degree of stability. We are all of course familiar with the type of personal trust between human beings which can develop as an attitude or 'state of mind' emerging from relationships. This is a psychological, micro-form of trust. To trust or to mistrust is learnt from infancy and is associated with the developing identity of a young person. Personal and social arrangements in which someone manifests trust are "symbolic complexes, which are especially sensitive to disturbance. Hence, one falsehood may be reacted to with great emotional intensity and [may] upset trust for ever" (ibid., p. 23). The highly emotional reaction when trust is betrayed is also mentioned by other authors, e.g., Vidovich and Currie (2011), who insist that trust can be destroyed by a single negative interaction or experience. It may take years to build but be destroyed in a day.

Social trust conveys the belief that most people can be accorded a reasonable degree of confidence and is developed by repeated experiences and interactions (Uslaner, 2018). It leads to better health outcomes, lower rates of mortality, fewer instances of suicide or traffic accidents, and more life satisfaction overall (ibid, p. 11). Uslaner (ibid.) stresses the pragmatic advantages of trust: in a climate of trust, there is less need for firms and individuals to divert resources of money or personnel (e.g., lawyers) that will shield them against deceit or malpractice, hence overall performance is raised and efficiency is maximised. Lane too (1998) states that trust is often regarded as a precondition for superior economic performance and competitive success in a business environment. Newton et al. (2018) claim that trust between citizens is an essential ingredient of social stability and peaceful government; they go so far as to state that trusting societies are prosperous societies and adduce the example of the "small wealthy and homogeneous welfare states of the Nordic region and parts of Northern Europe [that] register high levels of social and political trust" (ibid.). At the top and bottom levels, studies indicate that Norway, Sweden and Finland have trust levels of over 65% on average, whereas the Philippines has a trust level of 3%; in the UK it is 30%, in the US 39% and in Germany 42% (Ortiz-Ospina & Roser, 2016).

Institutional trust is a macro-form that draws on specific impersonal arrangements in the organisational environment within which a business or body is embedded (Bachmann & Inkpen, 2011). Where institutional trust exists, all parties may benefit from its safeguards and can thus repose trust without having any prior personal experience in dealing with one another. The authors make the point that particular industries develop in some countries, but not in others; they suggest that this is connected with how trust has evolved in specific business environments, sometimes emanating from ancient traditions going back to the Middle Ages, as in Germany or certain other continental European countries (ibid, p. 296). These associations are very conducive to developing institutionally-based trust, as for example in continental European business environments. Bachmann and Inkpen (ibid., p. 281) believe that "The ability to create trust has been widely recognized as hugely valuable because it can significantly reduce transaction costs and lead to the creation of new ideas, for example when knowledge is pooled in inter-organizational relationships". They add that the sanctioning process for breaking trust is usually costly and time-consuming – which is why it is best if trust remains implicit without too many rules and prohibitions.

Political trust is directed at government and is associated with the state of the economy. It is more volatile and changeable than social trust. People's trust in, for example, the criminal justice system depends on their experience with police and the courts. Individuals need to feel that they and their social group are affiliated with those institutions (Uslaner, 2018). High political trust leads to better voter turnout, more tax compliance and more confidence in government (ibid, p. 11). As shown above, trust can be interpersonal or impersonal: a form of human interaction or a reaction to how one is impacted at the systemic level. Putnam (1993) argues that in social capital theory, the link between social and political trust is a centrepiece of healthy democracies. The scholarly consensus is that trust is a highly desirable social and political trait, a force for public good which has often been negatively impacted by neo-liberalism (see Broucker et al., 2016). In the UK, 40% think that major forms of corruption are widespread in Britain (Richards, 2015). This is especially so in perceptions of political parties (59%) but much less so for education (15%), the military (18%) and NGOs (19%); several big banks have been caught manipulating borrowing rates, editors of major newspapers have stood trial for phone-hacking, politicians have been caught falsifying expenses.

Trust and higher education. The varying types of trust described above are not mutually exclusive. They may co-exist, conflict or overlap; but sometimes they also enrich one another with formal and informal structures working together. Stensaker and Maassen (2015) are convinced that trust is a central issue in HE. They say that the two main bases for such trust are a) rational-instrumental and b) normative-cognitive. The former relies on governance with its associated procedures, standards and regulations. Especially in neo-liberal societies, trust involves accountability, for example by means of regulation which may actually militate against trust by seeking to control every aspect of an operation or organisation. The second basis for trust is more diffuse and instinctive: strong values and beliefs govern the behaviour of those involved, and the assumption is that everybody will adhere to shared norms and do a good job. Trust is established over time when accountability is demonstrated, and reputation (even ranking) often acts as a proxy for trust. However, trust is bigger than accountability. If trust were fully actuated, formal accountability would hardly be necessary; it would have become implicit and embedded. Trust carries an element of risk, because it may be abused if it is not combined with quality and competence; and also because *a priori* decisions to trust or not to trust often have to be taken at an *early stage of development* before an evidential basis for trusting has been established.

Curzon-Hobson (2002) argues that trust is a fundamental, integral element in the pursuit of higher learning for it is only through a sense of trust that students will embrace an empowering experience of freedom; the exercise of this freedom requires a risk on behalf of students and their teachers. Trust, he believes, is characterised by a transforming, dialogical learning environment that challenges students to think and act according to their own perceptions without recourse to recitation or transcending ideals. It is a delicate process: "[A] relationship … that accentuates the perception of the teacher and his or her knowledge as also becoming, incomplete and unfinished" (ibid., p. 269). "It provides a sensation of collegiality that rebels from the bland acceptance of the ideas and values of the 'public' and challenges each student and teacher to formulate, discover and test, through dialogue, their personally transforming relationships to knowledge, self and the other" (ibid., p. 268). This recalls the Humboldtian concept of the unity of teacher and learner: both are equal in their search for knowledge; neither "possesses" it and both are there for it, "Beide sind für die Wissenschaft da" (Pritchard, 1990, pp. 44–46).

In linking higher education and trust, we must ask how individuals align themselves to institutional structures in which they work; these in turn are

embedded in a larger social structure that is part of a *politicum*, both nationally and internationally. Context is therefore essential to understanding what
Tierney (2006, p. 57) calls "the grammar of risk and faith". Tierney adds that
rational-choice theorists react against an overly individualistic or psychological
view of life, and that "Trust comes about when individuals hold similar views
of the world that are in sync with the structures in which they reside" (ibid., pp.
54–55). This makes trust a highly contingent concept rather than an inherently
logical one. It is of course different in different jurisdictions and cultures. Trustworthy behaviour may be influenced by the employment circumstances within
which academics work, and this is true of early career researchers, especially in
Germany. They may be pressurised for frequent publication and have to accept
without complaining the unwelcome fact that superordinates sometimes insist
on having their names included as co-authors in publications, even though their
contribution may be minimal or absent (Krempkow, 2016; see also BuWiN, 2021).

3 The Personal Impacts of COVID-19 on Students and Staff in an Era of Online Learning

Jong-Sung You (2018) emphasises the need for integrity and fairness in maintaining institutional trust. He discerns a generally strong correlation between
inequality and corruption; inequality may fuel corruption, especially in
democracies, by increasing patronage, cronyism, and "elite capture" (in which
certain groups experience reduced access to public goods compared with others of higher standing). The present section will report on research findings
covering the UK student population generally in the era of COVID-19; it will
also deal with gender and with some minority groups in academe, having in
mind Lenard and Miller's statement (2018) that ethnic and cultural diversity
has a mainly negative effect on levels of trust.

3.1 Students' Satisfaction with Their Education
So how fairly do British students feel that the universities have treated them
since the advent of COVID-19? First of all, it should be pointed out that many
of them did not feel at all well equipped to cope technically with online learning. A poll conducted by the Office for Students (OfS) showed clear evidence
of digital poverty and inequality in access to technology (OfS, 2020). In an OfS
follow-up survey (2021), it emerged that around 30% of the students lacked
adequate internet access, and 30% did not have access to proper study space.[4]

As is widely-known, British universities charge very high fees that vary
across the four regions that make up the UK. Undergraduate fees may cost up to
£9,250 per annum in England, £9,000 in Wales and £4,395 in Northern Ireland.

Scottish students studying in Scotland do not pay undergraduate fees at all.[5] Most universities have not reduced their fees during the period of COVID-19 despite the fact that tuition has been mostly online. The human impact of such factors has been studied by Neves and Hewitt (2021) who have produced a Student Academic Experience Survey under the auspices of the Higher Education Policy Institute (HEPI) and Advance Higher Education. This is a major piece of work based on the views of 10,186 full-time undergraduate students studying in the UK; it continues a series of such surveys that began back in 2006. The authors regard 2021 as a unique year, and have included extra questions and some open-ended items designed to probe the COVID-19 impact.

The Student Academic Experience Survey (SAES) of 2021 indicates that students' perception of their present course's value-for-money has fallen to the lowest ever level this year.[6] The students were asked: If there were no pandemic restrictions, how would you prefer to learn? The majority (57%) wanted in-person learning. Only just over one-in-ten (12%) preferred online learning with nearly one-in-three (31%) endorsing a blended approach. The online learning experience is not regarded as providing adequate Value-for-Money (VFM) compared with face-to-face (F2F) teaching; and this is felt particularly intensely by people studying subjects that require practical placements, experiments and fieldwork. Just over one-in-four students (27%) claim that they have received good or very good value against 44% perceiving poor or very poor value. The proportion of respondents whose experience has been mainly *worse* than expected has doubled from 13% to 27%; by contrast, there has been a fall in the number of students whose experience has been *better* than expected (down to just 13% from 26% last year). Quotations from the open-ended responses convey these students' feelings vividly.

> The course is great ..., but considering it's all online, I think £9,250 is too much. [As stated above, £9,250 is the annual undergraduate fee in England]. (Neves & Hewitt, 2021, p. 15)

> Working for free as a student nurse while also paying to go to uni, I am essentially paying to work. (Neves & Hewitt, 2021, p. 15)

> Fieldwork ... was meant to be included in the course but didn't happen due to coronavirus. The ability to go to a uni with free field-trips was one reason I chose [it]. (Neves & Hewitt, 2021, p. 15)

Almost one-in-three had considered leaving their course. The main reason for leaving is poor mental health.

I think that the institution could support students' wellbeing/ mental health better. I have been stuck in halls [of residence] and no form of earning money and there is no way for me to apply for funds. I think there should be more support. This would help my academic experience as I wouldn't be worrying all the time about whether or not I can afford food the next week. (Neves & Hewitt, 2021, p. 29)

Listen to students when we say that the money we pay for tuition does not reflect what we receive. Be honest about whether it was/is safe or right for students to move around the country for university, and not just for profit reasons. Have an open dialogue about online learning, recognise that it is not the same quality as in-person learning. (Neves & Hewitt, 2021, p. 30)

Think about student mental health. Yes, there are counselling services in place, however with the impact of COVID I have seen a massive decline in my mental health and the mental health of everyone around me. The staff are still expecting students to get work completed on time and to a high standard and very few are taking into consideration external factors that could impact student life. (Neves & Hewitt, 2021, p. 31)

The negative perceptions seem to have been intensified by diversity. The ethnic minority population of the UK was around 13% at the time of the last census in 2011. It is already known that there is a higher observed incidence and severity of COVID-19 in minority groups; and that such groups tend to be suspicious of vaccination (PHE 2020, section 4.1). This is true both in the UK and in the USA. Illness may be associated with socioeconomic, cultural, or lifestyle factors, genetic predisposition, or physiological differences in susceptibility to infection (Khunti et al., 2020). Cook and Santana (2018, p. 272) note that in cases of disaffection, "[T]he powerless can use distrust of the powerful as a check on their exercise of authority" and they claim that democracy fosters strategies which can reflect fundamental distrust of a too-powerful government. Freeman et al. (2020) write: "Over the longer term, we need to rebuild trust in public institutions and experts – a task that will require society to address the sense of marginalisation that has led many people to question the value and veracity of science and other forms of expert knowledge. *As crises like the current pandemic make clear, trust is the foundation stone of our community. Without it, even the most significant medical breakthroughs can seem like cause for suspicion*" (emphasis added).

In the SAES 2021 study, chapter 8, we find that under one-in-four Black, Asian, and Minority Ethnic (BAME) students believe that they have received good VFM and learnt a lot during lockdown. In almost all cases, White students report more positive findings, and for some of the measures, the gap between BAME and White students is high; e.g., for a question about whether they would choose the same course and university again, there is a negative difference of 14% on behalf of BAME students (Neves & Hewitt, 2021). A very large proportion of Trans students – 64% – had considered leaving their course; and only one-in-four would make the same choice again.

So, evidence shows that VFM and satisfaction with online education are lowish for all groups, and especially for minorities. In the longer term, this is not good for society as a whole. The UK charges high fees for HE; institutional trust may have been adversely affected by this apparent institutional "greed" in circumstances when the student experience is much less satisfactory than it would normally have been even though great efforts were made to replicate the in-class experience through the introduction of online tools. Because of the high cost of British university study, student resentment may be felt more intensely than in other countries, for example in Continental Europe. The Office of the Independent Adjudicator for Higher Education (OIAHE)[7] is the student complaint ombuds-service for higher education in England and Wales. In 2020 it received 2,604 complaints. Many students have suffered financial hardship exacerbated by COVID, and by December 2020, the Government had made £70m available for student support in such cases.[8] In Northern Ireland payment of compensation to students under the COVID-19 Study Disruption Payment Scheme was a *de facto* recognition of shortcomings encountered.[9]

Traditionally the ability to form associations has been vital to social and political trust. It has many advantages for democracy and indeed for students' life-paths. Paxton and Rossler (2018) state that participation in social life leads to increased trust; and that membership of connected associations broadens one's sphere of influence and concern. It also promotes inclusivity by expanding the category of "us" and helping to build social capital. Networks have the potential to generate trust especially during times of uncertainty (Cook and Santana, 2018). However, networks have been negatively impacted by COVID. A survey carried out by Harvey and Karzunina (2021), covering 12,000 British students in 140 universities, shows that 55% feel lonely on a daily or weekly basis; and 45% say that they have been avoiding socialising in person or online with others. The Office for National Statistics (2021) conducted a Student Covid Insights Survey (SCIS) in November 2020; 57% of students reported that their well-being and mental health had become slightly or much worse since the start of the autumn term. Further, students responding to the SCIS reported lower levels of life satisfaction and happiness; also higher levels of anxiety, compared with the general population.[10] This is more than an immediate problem, serious though it is for students at the present time. Their negative experience threatens to reduce their opportunity for building social capital that will sustain them in their future lives to come. Tierney (2006, pp. 92–93) stresses that "[A]ll networks have the ability to create and maintain trust" and that an organisation "without opportunities for social capital is an organization at risk".

Germany forms an instructive contrast with the UK in its cultivation of community associations. Kampfner (2020) in his book *Why the Germans Do it Better* notes that Germany puts social cohesion as one of its top priorities, and that its social capital (viz. Putnam, 1995) is not declining as fast as elsewhere. The Federal Ministry of the Interior consciously seeks to promote vigorous and democratic communities through long-term support for associations. Nearly every second German is a member of at least one club, and in 2016, there were about 400,000 of such organisations nationwide. By contrast, in the UK, membership of voluntary associations has declined significantly; the percentage of the UK population that is active in one or more organisations fell from 52% in 1993 to 43% in 2012 (Ortiz-Ospina and Roser, 2021). Such associations form part of communities that are critical in rebuilding trust and cohesion after a crisis. As Newton et al. (2018: 41) say, voluntary associations nurture a sense of trust and may span cleavages of ethnicity, sex, generation and language. So, they help to manage diversity which can be a problem within higher education sometimes resulting in culture wars.

3.2   *COVID-19 and Staff*

The most widespread strategies for coping with COVID-19 were the closing or partial closing of campuses and the pivoting to online teaching and learning. This was often combined with extreme isolation or quarantine of staff in a domestic setting. In her paper on "Time as the Fourth Dimension in the Globalization of Higher Education", Judith Walker (2009) claims that academics suffer particularly severely from the cult of speed and pressure of time. Space, movement and place form the basis of academic capitalism; and to these Walker (ibid.: 484) adds the dimension of time which impacts on the other three dimensions. Time and space have become compressed. "[W]hile modernity sought to distance time from space, globalization is said to seek to annihilate space through time" (ibid., p. 487). Walker states that both staff and students need to justify their time and be smart in their use of it. There is also a moral dimension to time – it must not be wasted.

All these time pressures have been intensified under COVID-19. Distortions of natural time due to working-at-home impose demands for constant availability; they expose staff (and often students) to surveillance. Here mistrust may recur. Staff are expected to be almost constantly available; and this is in line with the Office for National Statistics' 2021 finding (Martin et al., 2021) that in the latter stages of the pandemic, workers-at-home have become increasingly likely to perform in longer and more varied patterns. Digital tools exist that can be used to take screenshots of staff desktops and laptops, noting login times and active screentime. Campaigns have arisen to protect workers from remote surveillance and to ensure their right-to-disconnect from work technology after hours, as is already the case in France and Spain. The Information Commissioner's Office (ICO) has been requested by MPs and academics to draw up new rules to protect home workers from potential surveillance software that could allow bosses to snoop on how many days the employees have been logging-on and sending emails (Proctor, 2020). The campaigners suggest that any use of personal data through monitoring software should be subject to a Data Protection Impact Assessment (DPIA) before it is introduced.

Gender inequality has been highlighted by the COVID-19 crisis. Academics need to manage high-level academic communication within a domestic context that distracts them from core HE activities. Women lecturers have been especially adversely affected by working from home under COVID-19 conditions, and feel that the expectations placed on them have increased. Females are reputedly good at multitasking, but Crenshaw (2008) regards this "skill" as a myth and as of limited value. What is really happening is the rapid *switching* of tasks in the face of constant disruption – for example by phone- or text-messaging, cooking, answering the door, emailing students, quelling children's quarrels, giving online lectures, attending meetings etc. Working parents' experiences of home-schooling their offspring during school closures can be harrowing, and is made more difficult by the pandemic, plus domestic tension plus the fear that their kids will suffer irretrievable educational loss. Witness the home-schooling mother who said "My husband seems to struggle to keep emotions low [i.e., he is not very successful in doing so!]. There's always crying when he 'teaches'" (Skinner et al., 2021, p. 12). The greatest need expressed in this study was for flexible working hours to conduct home-schooling. In this connection, it should be noted that in the second lockdown, university lecturers were identified as key workers, so for some there was the opportunity for their children to continue to attend school.

McKie (2021) reports on a study carried out for the *Times Higher* relating to the impact of the pandemic on female academics. Three-quarters of the sample of 2,888 mothers agreed that their workload increased during the pandemic, but only 17.5% felt that their duties had been properly adjusted to accommodate childcare responsibilities of which they bore the brunt; though most people's immediate colleagues had been supportive, one in three felt that senior managers had not been supportive. The majority, almost 60%, felt that the quality of their work had declined, and three quarters said that their output had shrunk. Trust was invoked in coping with these problems. Nicole Westmarland, Professor of Criminology at Durham, emphasised that what mattered in the end was "compassionate leadership and trust in your staff"; however, this is from the managerial point of view, and Tierney (2006, p. 74) stresses that individuals may trust at the unit level (e.g., their own colleagues) but not at the organisational level. When the demands for communication processing become overwhelming, people often just shut down and withdraw: "Fragmentation and the impoverishment of trust results" (ibid., p. 97).

Berg and Seeger (2016) analyse the condition and process of belonging to an academic community. They are deeply convinced that affective and cognitive functions are indissolubly linked, and that new technologies need to consider emotional intelligence. In distance and blended learning, they argue, emphasis on the visual reinforces a mind/body split along with a subject/object dichotomy. In the end, job satisfaction is experienced in terms of feeling, and well-being is an inter-subjective rather than an individual achievement (ibid.). Berg and Seeger (ibid.) insist that if learning were purely or even predominantly cognitive, then computers would be adequate and there would be no point in gathering people together in a room. For them, as for the psychologist, Carl Rogers, the essence of academia is the personal relationship between student and teacher. This recalls the unity of teacher and learner that is characteristic of the Humboldtian university (Pritchard, 1990).

4   Trust, Society and Politics

Trust is neither intrinsically good nor bad. High levels of trust do not necessarily mean that an individual will be honest or virtuous – after all there is honour even among thieves. As we have seen above, a deficit of trust has negative civic and personal effects, but an *excess of trust* can also be dysfunctional. The latter can lead to naivety and complacency; it can also suffocate creativity and innovation by making people too satisfied with the status quo. Trust varies from one nation to another. It is not static and it does change over time. It is experienced differently in different countries because it is situated in particular contexts. In fact, contextual understanding is essential to a comprehension of trust (Tierney, 2006).

In most OECD countries, trust has fallen every year during the period 2009–2014, and in the USA it has now reached historically low levels.[11] Barack Obama (2020) in the first volume of his autobiography, A Promised Land, deplores the loss of trust in American society: he writes that "it had become axiomatic among political consultants that restoring trust was a lost cause" (ibid., p. 276). An effect of COVID-19 has been to tip the direction of influence from the international to the national and the local, even hyper-local, domains (Van der Wende, 2020).[12] This is partly because people have been confined to their neighbourhoods by the pandemic, and partly because effective action such as vaccination has been undertaken locally (see Deutsch and Wheaten (2020) for a critical but factual discussion of this issue in relation to the EU; also Irwin (2020)). The nation state is, once again, important. Green (1997) believes that the national state is currently the only viable site of democratic representation, accountability and legitimation; and that supra-national bodies enjoy only weak democratic legitimacy. The renewed emphasis on the nation states justifies nation-specific scrutiny of each country's trust mechanisms and norms.

Mayer et al. (1995) state that trust emanates from ability, benevolence and *integrity* [emphasis added]. It is important that honest values should be modelled by the highest in the land. Yet during his election campaign, the current British Prime Minister (PM), Boris Johnson, claimed that by leaving the EU, the UK would save roughly £350m per week that could be spent on the National Health Service. This was dismissed as "a clear misuse of official statistics" by the UK Statistics Authority.[13] The PM has been openly accused by the EU President of breaking trust in relation to Brexit (Burchard, 2020).[14] In November 2021, a You Gov poll discovered that only 21% of its respondents thought Boris Johnson trustworthy.[15] In 2021, parties were reportedly held in Downing Street (residence of the PM and other senior staff); government personnel had established lockdown rules that they were breaking themselves and this greatly angered the population. An advisor to the PM, Dominic Cummings, drove 260 miles to Durham during the strictest phase of lockdown. Initially the PM defended him and would not dismiss him – that happened later. But the Cummings incident adversely affected trust in England. Dr Daisy Fancourt (University College London (UCL) Epidemiology & Health Care), lead author of UCL Covid-19 Social Study referencing the affair, said: "Trust in government decisions and actions relating to the management of COVID-19 is a major challenge globally and these data illustrate the negative and lasting consequences that political decisions can have for public trust and the risks to behaviours".[16] There is a relationship between social trust and good government. The former makes it possible for the latter to flourish, so there is a mutual cause and effect relationship between the two: a virtuous circle instead of a vicious circle (Newton et al., 2019, p. 49).

The British Academy (BA) has produced a number of reports on the pandemic (see Lalot et al., 2020; BA, 2021b, 2021c). Broadly, they are intended to help answer the question: What are the long-term societal impacts of COVID-19?

Long-term means up to about 2030 and includes education in a whole-society context. Together, these policy reports and the evidence on which they are based represent the most substantial review ever undertaken by the British Academy. All in all, there is a deep consciousness that declining trust is a serious problem because it undermines the government's ability to mobilise public behaviour for wider social and health benefits. Low levels of trust will lead to division and the targeting or scapegoating of particular groups: they mean more inequality too which is likely to become an even more problematic issue within higher education since the advent of COVID-19.

Lalot et al. (2020) writing for the Academy specifically address the issue of trust and social cohesion in Britain during the pandemic. In tracing the trajectory of trust, they reveal that though it has oscillated, from June 2020 onwards a higher percentage of respondents *distrusted* than trusted the British government and its political leadership. Moreover, people felt that the country was more *divided* than united, and they had more confidence in levels of *local unity* than of national unity. Over the course of 2020, the use of news declined and belief in conspiracy theories increased; women engaged with news less than men; the poor and the disabled engaged with news least of all. These demographics are "infodemically vulnerable" to fake news and lack of COVID-19 information, leading to an erosion of trust in government and the news media (Mayhew, 2020; Krempkow & Petri, this volume).

The Academy's major report on *Understanding COVID-19* (British Academy, 2021c) is extensive and well-evidenced. It covers Health, Communities and Knowledge, but the section on Further and Higher Education only extends to seven pages out of 173. It repeatedly emphasises that trust and societal cohesion are linked, and that these links are currently under serious pressure due to governance issues. As we have seen above, COVID-19 has exacerbated aspects of inequality within higher education, and the BA 2021c report emphasises that the long-term effects of COVID-19 are likely to "... entrench aspects of existing inequality, impede intergenerational mobility and constrain young people to education and career binary paths, limiting their options and reducing the agility of the labour market" (ibid., p. 93). It states that: "In higher education, the financial impact of the pandemic, coupled with changing student demographics, challenges the sector's ability to deliver benefits to students, communities and the economy" (ibid., p. 98). The authors continue: "Looking forward, there is a real risk over the coming decade that *trust in government will continue slowly to erode* [emphasis added], in line with trends before the pandemic, and that national unity will continue to fragment" (ibid., p. 128).

Though there is mention of HE, this BA 2021c publication lacks a real vision for universities that might provide future inspiration. The section on

HE consists mostly of information on the "nuts and bolts" of income, funding, recruitment and grades. Reflective analysis has taken place in the UK Government Office for Science in the series "Rebuilding a Resilient Britain" (ARI, 2020). A section on Trust refers to "science", but conveys a pragmatic, utilitarian view of research. It dismisses "questionable research practices (…) that don't always match with *practical requirements*" [emphasis added]. The concept of science is understood as predominantly service-based.

Last to be mentioned here is the Academy's report on what is to be done: *Shaping the COVID Decade* (British Academy, 2021b). The document stresses the importance of voluntary associations in supporting sustainable development (this recalls the encouraging example of German culture, mentioned above). It is greatly concerned about inequality which is exacerbated by lost access to education at all levels, especially as a consequence of COVID. It emphasises that the societal impact of the pandemic cannot be mitigated by medicine, science, and technological innovation alone; mitigation requires the combined weight of the social, cultural, political, economic, and historical perspectives that the arts, humanities and social sciences (AHSS) offer. Though AHSS subjects are as important as science, technology, engineering, and mathematics (STEM) subjects, they receive little block funding and are largely dependent on student fee income (Baker, 2021); and in the United Kingdom, cuts of 50% have recently been made in funding for "non-strategic subjects" such as the performing & creative arts and media studies. This has been called an "act of vandalism" by Jo Grady, general secretary of the University and College Union (Weale, 2021). The British Academy (2021a) has pointed out that the "creative economy" is one of the most dynamic, productive and profitable sectors of the UK labour market and that these industries are now worth £84.1 billion to the UK economy.

A certain consensus is emerging internationally about how the COVID-19 environment needs to be handled, and it has implications for the whole of society as well as for higher education. The OECD is hosting a *Trust in Government* project to advance the measurement of public trust.[17] It lists five policy dimensions influencing trust in public institutions. These will be tabulated in Table 10.1 and compared with seven points given by the British Academy (2021b) and seven points given in a report by the Finnish Academy of Sciences and Letters (2021, 36 pp. "Bending not Breaking"). Finland is a high-trust country which for the fourth year in succession is at the top of the World Happiness Report.[18] It is, as might be expected, impossible to establish *exact* international similarity between all of the points, but a broad functional and thematic equivalence can be postulated.

There is a strong degree of international consensus about what issues need to be addressed and how governance needs to change in order to address these issues. Just one item in the Finnish report was not tabulated above: "Finland

TABLE 10.1   Policy points to promote trust in government. UK, Finland and OECD compared

British academy: Shaping the COVID decade	Finland: Academy of Sciences and Letters	OECD trust in government
1. Build multi-level governance structures based on empowering participation, engagement and cooperation to strengthen the capacity to identify and respond to local needs.		1. Provide or regulate public service.
2. Strengthen and expand community-led social infrastructure that underpins the vital services and support structures needed to enhance local resilience, particularly in the most deprived areas.		
3. Create a more agile, responsive education and training system capable of meeting the needs of a new social and economic environment and acting as a catalyst to develop and enhance our future.	1. Education needs to be reformed at all levels to promote diversity and wide variety of skills. Experiencing and creating art improves people's well-being and creativity. 2. A scientific advisory mechanism based on the expertise of the independent scientific community must be established in Finland. This will improve our crisis resilience and ability to act quickly when necessary. The coronavirus pandemic has shown that the current national scientific advisory arrangements are inadequate. 3.Finland must take a more assertive approach to international cooperation and commit itself to proactive cooperation in the fields of politics, the economy, science and resolving the environmental crisis. The existing permanent national scientific advisory mechanisms are both insufficient and ineffective in drawing on the expertise of the scientific community.	

(cont.)

TABLE 10.1   Policy points to promote trust in government. UK, Finland and OECD compared (*cont.*)

British academy: Shaping the COVID decade	Finland: Academy of Sciences and Letters	OECD trust in government
4. Improve the way we develop, share and communicate knowledge, data and information to enable all decision-makers to work from shared understanding of the facts.	4. Communication capabilities must be developed, and more education should be provided in this field. A clear plan must be created to eradicate disinformation.	2. Listen, consult, engage and explain to citizens.
5. Reimagine urban spaces to support sustainable and adaptable local businesses, amenities, and lifestyles.	5. Economic incentives must encourage stronger commitment to the principles of sustainable development.	3. Improve living conditions for all. 4. Use power and public resources ethically.
6. Empower a range of actors, including business and civil society, to work together with a sense of social purpose to help drive a solid strategy for recovery across the economy and society		5. Anticipate change, protect citizens.
7. Prioritise investment in digital infrastructure as a critical service to eliminate the digital divide, improve communication and joint problem solving, and create a more equitable basis for education and employment. Note: the UK has pledged £22bn for R&D.	6. The share of Finland's GDP that is directed to research, development and innovation must be increased to 8% by 2035. "To strengthen crisis resilience, we need, among other things, research into people's behaviours, aspirations and motivations – and their consequences. This research must be secured permanently in case of future crises."	

must take more effective action to improve the climate and the environment".[19] To the Finnish authors, climate and environmental crisis are clearly implicated in the pandemic, for example in the destruction of nature and in zoonoses that come from animals and develop into human diseases. They believe that their country has been too slow to act in stopping the increase of carbon dioxide and progressing towards climate neutrality. Global crises do not recognize the borders between countries, and this is why international cooperation is so important to a small country like Finland.

It can be seen from Table 10.1 that for the Finns, education and science have a specially prominent role to play whereas the British Academy seemed to under-emphasise them. Finnish stress on education is understandable not just in terms of crisis response, but also historically, because education was a major factor in helping Finland to define itself as a nation (see OECD Country Report on Finland).[20] Finland is one of the homogeneous high-trust, high-tax, high-welfare states of the Nordic region that was mentioned at the beginning of this essay. As Jong-Sung You (2018) points out, universal welfare programmes are more likely than means-tested approaches to increase social trust. Finland's population consists 93% of Finns, so diversity is much less of a challenge than in the UK (13% BAME); in religious makeup, 70% are Lutheran and, generally speaking, religious affiliation is conducive to trust (ibid.; also Ospina-Ortiz & Rosen, 2016). Finland is rated third "cleanest" on the world Corruption Perception Index (85/100).[21] The country, thus, has several characteristics that tend to make trust truly "normative-cognitive" (Stensaker & Maassen, 2015). Trust runs like a *Leitmotif* through the Finnish Academy's text. It is emphasised that trust needs to be built up on a long-term basis even when affairs seem normal; and even when there is no obvious crisis.

> The solid standard of education in the Finnish society and *trust* between the Finnish people allowed Finland to navigate the pandemic crisis relatively successfully.

> *Trust* and interaction between different actors and individuals are the easiest to maintain during crises if their foundations are built patiently when there is no sudden crisis.

Not all countries can replicate the conditions in Finland. However, trust in all its complexity functions as a portfolio word for the good society: the sort of society that will be resilient in future crises – which will definitely occur. Higher education has an important contribution to make to the public good. Though it is only part of the whole, it is a vital enabler of solutions. A survey by UPP (2021) shows that most people believe the university system is moving in the right direction and would like their children to attend an HEI. In the desperate search for a vaccine against COVID-19, the University emerged as cultural hero. Science emerged as heroic too. Sarah Gilbert, Saïd Professor of Vaccinology at the University of Oxford and co-creator of the AstraZeneca vaccine, was invited into the Royal Box at Wimbledon Tennis Tournament on 28.6.2021 and given a standing ovation for her work. In her book (Gilbert & Green, 2021) she states: "[T]he pandemic has … driven an interest in and respect for scientists that I hope will endure. I would love to think that, once the immediate crisis has subsided, we will continue to see scientists held up as inspirational role models". She deplores how precarious scientific careers are and calls for them to be better supported. The benefits of scientific knowledge are easy to understand. But the Finnish Academy praises art too because it "invites us to imagine thus allowing us to examine different futures in a deeply human way" (Finnish Academy, 2021, p. 29). There is a recognition that the whole person matters and that social distancing can "shatter" social interaction: "Human behaviour is often based more on feelings, emotions, and experiences than knowledge in itself. This should be considered more often, both in decision-making and in the scientific community. Crisis resilience is built through education – and it must be increasingly equal" (ibid., pp. 24, 27).

In terms of theory, the various dimensions of trust – interpersonal, social, institutional and political – intersect and overlap; it is hardly possible to discuss one dimension in isolation from others. Students and staff in higher education stand at the centre of an immense and complex field of force exposing them to influences far beyond their control. They are vulnerable, sometimes powerless, in the face of these pressures. Particularly in a system that is so costly to the individual as the British one, COVID-19 has strained the trust between the institutions and the students. Some British politicians have shown themselves untrustworthy, and this has strained the relationship between the citizens and their government. The British Academy (2021c) feels that long-term management of the pandemic and its consequences may need a more active state, different models of fiscal devolution and interventionism, and different kinds of social security systems: in other words a deep reform of governance structures in the United Kingdom. For trust to be reconstituted, the political culture needs to change. Finland shows what can be achieved, though it is far from complacent about its own civic culture. It is for British politicians now, as well as the universities, to help their country along the way that has been signposted. The COVID-19 crisis may even become a catalyst for positive change.

Notes

1   https://www.google.com/search?q=how+many+people+have+died+from+covid+in+the+wh ole+world&rlz=1C1SQJL_enGB877GB877&oq=How+many+people+have+died+from+covid+ &aqs=chrome.7.0i271j0j0i433j69i57j0l5j0i457.13609j0j15&sourceid=chrome&ie=UTF-8
2   https://en.wikipedia.org/wiki/Economic_impact_of_the_COVID-19_pandemic/, accessed 11.8.2021.
3   Saudi Arabia hosted 2,489,406 pilgrims in 2019; it imposed a limit of 10,000 in 2020 due to COVID-19. See https://www.google.com/search?rlz=1C1SQJL_enGB877GB877&sxsrf=ALeKko

ojxnH6byAdjnwUfDciV92_jSYtpw:1621514240258&q=hajj+attendance&sa=X&ved=2ahUKE
wikl6eio9jwAhW2_rsIHR-RDHcQ6B/M0ADApegQIJRAC/, accessed 11.8.2021. See also Javier
C. Hernández and Alexandra Stevenson for information on Chinese New Year.
https://www.nytimes.com/2021/01/28/world/asia/china-coronavirus-new-year.html, published January 28, 2021.

4   For a similar study in Germany, see Senkbein et al. (2019) who found that substantial pro-
    portions of first-year students (20%) as well as students in the sixth semester (52%) do not
    meet the foundational levels of ICT use; furthermore, for both groups of students there are
    considerable differences in their ICT-related competencies depending on areas of study
    and gender. See also Krempkow and Petri, this volume, in which they apply the European
    Reference Framework DigComp2.1.de to Germany; they find that students do not (or cannot)
    necessarily transfer skills acquired in their leisure time to the study context.

5   https://www.ucas.com/finance/undergraduate-tuition-fees-and-student-loans#how-much-
    are-tuition-fees

6   In Germany, see Marczuk et al. (2021) who found that 41% of their student sample were satis-
    fied with their academic experience, though 28% tended towards being dissatisfied.

7   www.oiahe.org.uk/

8   https://www.bbc.co.uk/news/education-55895334

9   https://www.economy-ni.gov.uk/articles/covid-19-study-disruption-payment-scheme-
    northern-ireland-2021/

10 The British government now appears to have recognised social isolation as an important
    issue: it appointed Tracey Crouch MP as its first Minister for Loneliness in the aftermath of
    the Cox Commission on Loneliness. Jo Cox, a female MP was murdered in 2016 by Thomas
    Mair, an extreme nationalist and neo-Nazi, who objected to Jo Cox's pro-Europeanism and
    pro-migrant stance. The murder took place a week before the EU Brexit referendum.

11 https://ourworldindata.org/grapher/oecd-average-trust-in-governments/

12 https://www.piie.com/blogs/realtime-economic-issues-watch/pandemic-adds-momentum-
    deglobalization-trend/

13 https://fullfact.org/europe/350-million-week-boris-johnson-statistics-authority-misuse/

14 https://www.theguardian.com/politics/2020/sep/09/brexit-claim-boris-johnson-responding-
    to-barnier-threat-called-fake-news-/

15 https://yougov.co.uk/topics/politics/trackers/is-boris-johnson-trustworthy/

16 https://www.ucl.ac.uk/news/2020/aug/cummings-effect-led-loss-confidence-uk-government/

17 https://www.oecd.org/gov/trust-in-government.htm

18 https://happiness-report.s3.amazonaws.com/2021/WHR+21.pdf

19 The environment received attention in BA (2021b) and in BA (2021c: 13) it was assumed that
    the environmental sustainability would be addressed by the general policy avenues and
    framework proposed.

20 https://www.oecd.org/publications/drivers-of-trust-in-public-institutions-in-
    finland-52600c9e-en.htm/

21 https://images.transparencycdn.org/images/CPI2020_Report_EN_0802-WEB-1_2021-02-08-
    103053.pdf

Acknowledgements

I wish to thank Bruno Broucker, Roddy Clarke, Nick Hillman, Brian McElwaine,
Michael Shattock and Sandra von Sydow for reading and commenting upon
earlier drafts of this paper.

References

ARI Working group 3. (2020). *Rebuilding a resilient Britain: Trust in public institutions.* ARI Report 3 [Online]. https://www.upen.ac.uk/go_science/RB3_TrustInPublicInstitutions.pdf/

Bachmann, R., & Inkpen, A. (2011). Understanding institutional-based trust building processes in inter-organizational relationships. *Organization Studies, 32*(2), 281–301.

Berg, M., & Seeger, B. K. (2016). *The slow professor: Challenging the culture of speed in the academy.* University of Toronto Press.

British Academy (BA). (2020). *Qualified for the future: Quantifying demand for arts, humanities and social sciences.* The British Academy.

British Academy (BA). (2021a). *Office for students – Consultation on recurrent funding 2021–22.* The British Academy.

British Academy (BA). (2021b). *Shaping the COVID decade: Addressing the long-term societal impacts of COVID-19.* The British Academy.

British Academy (BA). (2021c). *The COVID decade: Understanding the long-term societal impacts of COVID-19.* The British Academy.

Broucker, B., De Wit, K., & Leisyte, L. (2016). Higher education system reform: A systematic comparison of ten countries from a new public management perspective. In R. M. O. Pritchard, A. Pausits, & J. Williams (Eds.), *Positioning higher education institutions: From here to there* (pp. 19–40). Sense Publishers.

Burchard von der, H. (2020). *Von der Leyen to UK: Thatcher would not break her word on Brexit.* https://www.politico.eu/article/eus-von-der-leyen-slams-britain-over-plans-to-backtrack-on-brexit-withdrawal-agreement/

BuWiN (Bundesbericht Wissenschaftlicher Nachwuchs). (2021). Authored by the consortium of the national report on early career researchers and based on "National report on early career researchers 2021 statistical data and research findings on doctoral candidates and doctorate holders in Germany". Federal Ministry of Education and Research.

Cook, K. S., & Santana, J. (2018). Trust and rational choice. In E. Uslaner (Ed.), *Oxford handbook of social and political trust* (pp. 253–278). Oxford University Press.

Crenshaw, D. (2008). *The myth of multitasking: How "doing it all" gets nothing done.* Mango.

Curzon-Hobson, A. (2002). A pedagogy of trust in higher learning. *Teaching in Higher Education, 7*(3), 265–276.

Deutsch, J., & Wheaton, S. (2021, January 27). *How Europe fell behind on vaccines. The EU secured some of the lowest prices in the world. At what cost?* https://www.politico.eu/article/europe-coronavirus-vaccine-struggle-pfizer-biontech-astrazeneca/

Finnish Academic of Sciences and Letters. (2021). *Bending but not breaking. From the Corona virus to strengthening Finland's crisis resilience.* Academy of Sciences.

Freeman, D., Loe, B., Chadwick, A., Vaccari, C., Waite, F., Rosebrock, L., & Lambe, S. (2020). COVID-19 vaccine hesitancy in the UK: The Oxford coronavirus explanations, attitudes, and narratives survey (Oceans) II. *Psychological Medicine*, 1–15. doi:10.1017/S0033291720005188/

Gilbert, S., Green, C., & Crewe, D. (2021). *Vaxxers – The inside story of the Oxford AstraZeneca vaccine and the race against the virus.* Hodder.

Green, A. (1997). *Education, globalisation and the nation state.* St Martin's Press/ Macmillan.

Harvey, B., & Karzunina, D. (2021). *University: The best time of our lives? A call to action to address the declining mental health of UK students.* Accenture and Cibyl. https://www.accenture.com/_acnmedia/PDF-158/Accenture-Student-Health-Research-Report.pdf#zoom=40/

Irwin, D. A. (2020). *The pandemic adds momentum to the deglobalization trend.* The Peterson Institute for International Economics (PIIE).

Kampfner, J. (2020). *Why the Germans do it better: Notes from a grown-up country.* Atlantic Books.

Khunti, K., Singh, A. K., Pareek, M., & Hanif, W. (2020). Is ethnicity linked to incidence or outcomes of Covid-19? *British Medical Journal, 369.*

Krempkow, R. (2016). *Wissenschaftliche Integrität, Drittmittel und Qualität in der Wissenschaft* [*Academic integrity, external funding and quality in academia*]. https://www.researchgate.net/publication/303945901/

Lalot, F., Davies, B., & Abrams, D. (2020). *Trust and cohesion in Britain during the 2020 COVID-19 pandemic across place, scale and time.* Report for the British Academy.

Lane, C. (1998). Introduction: Theories and issues in the study of trust. In C. Lane & R. Bachmann (Eds.), *Trust within and between organizations: Conceptual issues and empirical applications* (pp. 1–30). Oxford University Press.

Lane, C., & Bachmann, R. (Eds.). (1998). *Trust within and between organizations: Conceptual issues and empirical applications.* Oxford University Press.

Lenard, P. T., Miller, D., & Uslaner, E. M. (2018). Trust and national identity. In E. Uslaner (Ed.), *The Oxford handbook of social and political trust* (pp. 57–74). Oxford University Press.

Marczuk, A., Multrus, F., & Lörz, M. (2021). *Die Studiensituation in der Corona Pandemie. Auswirkungen der Digitalisierung auf die Lern- und Kontaktsituation von Studierenden* [*Studying in the Corona pandemic: Effects of digitalisation on learning and the (social) contact situation of students*]. Deutsches Zentrum für Hochschul- und Wissenschaftsforschung (DZHW).

Martin, J., Haigney, V., Lawrence, B., & Walton, A. (2021). *Homeworking hours, rewards and opportunities in the UK: 2011 to 2020.* Office for National Statistics.

Mayer, R. C., Davis, J., & Schoorman, D. (1995). An integrative model of organisational trust. *The Academy of Management Review, 20*(3), 709–734.

Mayhew, F. (2020, October 27). Proportion of infodemically vulnerable people in UK grew under lockdown. *PressGazette*. https://www.pressgazette.co.uk/proportion-of-infodemically-vulnerable-people-in-uk-grew-under-lockdown-survey-finds/

McKie, A. (2021, June 10). "Business as usual" took toll on mums in pandemic. *Times Higher*.

National Academies of Sciences, Engineering, and Medicine. (2018). *The integration of the humanities and arts with sciences, engineering, and medicine in higher education: Branches from the same tree*. The National Academies Press. https://doi.org/10.17226/24988

Neves, J., & Hewitt, R. (2021). *Student academic experience survey 2021*. Higher Education Policy Institute (HEPI) and Advance HE.

Newton, K., Stolle, D., & Zmerli, S. (2018). Social and political trust. In E. Uslaner (Ed.), *The Oxford handbook of social and political trust* (pp. 961–976). Oxford University Press.

Obama, B. (2020). *A promised land*. Crown.

Office for National Statistics (ONS). (2021). *Coronavirus and the impact on students in higher Education in England: September to December 2020*. https://www.ons.gov.uk/peoplepopulationandcommunity/educationandchildcare/articles/coronavirusandtheimpactonstudentsinhighereducationinenglandseptembertodecember2020/2020-12-21/

OfS – Office for Students. (2020). *Digital poverty is leaving students behind in an age of online learning*. https://www.google.com/search?q=Digital+poverty+is+leaving+students+ behind+in+an+age+of+online+learning.&rlz=1C1SQJL_enGB877GB877&oq=Digital+poverty+is+leaving+students+behind+in+an+age+of+online+learning.++&aqs=chrome..69i57.2188j0j15&sourceid=chrome&ie=UTF-8/

OfS – Office for Students. (2021). *Gravity assist: Propelling higher education towards a brighter future*. https://www.officeforstudents.org.uk/publications/gravity-assist-propelling-higher-education-towards-a-brighter-future/executive-summary/#edn1/

Ortiz-Ospina, E., & Roser, M. (2016). *Our world in data*. https://ourworldindata.org/trust/

Paxton, P., & Ressler, R. W. (2018). Trust and participation in associations. In E. Uslaner (Ed.), *The Oxford handbook of social and political trust* (pp. 149–172). Oxford University Press.

PHE – Public Health England. (2020). *Disparities in the risk and outcomes of COVID-19*. PHE.

Pritchard, R. M. O. (1990). *The end of elitism: The democratisation of the West German university system*. Berg.

Proctor, K. (2020). *ICO (Information Commissioner's Office) urged to protect workers from Surveillance Software*. https://www.publictechnology.net/articles/news/ico-urged-protect-workers-surveillance-software/

Putnam, R. (1993). *Making democracy work: Civic traditions in modern Italy*. Princeton University Press.

Putnam, R. (1995). Bowling alone: America's declining social capital. *Journal of Democracy, 6*(1), 65–78.

Richards, L. (2015). *Is Britain becoming more corrupt?* CSI 14. http://csi.nuff.ox.ac.uk/wp-content/uploads/2015/06/CSI-14-Corruption.pdf

Senkbeil, M., Ihme, J. M., & Schöber, C. (2019). Wie gut sind angehende und fortgeschrittene Studierende auf das Leben und Arbeiten in der digitalen Welt vorbereitet? Ergebnisse eines Standard Setting-Verfahrens zur Beschreibung von ICT-bezogenen Kompetenzniveaus [Are first-semester and advanced university students ready for life and work in the digital world? Results of a standard setting method to describe ICT-related proficiency levels]. *Zeitschrift für Erziehingswissenschaft, 22*(6), 1359–1384.

Skinner, B., Hou, H., Taggart, S., & Abbott, L. (2021). Working parents' experiences of home-schooling during school closures in Northern Ireland: What lessons can be learnt? *Irish Educational Studies*, 1–20.

Stensaker, B., & Maassen, P. (2015). A conceptualization of available trust-building mechanisms for international quality assessment of higher education. *Journal of Higher Education Policy and Management, 37*(1), 30–40.

Tierney, W. G. (2006). *Trust and the public good: Examining the cultural conditions of academic work*. Peter Lang.

UPP (University Partnerships Programme) Foundation and Higher Education Policy Institute. (2021). *Public attitudes to higher education survey*. UPP and HEPI.

Uslaner, E. (Ed.). (2018). *Oxford handbook of social and political trust*. Oxford University Press.

Van der Wende, M. (2020). *Neo-nationalism and universities in Europe*. Centre for Studies in Higher Education.

Vidovich, L., & Currie, J. (2011). Governance and trust in higher education. *Studies in Higher Education, 36*(1), 43–56.

Walker, J. (2009). Time as the fourth dimension in the globalization of higher education. *The Journal of Higher Education, 80*(5), 483–509.

Weale, S. (2021, July 20). Funding cuts to go ahead for university arts courses despite opposition. *The Guardian*.

You, J.-S. (2018). *Trust and corruption*. In E. Uslaner (Ed.), *Oxford handbook of social and political trust* (pp. 473–496). Oxford University Press.

CHAPTER 11

Innovative Higher Education Institution or Innovator in the Higher Education Institution?

An Analysis of the Influence and Interplay of Frame Conditions and the Person-Specific Innovative Ability

Cindy Konen

Abstract

Based on a case study, this contribution provides HEIs with an ideal type model for assessing their innovative ability for cooperative innovations with enterprises. While previous approaches mainly focus on analysing innovation-supporting frame conditions and, on this basis, try to determine the extent of innovative ability, this contribution looks onwards. Therefore, it equally takes the professor acting as an innovator into focus. This creates a bottom-up perspective that shows that different ideal types can usually be found within one HEI since the professors' individual innovation ability and willingness to innovate can vary significantly from another. The case study results further show that innovative ability often does not arise due to the combination of innovation-supporting frame conditions and the professor acting as an innovator, but simply by the professor acting as an innovator without support. However, acting as an innovator without support leads to dissatisfaction with the HEI and a medium to long-term decline in innovation cooperation activities. Only by analysing both the innovation-supporting frame conditions and the person-specific innovative ability as well as their interplay, the HEI gets a realistic picture of its innovative ability.

Keywords

innovative ability – innovation cooperation – ideal types – case study – governance – bottom-up perspective

1 Motivation

The innovative ability, or in other words, the capability to generate innovations, is maybe one of the most used words in the context of managing new challenges, securing the survival of organisations or ensuring a competitive advantage (Smith et al., 2008; Hutterer, 2012; Wördenweber et al., 2020). Previously primarily discussed in the context of economic institutions, it is increasingly becoming the focus of Higher Education Institutions (HEIs) in Germany (Konen, 2020). One of the biggest drivers is the increased importance of the so-called third mission of HEIs. The third mission calls on HEIs to strengthen their engagement with society. One of these intensified engagement strands is to extend collaborations with enterprises to develop cooperative innovations (Henke et al., 2015). For this purpose, HEIs need a distinctive innovative ability. Innovative ability is here understood as the ability to create the intra-institutional prerequisites for innovations in innovation cooperations with enterprises (Konen, 2020).

Within the last few years, the wish for a robust innovative ability of German HEIs has been formulated by external sources like politics, society, and enterprises and by internal sources themselves. For example, in 2014, 93% of all rectors questioned in a survey wished for more cooperation with enterprises (Stifterverband, 2014). In this contribution, these cooperative innovations are defined as the complete process from the initiation to the conclusion of cooperation between at least one HEI with at least one enterprise and possibly other partners, such as non-university research institutes, with the aim of producing innovation. During the cooperation, the HEI contributes suitable resources as well as knowledge and skills (Konen, 2019). Furthermore, HEIs pursue several motifs with such cooperations. Typical motifs are the generation of third-party funds, gains in reputation, satisfying intrinsic motivation, and the wish to solve social and enterprise problems (Stifterverband, 2014; Konen, 2020).

This contribution provides interested HEIs with an approach to face that new challenge.[1] Therefore, it is necessary to understand the complexity of the construct of innovation ability. Only by understanding it scarce resources can be inserted meaningfully to increase the innovative ability. Furthermore, by knowing the construct of innovative ability synergies with the goals 'research' and 'teaching' can better be achieved (e.g. cooperative teaching projects or application-oriented research projects with benefits for all cooperating partners). Thus, managing the innovative ability gives an HEI many possibilities for a competitive advantage.

2   Theoretical Framework

By analysing the innovative ability within German HEIs, first of all, it has to be asked if all HEIs are provided with a similar extent of innovative ability. An initial assessment can be obtained by analysing rankings that include innovation output indicators like the CWUR, US News Ranking, QS World Ranking,

Shanghai Ranking, Times Higher Education Ranking, Reuters most innovative Universities Ranking and the U-Multirank. Relevant information can also be gained by analysing the participation on specific state third party subsidies and (if available) the third party funds per HEI and the average third party funds per professor. This number-based analysis shows a considerable range of potentially innovation-relevant activities and success. However, does this include an equal extent of innovative ability within the same HEI? There must be a deeper look at the influence factors of innovative ability to answer this question. Most detailed studies of the influence factors of innovative ability mainly focus on the sector of economic institutions (e.g. Lawson & Samson, 2001, Smith et al., 2008, Stern & Jaberg, 2010). However, if these studies are deeply analysed, it can be pointed out that innovative ability consists of the three levels causes (e.g. structure, culture, leadership), manifestation (e.g. ability to identify application potentials, ability to manage innovation processes) and results (different types of innovation).[2]

Nevertheless, these studies often focus mainly on the design of innovation-supporting frame conditions. Even if these studies comprehensively describe the construct of innovative ability, they cannot depict the particularities of the HE sector. An essential point of criticism is that often they are unnamed, assuming that innovation-supporting frame conditions automatically lead to innovation-oriented actions of the organisational members. Therefore, also findings from HE research have to be analysed. Hitherto, HE research mainly provides studies on individual aspects of innovative ability (e.g. leadership, structure and processes, the allocation of resources or culture). Studies focusing on the complete construct of innovative ability often analyse it from a holistic, little detailed perspective.

However, from the 1970s on, HE research provides several description models that work out the specifics of HEIs in contrast to enterprises and are to be used in the context of this contribution. Early significant work is provided by Weick (1976) with the model of loosely coupled systems, Cohen, March, and Olsen (1972) with the model of organised anarchy and Mintzberg (1979) with the HEI as an expert organisation. According to Weick's theory, an HEI consists of subsystems that often rarely depend on each other and contain different self-conceptions and cultures. Pursuant to Cohen, March and Olsen, HEIs are characterised through unclear goals as well as poorly known structures and decision-making processes. HEI members' willingness to participate in activities like cooperative innovations quite differ. Mintzberg accentuates HEIs as expert organisations that provide professors with high autonomy. Therefore, professors meet goals mainly on their preferences while HEI-leaders only have restricted possibilities to steer. The rules of the scientific community often play a more critical role for the professors.

Against the background of changed political and societal expectations as well as the increasing importance of the third mission, newer description models partially modify these core statements.

Therefore, Brunsson and Sahlin-Anderssen (2000) and Thoenig and Paradeise (2016) consider through the building of ideal types models if HEIs can develop a collective identity with accepted leadership mechanisms. They conclude that some HEIs succeed, while autonomously acting individuals with varying goals still drive most HEIs. According to Thoenig and Paradeise, a collective identity can arise if the subunits are integrated into an HEIs strategic development and decision process and thus, connectivity with the HEI goals emerges. This works particularly well when the framework conditions satisfy the professors' motivations (Scherm & Jackenroll, 2016).

There are several reasons why HEIs often fail to develop a collective identity. One influence factor is the shared loyalty of the professors. Though, they are both members of the HEI and their peer groups provided with specific requirements (Thoenig & Paradeise, 2016; Meyer, 2019). Related to this is the influence of intrinsic motivation. According to Etzkowitz's (2013) entrepreneurial university model, only a few professors are interested in innovation cooperation – even though being based in potentially application-oriented disciplines. A third factor is the still restricted influence of leadership in German HEIs (Badillo Vega, 2018). According to Hüther and Krücken (2013), possible leadership actions are only leadership by granting incentives (reward power) and leadership by restricting resources (coercive power). However, due to the HEIs nature, coercive power is only enforceable to a limited extent. On the one hand, professors can avoid this restriction by generating third party funds. On the other hand, HEI-leadership has to ask itself if it makes sense to block a professor's possibility for research by restricting resources (Hüther, 2013). Because of Germany's system of livelong and nearly non-redeemable professorship positions, the leadership has nearly no possibilities to affect the professors' behaviour against their personnel agenda.

By summarising, four aspects can be noted:
- Frame conditions do not automatically lead to desired actions. That means a professor does not automatically enter into cooperative innovations just because the HEI provides innovation-supporting frame conditions.
- Individuals and their specific goals massively drive HEIs.
- Leadership and targeting goals from leadership positions are only possible to a limited extent.
- Professors' interest in cooperative innovations varies greatly. While it is a primary goal for some professors, it has no relevance for other professors. This interest is not only driven by the extent of the application-orientation

of a discipline. Furthermore, differences are also expected among professors in the same discipline due to their intrinsic motivation.

On this basis, two assumptions can be proposed. They are called:
- Assumption I: The extent of innovative ability varies not only within the
  same HEI but also within the same discipline within one HEI.
- Assumption II: Innovative ability results from the interplay of innovation-
  supporting frame conditions and the professor acting as an innovator.

These assumptions will be analysed about their applicability in the German
HE sector in the further course. For this purpose, first, the design of a conducted cases study is described. Afterwards, selected results are presented.

3 Empirical Design

To examine these assumptions, a case study was conducted. This case study
followed the approach of Yin (2014). Therefore, single and cross-case studies
in eight German HEIs were conducted. Three state universities (state univ.),
three state universities of applied sciences (state UAS) and two private universities (private univ.) were analysed (for a more detailed analysis of the German
HE-sector and the differences between the forms, see Konen, 2019). To select
suitable HEIs, all German HEIs were first subjected to a data-based analysis of
their innovative ability. As can be seen in the following table, the selected HEIs
provide different levels of innovative ability according to data analysis.

In further context, the innovative ability of each selected HEI was in-depth
analysed using data triangulation. Therefore, a documentary analysis was
performed for every HEI. Analysed documents were, e.g. strategy papers, target agreements, transfer documents, monetary indicators, reports about the
HEI or specific marketing documents. In addition, 29 expert interviews were
conducted as part of the case study. As experts, leaders of transfer supporting
units, as well as professors from the departments of economics and mechanical engineering, were asked.

The leaders of the transfer supporting units were chosen because, on the one
hand, they are (typically) well informed about the innovation efforts driven by
the leadership and are, on the other hand, in daily interaction with the innovat-
ing professors. This point of view enables them to report well on the HEI-wide
challenges in the context of innovation by using a top-down point of view.

The professors were interviewed as experts with a bottom-up perspective.
Professors with high, medium and low innovative abilities were deliberately

TABLE 11.1   Extent of the innovative ability of the analysed HEI s according to data analysis

Denomination	HEI_A	HEI_B	HEI_C	HEI_D	HEI_E	HEI_F	HEI_G	HEI_H
HEI type	state univ.	state univ.	state univ.	state UAS	state UAS	state UAS	priv. univ.	priv. univ.
Estimated innovative ability	strong	mode-rate	mode-rate	strong	mode-rate	mode-rate	N/A[a]	

a   Statement not possible because of low data situation

selected. On the one hand, the influence factors that were individually decisive for entering into or not entering into innovation cooperations were to be determined. On the other hand, differences in the effectiveness of the influencing factors were to be recognised. The departments economics and mechanical engineering were chosen because they are both application-oriented. Therefore, it can be assumed that the professors have a higher intrinsic motivation to produce innovations than in less application-oriented subject areas like ancient literature or archaeology. It can also be assumed that the influence of external forces (e.g. peer groups, political and societal expectations) on the members of the same department is often roughly the same in principle. By looking at the individual actions of a professor, this influence is thus implicitly considered. Nevertheless, due to the diversity of the research discipline, the internal self-conception differs, e.g. in the area of publication or the extent of copyright protection. The results in the following section have to be interpreted under these conditions.

The examination of the case study results occurred systematically based on the content analysis of Mayring (2015).

4   Results

4.1   Criteria of Innovative Ability

One result of the case study is a detailed overview of the criteria of innovative ability on the level of causes, manifestation and results.[3] Innovative ability presented itself as a construct with sixty-five criteria. Fifty-two of these criteria can be found on the level of causes, eleven criteria on the level of manifestation and two criteria on the level of effects. However, the research contribution does not only refer to the provision of the derived criteria. Contrary to previous studies that deal with the innovative ability or related research areas such as transfer or third mission, it not only focuses on the design of the frame conditions but also on how these interact with the professor as an innovator. This means that it further divides the criteria of innovative ability into those that affect the actions of an HEI as an organisation through the design of innovation-supporting frame conditions (31 criteria) and those that focus on the professor's actions as an innovator (34 criteria). The professors' actions as an innovator can further be broken down into their willingness to accept the frame conditions (16 criteria) as well as their willingness to innovate and their resulting activities in innovation cooperations (18 criteria). The action of the HEI as an organisation determines the professors' action as an innovator. However, the design of innovation-supporting frame conditions is not solely responsible for the professors' actions as an innovator (see assumptions I and II). Instead, the professors' actions as an innovator are significantly influenced by several other individual influence factors (e.g. motif situation, the liability of other tasks).

Table 11.2 gives an overview of the discovered criteria of innovative ability.

4.2   Developed Ideal Types

The sixty-five criteria of innovative ability form the basis for a developed ideal type model. Each criterion is an integral part of each ideal type. Which ideal type arises depends on how the respective criteria are specified.

While hitherto existing ideal type models for HEIs (e.g. Brunsson & Sahlin-Anderssen, 2000; Thoenig & Paradeise, 2016) assign the complete HEI to the same ideal type, the here presented conception differs. Assumptions I and II put the individuality of the professor into focus by analysing their individual goals and motif situation as well as, as a result, the different estimation and acceptance of the implemented innovation-supporting frame conditions. Therefore, it seems impossible to classify the whole HEI from a top-down perspective into just one ideal type. Instead, it assumes that the ideal type of the HEI is always person-specific and therefore, by using a person-specific view, different ideal types can be found within one HEI.

However, this does not mean that the fundamental characteristic of the formation of ideal types, namely the abstraction of reality to a generalisable structure, is reduced to ad absurdum. Instead, this approach assumes that the differences within an HEI can be much better carved out by taking the individual perspective into account. This means different ideal types can be found in an HEI based on the individual. Nevertheless, the number of overall ideal types is still limited. Therefore, a limited number of possible ideal types occur with varying frequency within the HEIs over the entirety of members. Individual innovation skills of the HEI members can thus also be analysed and explained beyond the basic application orientation of a subject.

TABLE 11.2   Criteria of innovative ability

Level/criteria	Implementation of frame conditions	Acceptance of frame conditions	Activities in innovation cooperations	Total number of criteria
Causes	31	16	5	52
Motif situation			1	1
Strategy	3	3		6
Leadership	4			4
Recruitment	2	1		3
Personnel development	3	3		6
Target system and incentives	2	2		4
Scientific cooperation structure	2	2	2	6
Transfer support	5	2		7
Supporting boards & commissions	1	1		2
Marketing & information for innovation coop.	2	1		3
Culture	2		1	3
Other resources	3			3
Methods for innovations	1		1	2
Coordination cause factors	1	1		2
Manifestation			11	11
Ability to acquire knowledge			1	1
Ability to recognize application potential			2	2
Ability to manage cooperate innovations			5	5
Ability to generate learning effects			2	2
Coordination of the abilities			1	1
Effects			2	2
Obtaining innovation-relevant performance			2	
Total	31	16	18	65

As described above, this contribution postulates that there must be a distinction between the dimension of steering the HEI and the dimension of an individual's actions. These two dimensions can pursue the same goals and thus act in the same strategic direction, but they can also differ in terms of their goals. Since the goals of the HEI members can also be different, it is insufficient to differ between the dimension of the HEI as an organisation and the dimension of HEI members as a totality. The HEI members have instead to be analysed under an individual person-specific view. Therefore, the ideal types are arranged in an axis system. The horizontal axis shows the extent to which a professor enters into cooperate innovations and lead them to success. This axis is the 34 criteria that refer to the professor acting as an innovator. Behind the vertical axis are the 31 criteria that focus on implementing innovation-supporting frame conditions.

On this basis, four different ideal types can be derived. The
- traditional HEI;
- ambitious HEI;
- part-innovative HEI;
- innovative HEI (real/fictional).

Figure 11.1 presents the below-described model. Please note that in the following description, the gender-neutral "they" is used to describe the actions of the professor as an individual.

The first quadrant represents the traditional HEI. In the traditional HEI, no or only a few innovation-supporting frame conditions are implemented, and the professor enters only a few or no innovation cooperations. This is because they do not expect desirable consequences of actions. The professor does not believe in satisfying their motifs by entering into cooperative innovations, as they do not receive appropriate incentives from the HEI. Nor do they assume that entering into innovation cooperations will further the recognition of their work or increase their reputation in their peer group. Furthermore, entering into innovation cooperations would not lead to the satisfaction of their intrinsic motivation (e.g. through the knowledge that they had contributed to solving practical problems).

The ambitious HEI can be found in the second quadrant. Here, innovation-supporting frame conditions are implemented to a large extent. Still, the professor does not enter into any or only a few innovation cooperations because they do not expect desirable consequences of actions. Two main reasons can be causal. First, the HEI offers the professor the wrong innovation-supporting frame conditions. This can be because either the leadership does not know which innovation-supporting frame conditions would affect the professors' wishes or it cannot fulfil them. For example, the HEI provides material

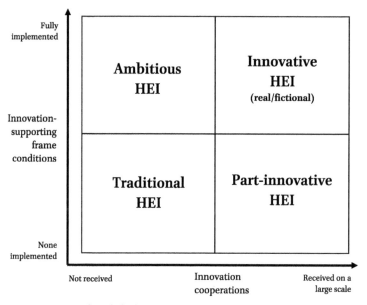

FIGURE 11.1   Developed ideal type model

incentives, but the professor wishes temporal freedom. Second, the HEI may not be able to incentivise the professor to enter into cooperative innovations. For example, the professor may be in a dilemma if cooperating partners wish for applicable research results and nondisclosure contracts while the peer awaits A-Publications. At least, entering into innovation cooperations may not satisfy their intrinsic motivation.

The part-innovative HEI is located in the third quadrant. Here no or only a few innovation-supporting frame conditions are implemented. Nevertheless, the professor enters into many innovation cooperations because they assume desirable consequences of actions – even without support from the HEI. Moreover, entering into cooperative innovations will satisfy their intrinsic motivation. Therefore, the professor may invest their free time in innovation cooperations without HEI support because they enjoy the project, believe in the importance of a problem-solving contribution, or expect an increase in their reputation.

In the fourth quadrant, the innovative HEI can be found. It has the particular characteristic to take on two forms – real or fictional. Within the real-innovative HEI, innovation-supporting frame conditions have been implemented on a large scale. The professor enters into many innovation cooperations because they assume desirable consequences of actions and satisfy their intrinsic motivation. It is characteristic for the real-innovative HEI that some of the desirable consequences of action result from the implemented frame conditions.

It has been emphasised that innovation-supporting framework conditions do not necessarily lead to cooperative innovations. This supposition has been found in the case study, too. Thus, the form of the fictional-innovative HEI has to be introduced. To better understand the form of the fictional-innovative HEI, it is necessary to look at the individual motif situation. In the fictional-innovative HEI, the professor enters into cooperative innovations because they assume desirable consequences of actions and thus also the satisfaction of their intrinsic motivation. However, the implemented innovation-supporting frame conditions are not causative. Maybe the professor sees them as inappropriate or does not know them because of a lack of information diffusion.

This clarifies how important it is for leadership to analyse the professors' motifs. If leadership does not profoundly analyse the reasons for the HEIs innovative ability, they classify the implemented innovation-supporting frame conditions as causative for high innovative ability. If the professors' intrinsic motivation disappears, the leadership may wonder why the innovative ability declines while nothing has changed on the dimension of innovation-supporting frame conditions. It is also possible that a professor who classifies their HEI as a fictional-innovative HEI migrates as soon as they find a job that better satisfies their motives.

As can be deduced, only the traditional HEI and the real-innovative HEI are balanced ideal types. Leadership goals and the professors' actions correspond. However, an imbalance characterises the other ideal types. The leadership goals and the professors' actions contradict each other within the ambitious HEI and the part-innovative HEI. Within the fictional-innovative HEI, the goals of the leadership and the professors' actions are rectified. However, a conflict field still exists due to the leadership's inability to satisfy the professors' motives.

4.3   Ideal Types within the Case Study

Following it is analysed if and how the examined HEIs are taking part. First, it can be stated that all identified ideal types can be found at the analysed HEIs. Figure 11.2 gives an overview of the occurrence of the ideal types.

Five analysis units classify the HEI as a traditional HEI and five as an ambitious HEI. Seven analysis objects classify the HEI as a part-innovative HEI. With twenty classifications, the innovative HEI has the most nominations. Nevertheless, only fourteen classifications assign the HEI to the real-innovative HEI, and six analysis units assign the HEI to the fictional-innovative HEI. Therefore, Figure 11.2 already shows that the extent of innovative ability varies within one HEI as formulated in the first part of assumption I. The question now arises whether there is also evidence for the second part of assumption I and if differences in

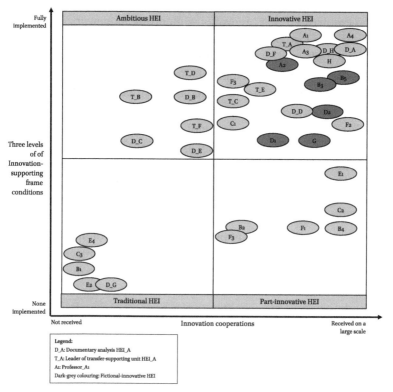

FIGURE 11.2   Occurrence of ideal types

the extent of innovative ability between the category of analysis units, especially in the category of professors' can be found. As shown in Figure 11.3, the
case study results clearly show that the category of analysis unit matters.

If the analysis unit documentary analysis is brought into focus, the ideal
type real-innovative HEI is highly important (five of eight documentary analyses). Furthermore, the documentary analysis leads to two classifications as an

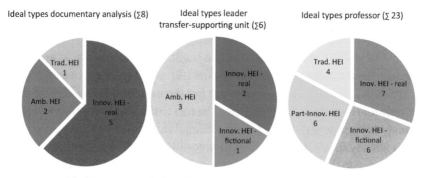

FIGURE 11.3   Ideal types per analysis unit

ambitious HEI and one as a traditional HEI. One reason why the real-innovative HEI can be found so often is due to the peculiarity of the document analysis. The strategy papers, the target agreement, transfer documents and specific marketing documents often show a high level of commitment to the subject of innovation. HEIs use them as instruments to express their wishes and develop a highly innovative image of the HEI. In this way, the HEI convey the image of fulfilling the state, society and enterprise expectations. Nevertheless, the documentary analysis also includes output indicators like third party funds or other monetary indicators. These indicators can be causative for the classification of the HEI as an ambitious HEI instead of a real-innovative HEI.[4]

The leaders of the transfer-supporting units, on the other hand, classify their HEI less often as a real-innovative HEI. From the six interviewed leaders of transfer-supporting units,[5] only two classify the HEI as real-innovative HEI, three as ambitious HEI and one as fictional-innovative HEI.

The classification as an ambitious HEI instead of a real-innovative HEI can be explained by the specific position the leaders of the transfer-supporting units have in the organisational structure. As a link between the leadership and the professors, they have sufficient knowledge of implementing innovation-supporting frame conditions. Furthermore, through the intensive contact with the professors, they also know the extent of innovation cooperations and the acceptance of innovation-supporting frame conditions.

In the group of professors, no ideal type dominated. This is partly due to the design of the case study. Within it, professors with a high, a medium and a low innovative ability were explicitly chosen. As described in the empirical design section, all interviewed professors come from the application-oriented mechanical engineering and economics departments. The results have to be interpreted against this background.

However, analysing the classification of ideal types in the group of professors produces relevant research output. By considering the dimension of the HEI as an organisation and the professor as an individual and the development of the ideal types fictional-innovative HEI and part-innovative HEI, a possibility to better explain the actions and motives of innovative professors is presented. If the developed model would not differentiate between the dimension of the HEI as an organisation and the professor as an individual, but rather, like previous approaches, almost exclusively focus on the implementation of innovation-supporting frame conditions, the six cases of the HEI as fictional-innovative HEI would not be correctly considered. Rather the HEI was only perceived as highly innovative. The reasons for the highly innovative ability – namely, the professor is acting as an innovator without perceiving suitable frame conditions would remain undiscovered.

Furthermore, if the developed ideal type model would only focus on the innovation output and not take the input factors (in particular, the frame conditions and the professor's motivation) into account, then the six cases in which the professor classified the HEI as a part-innovative HEI would also be misjudged. Here, the innovative ability also arises by the professor acting as an innovator without innovation-supporting frame conditions. It is now comprehensible to ask whether this is problematic if the professor nevertheless works as an innovator. However, the case study results clearly showed that professors who assign their HEI to the part-innovative HEI are often dissatisfied. As a result, the risk of leaving the HEI if a better job is offered arises. In addition, this dissatisfaction and the excessive demands that result from entering into innovation cooperations without suitable frame conditions often reduce innovation cooperation activities in the medium to long term.

To make it even more concrete, these results show that twelve of the twenty-three interviewed professors describe themselves as innovators who act without suitable frame conditions. They are employees in an imbalanced ideal type.

Figure 11.2 and the following explanations have already shown evidence for assumption I. Figure 11.4 is intended to emphasise this with all clarity. Comparing the ideal types according to each HEI shows that the extent of the innovative ability generally varies within the HEIs.

As can be seen, in most HEIs, three to five ideal types can be found. Exceptions are the HEIs A, G and H. However, these HEIs G and H were the private HEIs. The private HEI only complemented the research design. Against this background, only one documentary analysis and one interview with a highly innovative professor was conducted in each private HEI. The main focus was

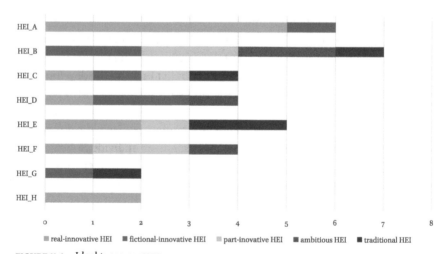

FIGURE 11.4   Ideal types per HEI

on the state HEIs. The private HEIs were included to get a basal overview of whether there are any significant differences to the state HEIs. This was because political and societal actors often formulate a competitive advantage of private HEIs against state HEIs because of strong innovation-supporting frame conditions and a high intrinsic innovation-motivation of all HE-members.

Against this expectation, only slight differences between the state and the private HEIs were found.[6] However, it must be taken into account that the results must be interpreted with extreme caution due to the small number of cases at private HEIs.

The other exception is HEI_A. Five of the six analysis units classified the HEI as a real-innovative HEI (three professors, the leader of the transfer supporting unit and the documentary analysis). Only one professor described it as fictional-innovative HEI. However, at the beginning of the case study, HEI_A was assumed as an HEI with strong innovative ability. Case study results confirmed this supposition. In building a strong innovative ability, HEI_A succeeds significantly better than the other analysed HEIs. The innovative ability arises from both: appropriate frame conditions and the professor acting as an innovator.

When taking a deeper look into what makes HEI_A a real-innovative HEI, it can be assumed that its innovative ability results from a complex interplay of a lot of the above mentioned sixty-five criteria of innovative ability.[7] Nevertheless, some criteria seem to be highly important for HEI_As innovative ability. First, this is a rector who highly involves themselves in innovation proceedings, creates innovation-supporting frame conditions and enforces innovations against resistance. Second, during the recruitment of professors', the innovative ability and the willingness to innovate play a significant role – a shortcoming at all of the other state HEIs examined. Third, HEI_A grants professors immense freedom to realise their innovation activities and relies on a diverse, subject-specific material and immaterial incentive system. Through the combination of innovation-oriented recruitment and a manifold incentive system, HEI_A addresses both the professors' intrinsic and extrinsic motivation. The example of HEI_A shows evidence for assumption II. It shows that a real-innovative HEI only arises through the interplay of innovation-supporting frame conditions and the professor acting as an innovator.

Within the other state HEIs innovative ability more often only arises through the professor acting as an innovator. The professors within these HEIs also described the extent and usefulness of innovative ability as more differentiated than the professors in HEI_A. Thus, it can be said that there is no collective identity within the HEIs B to F. In particular, most professors classify the HEI to another ideal type compared to the documentary analysis. This makes it impressively clear that the person-specific classification of the HEI into an

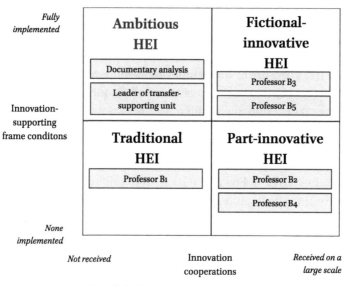

FIGURE 11.5   Spreading of ideal types in HEI_B

ideal type is essential if an HEI wants to get a realistic picture of its innovative ability.

On the example of HEI_B, the following section provides even more detailed proof for the relevance of assumption II. HEI B was selected because it has the most significant spread among ideal types of all the HEIs examined.

For reasons of presentability, the classification to an ideal type is presented based on particularly appropriate quotations. However, as part of the data analysis, all criteria of innovative ability were analysed for each analysis unit.

Figure 11.5 gives an overview of the ideal types found in HEI_B. They are described below.

The strategy paper of HEI_B formulates:[8]

> Innovation is one of the essential powers of our university. Therefore, our university does everything necessary to strengthen it.

Nevertheless, further documents showed there is only poor innovation-oriented recruitment and a target system with nearly no orientation on innovations. Moreover, the effect indicators show only moderate innovation output. So, if only the documentary analysis is focused, HEI_B is classified as an ambitious HEI.

The leader of the transfer-supporting unit classified HEI_B as an ambitious HEI as well. They said:

> The rectorate is trying to build innovation-supporting structures. Nevertheless, like most HEIs, our HEI sometimes has a rigid and slow structure. It also has a lot of internal communication leaks.

And further

> This innovation strategy paper is our first one. Right now, the acceptance is only moderate. Professors are often more anchored in fundamental research than in applied innovation-oriented research.

If now the professors are taken into focus, a much more differentiated picture arises.

Professor B1 (mechanical engineering) classifies HEI_B as a traditional HEI. Therefore, they said:

> Due to my specific research area, I'm active in fundamental research and not in cooperative innovations.

And further

> The main focus of my HEI is to gain third party funds. I don't think they are focussing a lot on innovation-oriented projects. In my opinion, they are very interested in excellent research and DFG funds.

Professor B2 (mechanical engineering) classifies HEI_B as part-innovative HEI. They formulate:

> Thank you for showing me this innovation strategy paper of my HEI. I have never heard from this before – and I can tell you: My HEI doesn't act in the here described way. There are no incentives for acting innovation-oriented.

And further

> Yes, I'm going into cooperative innovations. However, I'm doing it without support from the HEI. And, yes, acting without support has a negative effect on the number of cooperative innovations.

Professor B4 (economics) also has the opinion that HEI_B is a part-innovative HEI. However, they are even more unsatisfied. They said:

> I've been very active in cooperative innovations for more than 20 years. Nevertheless, I initiate them all by my power. Unfortunately, the HEI doesn't support me in any way. Even worse, the actions of the transfer supporting units are the most significant restraint in being innovative. I really like my job, but I'm very unsatisfied with my HEI as an organisation.

Professor B3 (mechanical engineering) and B5 (economics) both classified the HEI_B as a fictional-innovative HEI.
Professor B3 said:

> Yes, cooperative innovations are playing a massive role in my daily business. I think the HEI has a high interest in cooperative innovations as well – and I know they implemented a couple of innovation-supporting measures. Nevertheless, there is much room for improvement. In reality, recruitment doesn't occur under innovative aspects, for example. Also, the target system is inappropriate to incentivise innovations.

Finally, Professor B5 gave the following statement:

> Since my first year as a professor, I've been very active in cooperative innovations. The support from my HEI differs. Previously the support activities were very moderate. Within the last years, the HEI implemented many measures. Some are really good and supportive, but others don't work very well, as the target system or the creation of spaces for internal collaboration. Therefore, my cooperative innovations are driven mainly by my intrinsic motivation.

The example of HEI_B clarifies that models that assess the innovative ability of HEIs must not assume a shared identity. This means that the complete HEI cannot be assigned to an ideal type – not even for reasons of complexity reduction. The resulting image of the HEI would be a significant distortion of reality. Instead, it shows that the person-specific application of defined ideal types shows a much more detailed picture of the actual innovative ability of an HEI. This innovative ability results from the sum of the individual innovative abilities of its members.

5   Conclusion

This contribution aimed to provide HEIs with a detailed model for analysing their innovative ability. Therefore, a case study in eight German HEIs was conducted. Within the case study, sixty-five criteria of innovative ability were deduced. The remarkable achievement of this contribution is that the criteria do not, as usual in previous studies, focus significantly on the design of innovations-supporting frame conditions. Instead, they equally focus on the professor acting as an innovator. Accordingly, thirty-four criteria could be assigned to the professors' acceptance of the frame conditions and their individual willingness and ability to innovate.

Based on the specification of the criteria for innovative ability, the HEI was assigned to ideal types. The used ideal type model was also developed due to the case study. Here, too, further development of the traditional view takes place. While existing ideal type models take a top-down view and aim to assign the HEI as a whole to an ideal type, this contribution follows the logic of an individual classification of the HEI depending on the analysis unit. This further development inevitably results from the professor acting as an innovator and the resulting bottom-up view on the innovative ability of the HEI.

When critically analysing the following results, it must be taken into account that the case studies were carried out in the application-oriented departments of mechanical engineering and economics. Therefore, the application possibility for other departments still has to be checked.

The analysis of the innovative ability from this point of view clearly shows that the innovative ability in one HEI is not equally strong – not even among professors of the same department. Instead, it is a result of the individual innovative ability of its members. Moreover, innovative ability can vary significantly from one another. Therefore, different ideal types can be found within one HEI.

Case study analysis further showed that innovative ability could arise through the interplay of the innovation-supporting frame conditions and the professor acting as an innovator or the professor acting as an innovator without supporting frame conditions. The first case described results in the ideal type of the real-innovative HEI. If the second case takes place, the HEI is classified as a part-innovative or fictional-innovative HEI. Results showed that only nine interviewed professors classified their HEI as a real-innovative HEI, while twelve saw it as part- or fictional-innovative HEI. Ideal type models that do not focus on the criteria assigned to the professors' acceptance of the frame conditions and their willingness and ability to innovate could not explain these twelve cases in a meaningful way. This is a dangerous situation for an HEI because acting as an innovator without support leads to dissatisfaction with the HEI and a medium to long-term decline in innovation cooperation activities.

By combining the analysis of the impact of innovation-supporting frame conditions as well as the professors' willingness and ability to innovate, leadership gets into a better position to use its potential to steer the HEIs innovative ability. Resulting, leadership can coordinate the innovation-supporting frame conditions in a more targeted manner. Thus, they can better support the professors' willingness and ability to innovate. This may increase the professors' satisfaction with the HEI and their extent of innovation cooperations. That impressively shows that future research has to put a lot more focus on the individual perspective and the interplay of innovation-supporting frame conditions and the person-specific innovative ability.

Notes

1 This contribution presents some selected results of the author's research on innovative ability of HEIs. Konen (2020) provides a detailed overview of the results.
2 For a detailed analysis of these studies, see Konen (2020, p. 62 ff.).
3 Specified for the German HE sector but adaptable for other countries under consideration of their individual frame condition (e.g. finance structure, possibilities of state control).
4 The quality and quantity of monetary indicators published by the HEIs vary. Therefore, the classification of the HEIs based on the results of the documentary analysis was occurring on different levels of detail.
5 The interviewed leaders of transfer-supporting units are located in the state universities and state universities of applied sciences. Private HEIs in Germany often do not have specific transfer positions. If for the analysed private HEIs information had been given whether they had implemented such positions, there would have been the risk of disclosure of their identity.
6 Konen (2020) gives a detailed overview of these results.
7 For a detailed analysis of the specificity of the criteria in all analysed HEIs, see Konen (2020).
8 The following quotes are summarised and not taken verbatim.

References

Badillo Vega, R. (2018). *Präsidale Führungsstile in Hochschulen: Vom Wandel zur Transformation.* Springer VS.

Brunsson, N., & Sahlin-Anderssen, K. (2000). Constructing organisations: The example of public sector reform. *Organization Studies, 21*(4), 721–746.

Cohen, M. D., March, J. G., & Olsen, J. P. (1972). A garbage can model of organizational choice. *Administrative Science Quarterly, 17*(1), 1–25.

Etzkowitz, H. (2013). Anatomy of the entrepreneurial university. *Social Science Information, 52*(3), 486–511.

Henke, J., Pasternack, P., & Schmid, S. (2015). *Viele Stimmen, kein Kanon: Konzept und Kommunikation der Third Mission von Hochschulen.* HoF-Arbeitsberichte 2/15. https://www.hof.unihalle.de/web/dateien-/pdf/01_AB_Third-Mission-Berichterstattung.pdf

Hüther, O. (2013). Alleinherrscher oder Halbstarke? Handlungsspielräume von Hochschulleitern. *Forschung & Lehre, 20*(10), 808–810.

Hüther, O., & Krücken, G. (2013). Hierarchy and power: A conceptual analysis with particular reference to new public management reforms in German universities. *European Journal of Higher Education, 3*(4), 307–323.

Hutterer, P. (2012). *Dynamic Capabilities und Innovationsstrategien: Interdependenzen in Theorie und Praxis.* Springer Gabler.

Konen, C. (2019). Innovativeness of higher education institutions: Pre-conditions for the development of co-operative innovations. In P. Teixeira, A. Magalhães, M.-J. Rosa, & A. Veiga (Eds.), *Under pressure? Higher education coping with multiple challenges* (pp. 125–145). Brill.

Konen, C. (2020). *Innovative Hochschule oder Innovateur in der Hochschule? Ein idealtypenbasiertes Modell zur Analyse der Innovationsfähigkeit von Hochschulen.* https://www.zhb-flensburg.de/dissert/konen/

Lawson, B., & Samson, D. (2001). Developing innovation capability in organisations: A dynamic capabilities approach. *International Journal of Innovation Management, 5*(3), 377–400.

Mayring, P. (2015). *Qualitative Inhaltsanalyse: Grundlagen und Techniken* (12th ed.). Beltz.

Meyer, F. (2019). Trends der Hochschulentwicklung: Der Weg zur wettbewerblichen Organisation. In B. Fähnrich, J. Metag, S. Post, & M. S. Schäfer (Eds.), *Forschungsfeld Hochschulkommunikation* (pp. 25–38). Springer VS.

Mintzberg, H. (1979). *The structuring of organizations: A synthesis of the research.* Prentice Hall.

Scherm, E., & Jackenroll, B. (2016). Liegt im Commitment der Professoren der Schlüssel zur Steuerung von Universitäten? *Hochschulmanagement: Zeitschrift für die Leitung, Entwicklung und Selbstverwaltung von Hochschulen und Wissenschaftseinrichtungen, 11*(4), 116–120.

Smith, M., Busi, M., Ball, P., & Van der Meer, P. (2008). Factors influencing on organizations ability to manage innovation: A structured literature review and conceptual model. *International Journal of Innovation Management, 12*(4), 655–676.

Stern, T., & Jaberg, H. (2010). *Erfolgreiches Innovationsmanagement: Erfolgsfaktoren, Grundmuster, Fallbeispiele* (4th ed.). Gabler.

Stifterverband. (Ed.). (2014). *Wie Hochschulen mit Unternehmen kooperieren: Lage und Entwicklung der Hochschulen aus Sicht ihrer Leitungen 2013.* https://www.stifterverband.org/download/file/fid/544

Thoenig J.-C., & Paradeise, C. (2016). Strategic capacity and organizational capability: A challenge for universities. *Minerva, 54*, 293–324.

Weick, K. E. (1976). Educational systems as loosely coupled systems. *Administrative Science Quarterly, 21*(1), 1–19.

Wördenweber, B., Eggert, M., Größer, A., & Wickord, W. (2020). *Technologie- und Innovationsmanagement im Unternehmen* (4th ed.). Springer Vieweg.

Yin, R. K. (2014). *Case study research: Design and methods* (5th ed.). Sage Publications.

CHAPTER 12

Community-Based Professional Development of Higher Education Teachers in Times of Transformation

Silke Masson and Tamara Zajontz

Abstract

Far-reaching and fast-paced transformations in higher education increase demand for continuous staff development and training. Community-based approaches to professional development, especially professional learning communities, can foster professional and institutional development and meet specific requirements on continuing education.

Based on evaluation data of six years and a recent survey on digital teaching during the COVID-19 pandemic, this paper discusses a community-based professional development initiative in higher education at a German university and assesses its features and effects. Our findings show an improvement of student-centred teaching skills as well as an intensification of dialogue and empowerment of university teachers. Through continuous occasions for dialogue and long-term cooperation, the initiative enables the development of mutual trust amongst participants and provides ways to transform academic teaching whilst ensuring academic freedom and freedom of teaching. However, successful implementation depends on external support and the necessary infrastructure for cooperation.

Our results suggest that community-based professional developments add value compared to individual formats of staff development, as they improve teachers' readiness to assume collective responsibility for the quality of teaching and student learning as well as for their own professional development.

Keywords

Professional Learning Community (PLC) – teacher cooperation – higher education teaching skills – professional development in higher education

1   Introduction

Growing demands for staff development are a widely recognised feature of ongoing transformations at universities; so is a growing need for cooperation at institutional level and also in relation to higher education staff and teachers (Gast et al., 2017). To investigate effects of cooperation, the paper employs an empirical approach and explores a community-based professional development initiative for teachers in higher education at a German university. We analyse promising ways of fostering collaboration and developing teaching skills.

2   Background

Community-based professional development, especially in professional learning communities (PLC), has become an established concept for professional development in primary and secondary education. PLCs refer to groups of teachers who cooperate to educate themselves, to share and jointly reflect on their teaching practices and to improve the quality of teaching and student learning (cf. Bonsen & Rolff, 2006; Hord, 1997). Several reviews of research have documented positive effects of PLCs on individual teaching quality as well as on student learning (e.g., Vangrieken et al., 2017; Vescio et al., 2008). Therefore, PLCs have been promoted as conducive to professional and institutional development in various other contexts. Though research in the field of higher education, especially in Germany, is still developing, the process is only gradual (e.g., Sekyra & Bade, 2020).

Scholarly debates about the concept of PLCs are still ongoing and there is no consensus on the core features that PLCs entail (Warwas & Schadt, 2020). Therefore, we initially discuss some of the theoretical strands as well as possible key characteristics of PLCs as described in the literature. There is a strong tradition which sees the institution as a whole as the appropriate unit of analysis (e.g., Bonsen & Rolff, 2006; DuFour, 2004; Hord, 1997). Using mainly quantitative data generated in large surveys among teachers, scholars have tried to assess the extent to which an educational institution "functions as a PLC" (DuFour, 2004, p. 6). The performance of the institution is compared with learning outcomes of students (e.g., Lomos et al., 2011) or teaching quality (e.g., Warwas & Helm, 2018) to investigate the effects of institutional development. In another tradition, which we refer to as small-group-approach, existing groups of teachers who collaborate and learn together are the unit of analysis (e.g., Bolam et al., 2005; Schaap & de Bruijn, 2018). Such research is concerned with the development and working routines of the identified groups.

In Germany, the operationalisation of PLCs by Bonsen and Rolff (2006), who draw on Kruse et al. (1994), has hitherto had the widest impact in the field. Bonsen and Rolff's five-component approach includes *shared norms and values* about one's role as a teacher and about teaching and learning as well as *collaboration*, i.e., the cooperation among teachers for instance in joint teaching projects or in the joint production of teaching material, as essential characteristics of PLCs (Bonsen & Rolff, 2006, p. 173). Their third dimension, the one of *student learning*, focusses on the extent to which activities are designed to promote and enhance student learning. The opening of one's own teaching for peer feedback and joint reflection is conceptualised as a distinct dimension and, to underline the contrast to the widespread view of teaching as a private matter, aptly termed the *de-privatisation of practice*. Finally, teachers should be engaged in continuous *reflective dialogue* about instructional practices.

With its rapid proliferation, concerns have been raised that the concept of PLCs is in danger of "losing all meaning" (DuFour, 2004, p. 6). Due to its ubiquitous use, there is an ongoing debate on what the key dimensions or characteristics of PLCs are. According to DuFour (2004, p. 7) there are three "big ideas" of PLCs that must be fulfilled in order to apply the concept:

– At the heart of the PLC model is the shift in focus from teaching to learning, which means the assumption that the primary goal of formal education for students is not to be taught, but to learn. In PLCs, therefore teachers must try to make all students learn and reflect jointly on what students should learn, how to determine whether learning content has been learned, and what strategies to use when learning difficulties arise (ibid., p. 8).
– To ensure that all students learn, educators must necessarily work together and create a collaborative culture. Nevertheless, he states that teachers still, for the most part, work in isolation. Characteristic for PLCs is thus a powerful collaboration and a professional dialogue, in which what has hitherto remained private is made public, e.g., teaching and learning materials, learning goals, learning problems (ibid., p. 9).
– According to DuFour (ibid., pp. 10–11) schools collect a lot of data but miss out on making effective use of it and deriving conclusions from it. At the same time, he sees a lack of data comparison between teachers due to the low level of cooperation. PLCs, on the contrary, must assess their effectiveness *based on results*, which means that the success of teaching efforts is verified by an increase in students' learning outcomes and is therefore data-driven (with data not only referring to test results but also to student understanding which is visible, e.g., through students' work). PLCs use the data that is collected anyway to generate important and relevant information for staff and the school.

Recently, Warwas and Helm (2018) as well as Warwas and Schadt (2020) introduced three core components of PLC s. The authors try to integrate previous models and, by concentrating on intersections between the existing heterogeneous models, name only indispensable core dimensions of PLC s. Accordingly, in most of the models sustainable *infrastructure* (structural dimension) is considered necessary in order to make cooperation in the group possible at all. This includes spatial, temporal and human resources, as well as successful work routines and transparency of responsibilities. Second, there is an ideational dimension: the *normative consensus* among the teachers with regard to the understanding of teaching or characteristics of good teaching, values and convictions shared within the group, as well as common goals. Ultimately, a behavioural dimension is proposed which, under the term "*cooperative development*", summarises the actual activities the group undertakes to improve their teaching. As examples for such activities, they name the joint planning, implementation and review of teaching units, regular reflective dialogues, the sharing of personal practice in peer review of teaching as well as data-based evaluation and decision-making (Warwas & Schadt, 2020, p. 43). With its integrating character and the clear distinction between group activities as well as an ideational and a structural dimension, the model seems well suited to inform the considerations discussed in this chapter.

Based on these remarks we can now specify our understanding of PLC s in the higher education context. Following the small-group tradition, we understand PLC s as groups of higher education teachers sharing a common purpose and establishing a focus on student learning. They convene on a regular basis to educate themselves, to share and jointly reflect on their teaching practices and to cooperate in improving the quality of teaching and student learning. To fully meet the standards of PLC s, the cooperation is results-oriented and uses various data on students' learning outcomes to assess the effectiveness of one's own teaching practice and group activities.

Following previous research efforts to fruitfully employ the concept of PLC s in the context of higher education, the paper explores a programme for community-based professional development called "Peer Coaching" and addressing higher education teachers at Johannes Gutenberg-University Mainz in Germany (JGU). The programme aims at an improvement of teaching skills, an intensification of exchange amongst teachers on teaching-related topics as well as the development of a new teaching culture; the establishment of a collective responsibility for teaching accompanies these endeavours. Established in 2010 and continued since then, the programme is carried out and evaluated by programme staff at the Centre for Quality Assurance and Development (ZQ) at JGU. Between 2012 and 2020 it was funded by the German Federal Ministry of Education and Research [Teaching Quality Pact] (BMBF, 2021). A total of 23 groups of university teachers from across a wide spectrum of academic disciplines, ranging from educational science and law to psychology, physics and dentistry, have participated in the programme, which is voluntary for all teachers at JGU. In contrast to widespread individualised offers for professional development, groups of eight to sixteen people work together for about three to four (or more) semesters to reflect on their teaching and develop their teaching skills. The initiative primarily addresses groups of teachers from the same discipline or study programme at our university. To structure the cooperation process, participating teachers can choose different training formats that are chaired by experts for teaching and learning: namely workshops, peer observation of teaching and peer advising. To best fit the group's needs, the programme allows the participating groups to choose various thematic foci and combinations. Workshops as well as peer observation of teaching can be completed either in a disciplinary or interdisciplinary variant and, like participation in the overall programme, remain voluntary for the teachers.

The *workshops* are intended to support teachers to develop teaching skills. They also provide an important platform to explore and reflect on individual approaches to teaching and to discuss these approaches with colleagues. Ideally, working materials or teaching units can also be co-created during these workshops. In order to support the needs of the different professional groups in the best possible way, financial resources are available to book external speakers (e.g., to provide subject-specific training). *Peer advising* as another possible programme element is a very resource-saving and solution-oriented format, in which the participants get the opportunity to consult collegially on challenging teaching situations. Peer advising follows fixed phases and has a set structure and predefined roles. Initially this element is guided by an expert for teaching and learning, but the goal is the continuation of peer advising after the end of the programme without any external support: just sustained within the group of colleagues by means of the available know-how. Another format which the teachers can select is the *peer observation of teaching*. This implies that two colleagues visit each other in their courses accompanied by programme staff based at our centre with expertise in teaching and learning. The observation aims to provide constructive feedback rather than evaluation, and thus much emphasis is placed on encouraging reflection and exchange through observation sheets as well as expert facilitation and advice. The observation in the courses is therefore prepared by a preliminary talk in which the colleagues describe to each other the process, the methods and the goals of their courses. The collegial visits in the courses are followed by a review meeting. In this meeting not only the teachers but also the programme staff give feedback. As a last step the university teachers formulate agreements on elements of teaching, they would like to change in the future. The topics discussed in this session are written up and made available to the teachers. An advantage of this element is that the teaching staff being observed gets direct and individual feedback within a real teaching situation. Furthermore, the university teachers can practise and implement the methods or strategies learned in the workshops. Peer observation of teaching also provides the opportunity to exchange experiences and to discuss challenges in teaching.

Conception and design of the programme examined here aim at initialising and supporting PLC s, as defined above. As Table 12.1 shows, it provides a supportive *infrastructure* for cooperation and reflection. For example, the programme staff organises and invites participating teachers to group meetings and moderates these events, when required. In addition, various templates are provided to stimulate reflection, including observation sheets and conversation guides. The programme aims at an improvement of teaching skills and establishing a shared focus on student-centred teaching. Therefore, it uses various measures to encourage a change towards a *normative consensus*, including a kick-off meeting, in which questions of "good teaching" are discussed within the group; an introductory workshop is provided in teaching and learning;[1] and standardized sheets record peer observation of teaching based on criteria of "good courses". To structure the *cooperative development*, different training formats are offered that resemble the activities typically ascribed to PLC s.

TABLE 12.1   Programme overview

Examples of programme offers	PLC dimensions adressed
– Scheduling and organisation of workshops and group meetings.	*Infrastructure*
– Provision of financial, spatial and human resources.	
– Provision of training and templates to support student-centred attitudes and teaching skills.	*Normative consensus*
	Shared norms and values
– Regular reflection opportunities within the group.	Focus on student learning
Choice of different training formats	*Cooperative development*
– Workshops and trainings tailored to the needs of the group	Reflective dialogue
	Deprivatisation of practice
– Peer observation of teaching	Collaboration
– Peer advising	

3   Approach

The programme is evaluated in all its phases with the help of a number of survey instruments of mixed-method design, combining quantitative data in a pre-post design and (guided) interview data. The evaluation, like the development and implementation of the programme, is the responsibility of ZQ staff.

Before the start of the programme, the actual situation is determined: The participants are asked to fill out *reflection forms* that address their previous understanding of teaching and learning, the extent of collegial exchange, and their expectations of participating in the programme. At the same time, an analysis of strengths and weaknesses is conducted with regard to the participants' own teaching. A *30-item questionnaire* (Winteler & Schmolck, 2003) is used to assess the individual teaching style.

About halfway through the programme, *guided interviews* are carried out to inquire about the progress of the programme and its initial effects.

At the end of the programme, an online-based *final survey* is part of the evaluation to explore effects of participation. A pre-post comparison of the data is realised by using individual codes. Additional items are included to obtain feedback on the quality of the process. In addition, all workshops are evaluated by the participants throughout the entire programme.

One year after the end of the programme, *follow-up guideline-based interviews* are conducted in order to be able to examine long-term effects on teaching and collegial exchange (for detailed evaluation see Leibenath et al., 2016).

Findings in this paper are based on results of eleven groups of university teachers who took part in the programme between 2012 and 2018. The final survey has a sample size of 57 university teachers, with 29 cases who were willing to provide an individual code and thus become suitable for a pre-post comparison.

To consider future development demands, data are reported from a university-wide online survey at JGU in Germany; they deal with specific challenges linked to the implementation of digital formats as well as on teachers' needs for professional development in summer 2020 (n = 572 teachers, response rate: 23.7%).

4   Results

Our findings concern teachers' satisfaction with the programme infrastructure, effects on attitudes and teaching practices of higher education teachers as well as insights on teaching during the pandemic.

4.1   *Infrastructure*

The results show a high level of overall satisfaction with the infrastructure provided by the programme. Of the 57 respondents, 83.3% chose the first two values on a seven-point Likert scale and classified themselves as "satisfied" or "very satisfied" with the entire programme. Only nine people were more critical and selected scale values between 3 and 5. The most negative values of 6 and 7 were not chosen at all.

The amount of time and the number of appointments during the programme met with broad approval from the teachers. Of the responding teachers, 74.1% considered the time frame to be "just right" (scale value 4; mean = 4.02), while only 14.9% felt that the amount of time was "high" or "too high" (scale values 5 to 7) and 11.2% "too low" or "low" respectively (scale values 1 to 3). The number of appointments, which is coordinated within the group and usually lies between one and three per semester, was rated "just right" by 65.4% (mean = 3.77); 23% of the respondents felt that the number of appointments was "(too) few" and thus wished for more appointments.

The participants were also very satisfied with the organisation of the offer. Of the 57 respondents, 80% found this "very good" or "good" (seven-point Likert scale) and only one respondent rated it "poor" (scale value 6, mean = 1.87). Similar results pertain to the accessibility of programme staff in cases where support was needed: 89.1% rated this as "(very) good" and only one respondent as "poor" (scale value 6; mean = 1.53). The interviews with teachers documented by Leibenath (2019, p. 25) revealed the importance of a continuous dialogue between the staff of peer coaching and participants. Programme staff schedule regular appointments and continuously discuss with the group how to proceed with the programme. In addition, one year after the end of the programme, the interviews point to the importance of conversation guides, reflection forms and structured preparations and follow-ups of the peer observations of teaching.

4.2   *Normative Consensus on Student-Centred-Teaching*

A pre-post-comparison of a standardised teaching style questionnaire showed an increase in the normative consensus concerning student-centred teaching and an improvement of teaching skills. The 30 items of the questionnaire are formulated approvingly in the sense of a student-centred teaching style or focus on student learning. All items showed a positive development with regard to the aspects examined which is thus interpreted as a development towards a normative consensus.[2] The strongest changes in the self-assessment of the teachers before and after participating in the programme were seen in the extent to which they attempt "facilitating the understanding of new issues by establishing connections and relationships to what is already known" (mean difference = 0.8) and "linking to the last course at the beginning of a new session" (mean difference = 0.7). Relatively large changes became apparent regarding the transparent communication of the learning objectives to students, emphasizing the relevance of the course for the overall educational goal, greater sensitivity towards students' prior knowledge and the encouragement of active participation (mean difference = 0.6 each). Lower, but still positive changes with mean differences of 0.1 and 0.2 were shown for example in the items "In my courses, I define new terms in an understandable way", "In my courses, I promote the social competencies of the students by means of cooperative learning methods" as well as "In my courses, I structure the material systematically". The comparatively marginal change in these items is partly due to the fact that they have already been rated very positively in the initial survey; a significant increase was therefore unlikely.

These results of the evaluation of the teaching style questionnaires are also consistent with the guided interviews as can be seen in this quote from an interview with participants:

> It has definitely changed, because I no longer talk through from the first to the last minute. [...] Just things like explaining content and learning objectives at the beginning. [...] For me, there is now always a form of summary at the end, and in between basically things that the students work out independently according to certain guidelines.

Irrespective of how the teaching style of the participants was characterised at the beginning of the programme, there is evidently a change to a shared conviction and a common consensus that the students have to be the main focus of teaching.

4.3   Cooperative Development

The data prove that there was an intensification of communication about teaching within the group of participants throughout the programme. However, the frequency of collegial exchange is only one indicator that can point to the establishment of a reflective dialogue among teachers. The development of a 'shared vocabulary', resulting from an increased familiarity with specialized terminology and concepts of teaching and learning, was another added value of programme participation. As the programme progressed, a common vocabulary concerning teaching increasingly developed within the groups, e.g., through the completion of several workshops in a fixed group context. A statement from the interviews one year after the end of the programme confirms this. According to this, *"a common tool set"* was created through peer coaching, *"on the basis of which one can then also talk"*. Another interviewee noted that they had already talked and exchanged ideas before participating in peer coaching, but that this simply could not take place in such a concrete and institutionalised way, because the group not only lacked the methodology but also the way of expressing it. Moreover, interview data showed that participants gained confidence in their own teaching practice. As a result, they reported of feeling unburdened. The fact that the programme is carried out over a longer period of time in the same group constellation also fosters the development of a sense of community and of a basis of trust. This goes hand in hand with greater mutual openness and empowerment of university teachers. The teachers meet regularly and thus have enough time to build up this dialogue in the protected space of the group. Challenging, difficult situations in teaching and in dealing with students can then be openly discussed.

One crucial part of cooperative development is the opening of teaching practice, which peer coaching fulfils by means of disciplinary and interdisciplinary observation of teaching. Although teacher groups sometimes rejected peer observation of teaching altogether when they entered the programme, in almost all cases at least some of the group members participated in this activity at the end. Where scepticism towards this form of observation was overcome, peer observation of teaching has proven to be the most profitable and rewarding programme element. When comparing the usefulness of formats offered, peer observation of teaching achieved the highest score at the end of the programme. Disciplinary observations were rated as "very helpful" or "helpful" by 94.7% of 38 respondents who experienced this format. Interdisciplinary observations were even approved by 100% of the respondents.[3] The value added by the observation results especially from receiving feedback in a real teaching situation (and thus in a situated context). Another benefit arises from gaining insights into other teaching styles, which on the one hand can broaden one's own view of teaching and on the other hand can also encourage one to try out teaching methods that are perhaps initially unfamiliar or not common in one's own discipline. Peer observation of teaching can therefore be considered pivotal to the programme, while at the same time best meeting the needs of academic teaching staff. The available qualitative data (material from interviews and open-ended questions in the final survey) also support this finding:

> I found that the best thing ever! For everything that can be done in the field of didactics, I found the peer observation of teaching the most exciting. Not because I learned such mind-blowing new things, but – ideas! Seeing how someone else does it!

In the final survey, the participants also indicated whether they would observe again in the future or would like to be observed by colleagues. Here, too, there was a high level of agreement. The university teachers apparently rated the mutual observation as so helpful that they would like to benefit from it even further. Thus, 37.9% of the respondents stated that they could imagine sitting in on their colleagues' courses in the future (scale values 1 and 2), while 10.3% thought this was rather unlikely (scale values 6 and 7). Another 51.7% were undecided (scale values 3 to 5). When asked about observational visits in their own teaching, agreement was even higher: 72.4% answered that they thought it was (very) likely that they would also be able to welcome colleagues to their courses in the future, and only 6.9% were not open to future visits. The desire for a continuation of peer observation of teaching is therefore evident. Crucial questions are thus whether continuous peer observation will be implemented in the future and whether peer observation, as well as preliminary and follow-up meetings, will be coordinated independently. This brings us back to the need for a sustainable infrastructure.

Another central part of cooperative development is the actual "collaboration". Joint projects or activities which are often mentioned as typical for PLC s (see above) were not directly promoted or initiated by the programme staff in our programme yet. Nonetheless, single groups initiated autonomous activities that went beyond the actual programme, and groups created their own projects to work on throughout the professional development programme. This happened in individual cases, e.g., in a participating group that linked the development of a catalogue of activating methods to the programme. One group revised several courses of different teachers after participating in a workshop dealing with a special teaching method. However, the conditions for success and the effects of this commitment have not been the focus of the evaluation design so far and thus cannot yet be assessed based on the data available.

4.4   Teaching during the Pandemic

In the university-wide online survey aimed at exploring the conditions of teaching and specific requirements for professional development during the COVID-19 pandemic, teaching staff stated that efforts were raised for preparing lessons, organising teaching infrastructure and providing feedback for students during the pandemic and the first digital semester; in some cases those efforts increased tremendously. Still, 70% of teachers saw no, or only minor, changes in the amount of collaboration with other university teachers (Schmidt et al., 2020). In addition, the use of open educational resources (OER) was at a very low level (mean = 5.78)[4] (ibid.). Despite severe time pressures and additional burdens on teaching staff (e.g., childcare), teachers did not share teaching materials, teaching continued to be closed and cooperation between teachers played a subordinate role in the concrete design of courses. Teachers in the pandemic therefore behave as if they understand teaching as an individual rather than a collective task that is best approached in cooperation with others.

Whilst throughout the pandemic much demand for support was concerned with technical matters, key issues around teaching and learning, such as student engagement and digital exams, came to the fore again when teachers were asked about future needs. Crucially, all results have differed significantly amongst teachers of different disciplines (ibid.). In addition, significant differences across academic disciplines were also evident in the implementation of teaching and learning scenarios in the first digital semester. The proportion of purely synchronous teaching in the natural sciences was comparatively high at 40%. Conversely, teachers in the social sciences in particular (46.8%) showed a stronger focus on exclusively asynchronous teaching formats (Schmidt et al., 2021). It is apparent that departments vary in their handling of digital teaching and their attitudes towards it. The support services and professional development programmes that follow on from this should be correspondingly multi-layered and take into account heterogeneous needs based on respective previous experiences and work situations. Overall, it is essential to provide a wide range of professional support for teaching and learning, which is sensitive towards subject-specific differences and needs (ibid., p. 47).

5   Reflections on the Findings

Based on evaluation data and a recent survey on teaching during the pandemic, this paper discussed a community-based professional development initiative for higher education teachers at a German university and assessed its features and effects. Our findings showed that the programme has positive effects on teaching practices as well as on attitudes of higher education teachers; these effects are in keeping with former research results gained in primary and secondary education contexts (cf. Cordingley et al., 2003). The opportunity to collaborate and exchange views with colleagues is highly appreciated and, as a result, has achieved high levels of satisfaction. We see an increase in inter-personal exchange amongst teaching staff on teaching-related issues for the duration of the programme as well as a move towards a common set of values and willingness to share one's own teaching practice. Thanks to continuous occasions for dialogue and long-term cooperation, the programme enabled the development of mutual trust amongst teaching staff, which is seen as a critical aspect for effective cooperation (Stoll et al., 2006). On this basis peer observation of teaching has proven to be an adequate format to share best practice as well as to foster reflection and dialogue on teaching-related matters. Participants gain confidence in their own teaching practice and generate ideas for developing teaching further. Participants report that the programme helped them to develop a 'shared vocabulary' on teaching-related affairs which can be interpreted as an element of empowerment. To tap into the full potential of cooperation via professional development, greater attention needs to be focused on precisely defined, time-limited cooperation projects. The cooperative creation and sharing of teaching materials and the dissemination of best practice thrive in well-established communities. Hence, future programme designs should stimulate this at an early stage of cooperation.

Despite the positive effects, the independent continuation of group activities beyond the programme period has proven to be difficult. As an earlier study on the programme (Leibenath et al., 2016) showed, effects on exchange and collaboration amongst teaching staff are in most cases limited to participating group members (and do not spread to the department as a whole) and to the duration of the programme. University teachers do not succeed in continuing the group independently after the end of peer coaching and, for example, in scheduling appointments for exchange, dialogue or further training without being prompted to do so externally. Outside of the programme, it is difficult for the groups to set up joint appointments on their own initiative and, for example, to conduct peer advising (ibid.). Accordingly, it is possible to initiate cooperation between the groups during the programme period. But the initiation and moderation of the group processes by the programme staff turns out to be the most important prerequisite for realizing a structured, systematic intra-faculty exchange on questions of teaching. Having dedicated contact persons in the different academic disciplines who are able to bring the participants together and drive the process forward have also proven helpful. These experiences coincide with the conditions for success already identified in the overview by Gast and colleagues (2017) which points at external moderation and successful team leadership as possible success factors. They are also in line with the experiences of other programmes at German universities, according to which the time required, but also the organisation, act as obstacles to the long-term use and establishment of the formats (Sekyra & Bade, 2020). The provision of adequate infrastructure for cooperation as well as the possibility of external organisational and content-related support are therefore core requirements for the successful implementation of cooperation measures not only in primary and secondary education (cf. Bolam et al., 2005) but even more so in higher education institutions which commonly have little tradition of cooperation in teaching.

The reported survey results, reflecting the experiences from 2020 (Schmidt et al., 2020), again showed that while we expect growing need for cooperation as a result of the rapid digitalisation of higher education, cooperation and the use of shared resources do not unfold automatically and face various challenges. Apart from this, they show substantial differences in the implementation of digital teaching as well as in future professional development needs reported in different disciplines. This encourages us in our already established approach to offer professional development for higher education teachers that is discipline-specific, needs-oriented and extends over a longer period of time. Community-based professional development, especially if it is targeted towards teachers of a specific department, unit or study programme, can be an alternative to highly differentiated offers to individual teachers. They provide additional benefits if they lead to enduring cooperation and teachers assuming responsibility for the quality of teaching and student learning as well as for their own professional development.

Today's professional development offers are commonly built to support the shift from teaching to learning and the orientation towards evidence-based teaching and learning. They therefore share the normative aspiration that is essential to the concept of PLC s. This makes the concept a fruitful theoretical basis for designing, as well as analysing the impact of professional development initiatives aiming at teacher cooperation.

With the attempt of a longitudinal training process in a constant group of teachers and the programme elements offered, including peer observation of teaching and reflective dialogues, the programme resembles PLC s. Against this background, we introduced our programme as a way of showing how community-based professional development can be successfully implemented in a university context. Nevertheless, the group activities promoted by the programme do not yet meet all the standards that are discussed in the literature on PLC s. Following DuFour's (2004) three "big ideas" of PLC s that we have introduced above, we see a close accord with the theoretical concept for the ideas of common purpose and collaborative culture. But there is a need to further strengthen the orientation towards results, meaning that the success of one's teaching efforts should be verified by an increase in students' learning outcomes and therefore be data-driven. Within the programme this aspect is best met through peer observation of teaching which lays a strong focus on generating observational data. To date, there has been no systematic use of student evaluations of teaching or data on student outcomes during programme implementation or evaluation. This may be a future enhancement. Community-based professional development programmes inspired by PLC s can then be a promising concept to complement more widespread approaches to evidence-based teaching at universities, such as Scholarship of Teaching and Learning (SOTL), that focuses on the individual teacher (cf. Kordts-Freudinger et al., 2018).

6   Conclusion

Future challenges intensify demands on staff development at universities. In this paper, community-based professional development was proposed as an adequate format to strengthen mutual trust amongst and empowerment of teaching staff and to transform academic teaching whilst ensuring academic freedom and freedom of teaching. They offer the opportunity to promote a student-centred teaching style and foster reflection of university teachers. However, PLCs and community-based formats in higher education, like the one described in this paper, need to be initiated externally, and particular care must be taken to ensure that professional development formats attend to discipline-specific differences in teaching as well as different professional development needs. Universities can help in creating an environment where the establishment of and participation in PLCs is promoted and rewarded.

Notes

1   The workshop gives an introduction to "Higher Education Didactics" and deals *inter alia* with principles of "good teaching", student-centredness, formulation of learning objectives, teaching and learning methods, assessment and feedback techniques.
2   Five-point Likert scale from 1 = "is completely true" to 5 = "not true at all". Against this background, low mean values are to be regarded as positive, high mean values as negative in the sense of student-centredness.
3   Seven-point Likert scale from 1 = "very helpful" to 7 = "not helpful at all".
4   Seven-point Likert scale from 1 = "OER were used to a very high degree" to 7 = "OER were not used at all".

References

Bolam, R., McMahon, A., Louise Stoll, L., & Thomas, S. (2005). *Creating and sustaining effective professional learning communities*. Research Report RR637. Universities of Bristol, Bath and London, Institute of Education. Retrieved August 16, 2021, from http://www.saspa.com.au/wp-content/uploads/2016/02/Creating-and-Sustaining-PLCs_tcm4-631034-1.pdf

Bonsen, M., & Rolff, H.-G. (2006). Professionelle Lerngemeinschaften von Lehrerinnen und Lehrern [Professional learning communities of teachers]. *Zeitschrift für Pädagogik, 52*(2), 167–184.

Bundesministerium für Bildung und Forschung (BMBF) [German Federal Ministry of Education and Research]. (2021). *Qualitätspakt Lehre* [*Quality teaching pact*]. Retrieved January 27, 2022, from https://www.qualitaetspakt-lehre.de/

Cordingley, P., Bell, M., Rundell, B., & Evans, D. (2003). *The impact of collaborative CPD on classroom teaching and learning.* Research Evidence in Education Library. Version 1.1. EPPI-Centre, Social Science Research Unit, Institute of Education. Retrieved August 16, 2021, from http://www.saspa.com.au/wp-content/uploads/2016/02/Creating-and-Sustaining-PLCs_tcm4-631034-1.pdf

DuFour, R. (2004). What is a "professional learning community"? *Educational Leadership, 61*(8), 6–11.

Gast, I., Schildkamp, K., & van der Veen, J. T. (2017). Team-based professional development interventions in higher education. A systematic review. *Review of Educational Research, 87*(4), 736–767. https://doi.org/10.3102/0034654317704306

Hord, S. (1997). *Professional learning communities: Communities of continuous inquiry and improvement.* Southwest Educational Development Department. Retrieved August 16, 2021, from https://files.eric.ed.gov/fulltext/ED410659.pdf

Kordts-Freudinger, R., Braukmann, J., & Schulte, R. (2018). Scholarship of Teaching and Learning – individuell-evidenzorientiertes Lehren [Scholarship of teaching and learning – individual evidence-based teaching]. In B. Szczyrba & N. Schaper (Eds.), *Forschung und Innovation in der Hochschulbildung. Vol. 1. Forschungsformate zur evidenzbasierten Fundierung hochschuldidaktischen Handelns* [*Research and innovation in higher education*] (pp. 213–229). Cologne Open Science.

Kruse, S. D., Louis, K. S., & Bryk, A. (1994). An emerging framework for analyzing school-based professional community. In K. S. Louis, & S. D. Kruse (Eds.), *Professionalism and community: Perspectives on reforming urban schools* (pp. 23–44). Corwin Press,

Leibenath, Y. (2019). *Evaluationsergebnisse zum Kollegialen Coaching am FTSK Germersheim* [*Evaluation results on Peer Coaching at the FTSK Germersheim*] [Unpublished report]. Zentrum für Qualitätssicherung und -entwicklung (ZQ), Johannes Gutenberg-Universität Mainz.

Leibenath, Y., Seipp, T., & Zajontz, T. (2016). Konzeption und Wirksamkeit kollegialer Formate in der Hochschuldidaktik. Das Projekt „Kollegiales Coaching" an der Johannes Gutenberg-Universität Mainz [Conception and effectiveness of collegial formats in university didactics. The project "Peer Coaching" at the Johannes Gutenberg University Mainz]. *Qualität in der Wissenschaft, 10*(3/4), 108–116.

Lomos, C., Hofman, R. H., & Bosker, R. J. (2011). Professional communities and student achievement – A meta-analysis. *School Effectiveness and School Improvement, 22*(2), 121–148. https://doi.org/10.1080/09243453.2010.550467

Schaap, H., & Bruijn, E. de (2018). Elements affecting the development of professional learning communities in schools. *Learning Environments Research, 21*(1), 109–134. https://doi.org/10.1007/s10984-017-9244-y

Schmidt, U., Schmidt, F., & Becker, N. (2020). *Ergebnisse der Befragung Lehren und Lernen im „digitalen" Sommersemester 2020. Befragungen Lehrender und Studierender an der Johannes Gutenberg-Universität Mainz* [*Results of the survey on teaching and learning in the "digital" summer semester 2020. Surveys of teaching staff and students at the Johannes Gutenberg University Mainz*] [Unpublished report]. Zentrum für Qualitätssicherung und -entwicklung (ZQ), Johannes Gutenberg-Universität Mainz.

Schmidt, U., Schmidt, F., & Becker, N. (2021). Perspektiven Lehrender und Studierender auf die Digitalisierung von Lehren und Lernen. Ergebnisse einer empirischen Studie an der Johannes Gutenberg-Universität Mainz. [Perspectives of teachers and students on the digitization of teaching and learning. Results of an empirical study at the Johannes Gutenberg University Mainz]. *Qualität in der Wissenschaft, 15*(2), 36–48.

Sekyra, A., & Bade, C. (2020). Professionelle Lerngemeinschaften als Chance für die Weiterentwicklung der Hochschullehre [Professional learning communities as an opportunity for advancing higher education teaching]. In K. Kansteiner, C. Stamann, C. G. Buhren, & P. Theurl (Eds.), *Professionelle Lerngemeinschaften als Entwicklungsinstrument im Bildungswesen* [*Professional Learning Communities as a development tool in education*] (pp. 276–285). Beltz Juventa Verlag.

Stoll, L., Bolam, R., McMahon, A., Wallace, M., & Thomas, S. (2006). Professional learning communities: A review of the literature. *Journal of Educational Change, 7*(4), 221–258. https://doi.org/10.1007/s10833-006-0001-8

Vangrieken, K., Meredith, C., Packer, T., & Kyndt, E. (2017). Teacher communities as a context for professional development: A systematic review. *Teaching and Teacher Education, 61*, 47–59. https://doi.org/10.1016/j.tate.2016.10.001

Vescio, V., Ross, D., & Adams, A. (2008). A review of research on the impact of professional learning communities on teaching practice and student learning. *Teaching and Teacher Education, 24*(1), 80–91. https://doi.org/10.1016/j.tate.2007.01.004

Warwas, J., & Helm, C. (2018). Professional learning communities among vocational school teachers. Profiles and relations with instructional quality. *Teaching and Teacher Education, 73*, 43–55. https://doi.org/10.1016/j.tate.2018.03.012

Warwas, J., & Schadt, C. (2020). Zur Modellierung Professioneller Lerngemeinschaften: Vergleich und Integration unterschiedlicher Ansätze [On modelling professional learning communities: Comparison and integration of different approaches]. In K. Kansteiner, C. Stamann, C. G. Buhren, & P. Theurl (Eds.), *Professionelle Lerngemeinschaften als Entwicklungsinstrument im Bildungswesen* [*Professional learning communities as a development tool in education*] (pp. 37–48). Beltz Juventa Verlag.

Winteler, A., & Schmolck, P. (2003). Teaching-Tipps. Tipps für effizientes Lehren und erfolgreiches Lernen [Teaching tips. Tips for efficient teaching and successful learning]. *Didaktiknachrichten (DiNa)*, *3*, 3–9.

CHAPTER 13

Rethinking Quality and Excellence in Teaching and Learning in Higher Education

Matt O'Leary, Tony Armstrong, Victoria Birmingham, Amanda French,
Alex Kendall, Mark O'Hara and Katy Vigurs

Abstract

"Quality" and "excellence" are omnipresent terms permeating all areas of higher education, particularly in the context of teaching and learning. The recent COVID-19 pandemic has further intensified debates about conceptions of quality and excellence, particularly regarding universities' ability to adapt from face-to-face teaching to virtual provision and to respond to the growing mental health needs of its students. In this chapter, we draw on evidence from three distinct projects undertaken in one university in England, each involving academic staff and students co-researching and collaborating on areas of curriculum, pedagogy and mental health. What links these projects is our participatory approach to rethinking notions of quality and excellence in practitioner education, which empowers students and staff to work collaboratively to improve the quality of teaching and learning experiences.

Keywords

higher education – teaching and learning – quality – excellence – collaboration – inclusive practice

1   Introduction

In this chapter, we share a series of innovations in practitioner education with the aim of opening up critical conversations about "quality" and "excellence" in higher education (HE) and interrogating what these terms might come to mean in the ruins of humanism and the aftermath of Black Lives Matter. We acknowledge the contested, contingent and heterogeneous nature of these terms and how they are subject to widely differing conceptualisations across HE (Harvey & Green, 1993). Collini (2012, p. 109) argues that there is a "vacuity" associated with words like "excellence" as there is "no such thing in the abstract". We also maintain that such terms have become 'colonised by an accountability agenda' in recent years, which can have 'disempowering consequences for those interested in understanding and improving HE teaching further' (Wood & O'Leary, 2019). With this in mind, we refrain from providing static definitions of "quality" and "excellence" and instead invoke our readers to explore new ways of conceptualising them. Added to this, we reflect on the implications of what real institutional change around the student experience could mean if educators were able to embrace more inclusive and democratic approaches in their practice. The three illustrative vignettes included in this chapter all focus on dimensions of practice development within our own HE setting, the Faculty of Health, Education and Life Sciences (HELS) at Birmingham City University (BCU) in the Midlands of England.

The UK HE sector has seen rapid growth over the past 50 years, with participation levels increasing from around 10% of the population in the 1970s to 50.2% by 2017/18 (Kershaw, 2019). Against the backdrop of this expansion, the HE policy and regulatory environment in the UK has grown increasingly competitive and marketised (McCaig, 2018; McGettigan, 2016). During this period, there has also been a shift away from student grants to student loans to cover tuition fees and living expenses, which has resulted in a repositioning of students as consumers. As a result of all these huge changes, HE managers and academics have found themselves under constant pressure to demonstrate "quality" and "excellence" in their provision, principally through various top-down government exercises such as the Teaching Excellence Framework (TEF), the Research Excellence Framework (REF), the Knowledge Exchange Framework and the National Student Survey (NSS). These frameworks have distorted teacher-student relations, positioning students as passive consumers and consolidating a pernicious hierarchy within and across universities. We argue, moreover, that they obscure the complexity of actual relations and interactions between students, their peers and staff as they participate in their learning and teaching.

The projects discussed in this chapter all emerged out of the Centre for the Study of Practice and Culture in Education (CSPACE), the education research unit in the Faculty of HELS. A distinguishing feature and commitment of CSPACE's work is its focus on "near to practice", participatory research, starting with our own staff, who are supported to become research-engaged, enabling them to interrogate and challenge dominant HE paradigms and ideologies. Practitioner research is the 'golden thread' that connects our research groups, specialisms and projects, impacting education policy and practice internally and externally across sectors. The work discussed in the three vignettes in this chapter exemplifies some of the practitioner research undertaken in CSPACE, along with the research interests of its staff.

2   Contextualising Birmingham City University

Birmingham, the UK's second city, sits at the heart of the region and is the largest metropolitan authority in Europe. Birmingham City University (BCU) is a
large, urban institution in the heart of the West Midlands. It is a "post-1992" or
"modern" university, a term commonly used in English HE to refer to former
polytechnics, institutes or colleges of higher education that were granted university status through the 1992 Further and Higher Education Act. The diversity
of BCU's local demographics is embraced by the University, which describes
itself as 'the University *for* Birmingham'. The emphasis on the word "for" here
relates to a core commitment that underpins BCU's overarching mission as a
locally engaging university that serves the needs and interests of its communities in the region. BCU's ethos reflects its position as the provider of choice for
students from so-called 'non-traditional' backgrounds. This includes students
who are often characterised in current policy discourses as first-generation,
students from low socioeconomic backgrounds as well as students of colour,
disabled and mature students.

     Nowhere is this more apparent than in BCU's largest faculty with nearly
9,000 students, the Faculty of Health, Education and Life Sciences (HELS),
in which the authors of this chapter all work. The HELS Faculty at BCU specialises in practitioner education in nursing and midwifery, teacher education
and social work, along with a wide range of professions allied to health (e.g.
speech and language therapy, physiotherapy, radiography and paramedic science). Our courses are endorsed by professional bodies, were co-designed with
employers, and have professional work placements built into them. It is also
worth noting that most teaching staff have dual professional identities, coming from professional/practitioner backgrounds in health sciences, social care,
nursing, midwifery and education. Some of them remain active professionals in these sectors as well as being university teachers and researchers. The
majority of the students in the faculty study vocational courses to qualify them
to become the health and education practitioners of the future.

     HELS is one of the largest providers of teaching and nursing education in
the UK and the majority of our students come from the West Midlands and
continue to live and practise in the region after graduating. Our student population closely reflects the highly diverse communities we serve, with over half
of our undergraduate students from black and minority ethnic (BAME) communities (55%). The majority of our students (84%) come from and continue
to live in the region. They are also from areas with high levels of deprivation,
as well as many being the first in their family to attend university (65%). We

also cater for a large population of mature students (46%). In addition, 11% are disabled (self-declared) 1.4% are care leavers.

BCU's diverse student body is largely due to the success of the widening participation initiative, which was originally created to promote an ideal of greater inclusiveness and accessibility in UK HE. The majority of widening participation students in England attend 'post-1992' institutions like BCU where there is consequently a much more diverse HE student population, (Waller, Ingram & Ward, 2017). However, there is evidence to suggest that the expansion of HE has given rise to the use of new deficit labels – such as the 'non-traditional student' and the 'commuter student' (Holdsworth, 2006) – which are connected implicitly to social class (Reay, Crozier & Clayton, 2010) and ethnicity (Alexander & Arday, 2015; Donnelly & Gamsu, 2018).

In this chapter, we challenge those student-based deficit discourses, seeking rather to explore how innovative institutional change can be adopted to meet the needs of this more diverse student body. Specifically, we focus on how particular difficulties adapting to the demands of HE arise because widening participation students have to fit into an education system not designed with their learning and development needs in mind (Ahmed, 2012; Reay, Crozier & Clayton, 2010). This is precisely the issue that the institutionally based projects described in this chapter seek to address in different ways by opening up new, discursive spaces and opportunities for different ways of thinking, being and doing about teaching and learning in HE. This chapter therefore adds to the important debate about how universities like BCU can meet the needs and positively address the issues of a political economy of difference in their student body. More positively classified as "post-traditional" (Aquino & BuShell, 2020), these different categories of students are 'complex individuals with multifaceted and multi-layered identities' (Kasworm, 2010) which engrained binary labels such as "traditional" and "non-traditional" fail to reflect. An illustrative example of this in relation to student-hood is the idea that the 'traditional' undergraduate student is someone who studies full-time and lives away from home. In contrast to this entrenched orthodoxy, the so-called 'non-traditional' student (i.e. studies part-time and lives at home) at BCU is actually the 'marginalised majority' (Fulford, 2020).

3   Introducing Our Vignettes

Our vignettes, which explore our commitments to building a more diverse community, paying attention to the mental health and well-being of our students, and reorientating the purpose and dynamic of observing teaching and learning, are shared as triggers for discussions about power, positionality and identity in the modern university. We reappropriate ideas about 'quality' and 'excellence' as opportunity spaces for rethinking the being and doing of practitioner education towards the urgent project of reimagining more diverse, inclusive and democratic possibilities that better equip practitioners and students for alternative futures. This reimagining conceptualises development in teaching and learning as an ongoing, dialogic process that emerges from a situated understanding of the complexity of teaching and learning environments.

Our central provocation is that rather than indexing a priori metrics and indicators of so-called "quality" (through the TEF, REF and KEF), excellence "in the ruins" (MacLure, 2011; St. Pierre & Pillow, 2000) is about acknowledging and embracing the more complex, nuanced work of "staying with the trouble" (Haraway, 2016). Haraway makes a call to arms for us to learn to think together to open up the possibility of a more "response-able" present: "learning to be truly present ... as mortal critters entwined in myriad unfinished configurations of places, times, matters, meanings" (Haraway, 2016, p. 1).

We draw on the illustrations of our practice below to explore what "response-able" practice might begin to mean in our context. For Bayley, these sorts of pedagogical questions are urgent ones, "no longer simply an "if" or a "why" but how. Simply HOW [sic]?" (2018, p. 243). And we situate this chapter as a response to that "HOW". We challenge ourselves to begin to reimagine practitioner education as an everyday, negotiated practice that resists traditional binaries, identities and positionalities (i.e. student/teacher, researcher/participant, observer/observee) of dominant humanist paradigms that have the effect of reproducing inequalities towards more 'entangled modalit[ies] of co-laboring [sic]' (Franklin-Phipps & Rath, 2018). We conceptualise practice as reciprocity, or the kind of 'odd-kin-making' that Haraway (2016) imagines, a becoming together beyond binaries. We have argued elsewhere that this may be particularly important in the context of education in countries like England that have entangled, present but often silenced and suppressed histories of empire and colonialism (Kendall et al., 2021). In our context in Birmingham, this may be particularly urgent – making kin with post-humanism argue Franklin-Phipps and Rath (2018, p. 270) refuses humanist stories of white exceptionalism 'that centre [sic] certain kinds of human subject and destroy others' and to stay with the trouble as "a sustained consideration of ideas that challenge us in an ethical encountering of and becoming response-able to and for suffering, dispossession, histories that hurt" (Franklin-Phipps & Rath, 2018, p. 271).

We therefore invite readers to interact with our three vignettes as starting points for re-imagining quality and excellence in the aftermath.

4   Vignette 1 – Reimagining Teaching-Learning Relationships in Higher Education: Towards the Development of a Radical and Inclusive 'Practitioner Learning Community'

4.1   *Introduction*

This vignette outlines one project's attempt to open up a new practitioner-researcher space for thinking differently (more inclusively and 'care-fully') about learning and teaching in HE. This involved a collective re-thinking about relations within academic learning communities and developed a process for creating a collaborative research team, comprising both undergraduate students and undergraduate teaching staff, of and for one faculty. This was an internal faculty research project, commissioned and supported by the faculty's leadership team in 2020–21, which stemmed from the UK National Student Survey (NSS) data that provided messages about the way that students experienced studying and everyday life in the faculty. Moving forwards, the faculty wants to foster and sustain an explicitly welcoming and supportive 'Practitioner Learning Community' amongst students and staff. It is hoped that the development of this concept will inform different ways of thinking about and practising learning and teaching and address the concerns illustrated in Figure 13.1.

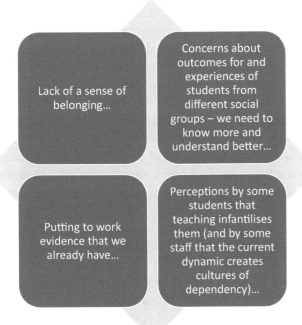

FIGURE 13.1   Rationale for the research

4.2   *Conceptualising the Aims and Theoretical Focus of the Project*

The main aim of this project was to recruit ten undergraduate students and ten undergraduate lecturers (along with two research facilitators) from across the faculty to create a diverse team of practitioner-researchers and to explicitly build a working example of an inclusive practitioner learning community over a period of six months. Many of the team members were new to social and educational research. Everyone within the team was considered and explicitly encouraged to identify as a co-researcher rather than as a member of staff or student, thus disrupting conventional roles and identities in HE. It is also important to acknowledge the wider context of the COVID-19 pandemic, as during the project's life, members of the team variously experienced personal loss and grief, loneliness and isolation, the pressures of juggling work, study and caring responsibilities and many were also working on the frontline in clinical health and education settings. It also meant that the entire project was conducted remotely using an online platform. We never met face-to-face.

In order to get to work as research facilitators, we started by considering our roles and how they differed to the co-researchers. As research-facilitators, we were positioned as having knowledge and skills to facilitate the research process but emphasised the importance and value of the knowledge which would be gained from our participant practitioners and students who were not researchers themselves. We were thoughtful about the philosophy and values that might need to underpin the development of this new and differently relational HE space, particularly during a global pandemic. We found it helpful to use a range of connected and overlapping theoretical ideas to set the project's intentions. These included the concepts of critical pedagogy (Freire, 1972; Apple, 2011; Crean & Lynch, 2011), "doing risk" (Kitching, 2011), "ethics of care" (O'Brien, 2011; Breeze & Taylor, 2020), border crossing and "little stories" (Cotton & Griffiths, 2007).

Critical pedagogy is a democratic process of education which encourages critical consciousness as the basis for transformative collective action. Here we invoked Paulo Freire's calls for justice and transformation *through* relationship, reflective dialogue and responsive practice. This required us to be aware, responsive and attuned to the conditions that we and others were experiencing. Weekly meetings and a flexible approach to the running of the project functioned as a "care-full" research community which adapted to the context of the researchers rather than being confined a traditional working pattern. There was also the concept of 'doing risk' which acknowledges that this sort of work is not neutral, rather it is critical and political and this can often be uncomfortable. It was possible that the practitioner-researchers would need individual and collective courage in order to think, feel and act differently. For example, by immersing themselves in new areas of literature, practitioner-researchers might encounter research which contradicted or made them question tacit assumptions of their practice.

The concept of "ethics of care" foregrounds the significance of emotions and relationships to the process of education. Emotional responsiveness and affective practices are crucial aspects of pedagogy. However, care and relationality are often not visible, recognised, valued, or given discursive space within the academy (Breeze & Taylor, 2020). The significance of border crossing is an idea about becoming critical through the act of seeing life from an altered perspective and building alliances across difference. And finally, the concept of 'little stories' means situating an individual's voice within collective narratives, making a connection between deeply personal, everyday stories and the profoundly political. In this project, it was in these theoretical threads that we felt 'radical' possibilities lay; by 'radical' we refer to moving away from conventional delineations between lecturers and students, replacing the "them" and "us" with just an "us" as an inclusive learning community. These theoretical ideas raised some key questions for the project. Some of the key ones we were immediately faced with were: How would we build trust and rapport between co-researchers? How would we create a supportive and safe space? What conditions would we need to create to build meaningful dialogue? What would we need to do to ensure a critical, reflective and reflexive environment? How would we identify and tackle issues of power and privilege? What needs to be in place to stimulate collective activity? Our feeling was that if we raised and tackled these questions, we would have a good chance at co-creating an inclusive practitioner learning community. We did not know whether it would work and at times it felt uncertain and risky.

4.3   *Developing Our Researcher Community and Collaborative Methodology*

Once the 20 co-researchers were recruited, building trust and rapport between the facilitators and each individual co-researcher was prioritised. The facilitators set up initial email conversations with each co-researcher to get to know them as individuals by asking questions like "What should we do to make sure the project is accessible and engaging for you?", "Is there anything about your involvement in the project that you are worried about?", "What main communities or groups do you feel you belong to?". These interactions were then incrementally followed up with individual one-to-one online meetings to welcome them to the team. Everyone was then asked to create a personal 'fact file' as a written document, picture or video to introduce themselves to the rest of the team. We then co-created a set of team values and communication ground rules. Everyone was asked to put forward their top three principles for achieving an inclusive and positive team experience. The 60 responses were transformed into 22 principles, which grounded our own bespoke, team micro-culture. Everyone also wrote and shared a reflexive position statement at the beginning of project, which was reviewed and updated at the end. This relational groundwork was crucial and allowed trust, understanding, empathy and rapport to be built quickly within the team.

We used Microsoft Teams to co-create an online team space to organise our work and communications. An inclusive and engaging digital space was achieved, with regular interaction encouraged and modelled by the facilitators. The facilitators set out to actively acknowledge and validate each person's contribution to the team space. Each week there was both a formal team meeting (recorded for those who could not attend) and an informal drop-in session. This approach ensured that participation was flexible and acknowledged the competing pressures and priorities being juggled by each person. As a research team, we conducted a collaborative international literature review on the following topics: students' experiences of time and space; student belonging and sense of identity; dynamics and communications between students and staff (themes that emerged from an analysis of the NSS data).

The team read and critiqued over 60 research papers and chapters. Research-informed PowerPoint presentations were created for each topic area to communicate what the team had learned and to identify questions that had arisen from the collective reading exercise. On the back of the literature review, the team then identified three areas for further research within our faculty: What does it feel like to walk in our students' shoes? Exploring what meaningful relationships look like between staff and students and investigating diversity and inclusion praxis. The team co-designed interview questions for undergraduate students. This was a supportive and iterative process. We piloted the student interview questions within our team during a formal meeting, which was a valuable research learning opportunity. On gaining ethical approval the team members conducted 25 in depth interviews by email with undergraduate students in the faculty to find out what it is like to walk in their shoes as a student. Our next steps are to present our findings back to faculty to explore ways this data can be utilised to move the student experience towards being more collaborative.

4.4   Conclusion

This vignette suggests we were successful in modelling a radical practitioner-researcher community in/for our faculty, by foregrounding positive relationships for practitioner learning, by explicitly striving for collaboration that is "care-full", and by moving from a culture of "them and us" to simply "us". Success also comes in the form of how this research will be used in the future. It raises the question of what might happen if relations of care (and its associated labour) between staff and students were visible, valued, resourced and equitably distributed within our universities? What would change? How might the quality of teaching and learning be affected? All these questions will be considered when working with faculty senior leadership to integrate the findings into future staff development. Additionally, from a methodological perspective, we anticipate that collaborative research between students and staff could be considered part of the continued journey on the path towards a culture of "us".

5 Vignette 2 – Postgraduate Mental Health Research Project

5.1 Introduction

This second vignette is an account of a research project that explored the quality of doctoral students' (both PhD and EdD) experience as it specifically related to mental health whilst undertaking their doctorate at BCU. In addition, the research also intended to contribute, through student and staff engagement, to institutional knowledge making and the imagining of new ways in excellent doctoral practice including alternative futures for doctoral students within the university. The research project took place between September 2018 and July 2020. The main period of data collection and analysis intriguingly captured the experience of the participants just before the onset of the COVID-19 pandemic and well before its mental health implications for students became apparent. The research therefore identified what was "normal" in the pre-pandemic phase rather than doctoral students' mental health challenges in *extremis* under the atypical pandemic conditions.

5.2 Research Aim and Context

The overall aim of the research was to examine and evaluate the mental health of doctoral students via a mixed methods approach which included an online survey for students and focus groups with both students and supervisors. Initial informal reconnaissance work was carried out by the research team before the research started. This informal fact finding and scoping exercise consisted of listening to student concerns and taking field notes within the everyday context of supervisions, seminars and at social learning gatherings. The reconnaissance work indicated that a significant number of students, probably around a third, were experiencing mental discomfort during their doctoral journeys and this was often triggered by milestone type events and periods of writing and assessment intensity, in addition to the pressure from longer term institutional policies, processes and procedures. However, these circumstances were far from unique to BCU students, as recent studies identified an emerging trend of disconcerting levels of psychological distress among postgraduates with 32% of PhD students at risk of having or developing a common disorder (Levecque et al., 2017).

BCU is a teaching intensive university with a focus on employment in the regional economy. As a former polytechnic, BCU also inherited a small and underdeveloped doctoral research culture and community. However, it is worth acknowledging that in the three years prior to the project, BCU experienced a 100% growth rate in its doctoral student numbers, reaching a total of 542 at the time of the research. Perhaps significantly though, this surge in recruitment was not matched by accompanying investment in provision and/ or infrastructure. Indeed, with the noted surge in student numbers, the distribution of doctoral students across the institution had also become increasingly uneven with the majority of part-time students, in particular, located in one of the four Faculties, which also had the lowest number of supervisors available. Full-time students tended to predominate in two of the four Faculties with a greater availability of supervisor capacity.

5.3   Theory and Methodology

On the theoretical and methodological level, the research project consciously focused on the ordinary lived experience of the everyday for the students in space and time, deploying the approach of Henri Lefebvre (2002, 2014) and rhythm analysis. This theoretical and methodological stance was a deliberate swerve away from the more conventional psychological approaches that are often applied to the investigation of doctoral students' mental health and focused instead on the doctoral rhythms of the participants. The rationale for the choice of a rhythm analytical approach was twofold. Firstly, it reflected the research interests of the research team. Secondly, it allowed the research team, all of whom were practising doctoral supervisors, to adopt an innovative lens through which to explore the student experience and doctoral rhythms as both an object for research and a mode of analysis.

The online survey deployed at the outset used a Likert-type scale of questions and free text responses, which was distributed to all registered BCU doctoral students. The survey produced a typical response rate of just over a third (34% – n = 186). This constituted a useful baseline for the data and stimulated further investigation. Following the survey, focus groups were carried out and facilitated by members of the research team, with a total of four sessions for students and two sessions for supervisors, all of which produced a substantial amount of qualitative data. The focus groups were conducted across the University's two main campuses at different times to enable attendance from both full-time and part-time students and supervisors.

5.4   *Key Findings*

It is perhaps worth saying that the research team certainly anticipated at least some troubling data from their early reconnaissance work but they were quite unprepared for and indeed unsettled by the poignancy and cathartic dynamics of much of the data, particularly from the focus group stage and accompanying evidence. The data identified the everyday rhythms of the doctoral student experience, including their negative embodiment for students, the pulse of unresolved relationship tensions with supervisors and others, and the relentless cycle of institutional antagonisms. For example, it was both concerning and surprising to the researchers that 65% of students felt anxious prior to supervision sessions. Students were also insistent that supervisors were poorly prepared or unresponsive to the growing level of mental health issues they experienced. In some cases, students experienced debilitating levels of anxiety expressed in terms of bodily pain, sleep deprivation, self-harm and eating disorders.

Another concerning and perhaps surprising finding was the seminal importance given to space for the students particularly those undertaking full-time doctorates. Some respondents claimed that the recent institutional removal of a dedicated student space at the central campus of the university had had a detrimental effect on student mental health as it had completely undermined any sense of belonging or community which had been carefully and slowly built up over the years. In short, some students felt that their specific needs, space and contribution were not a priority within the University. In a similar way, it was also felt that the internal university systems presented significant barriers to research development and tended to be disablers rather than enablers to progress. For example, this was particularly the case it was claimed with the research integrity and ethical review processes and the institutional pulse and pressure of progress assessment panel events which were requirements for all doctoral students.

What emerges from the research is therefore a certain rhythm of pained resentment from those who felt marginalised and trivialised within their own organisation. However, this was not simply a consequence of growing student numbers but also related to the increased diversity of needs. For example, 81% of students found balancing other pressing commitments in their lives, such as paid work and family responsibilities with their doctorate either difficult or very difficult. This was a particularly noticeable issue with part-time students who were often employed in all education sectors locally. Indeed, those part-time students employed at BCU itself felt that they did not have the quality and depth of appropriate time made available by the institution to dedicate to their research and their researcher development. Furthermore, this group regarded themselves as being caught up and entangled in a particularly pernicious doctoral rhythm which impacted on their everyday. This rhythm consisted of anxieties around rising career expectations in HE of doctoral engagement within a context of heavy and unsustainable teaching workloads and a low functional level of institutional sensitivity or even awareness about their position.

5.5 *Recommendations*
The research explored the quality of the doctoral student experience at BCU as it related to a growing concern with mental health and undertaking a doctorate. The research was also an example of and a contribution towards institutional knowledge making and the rethinking of excellence in doctoral practice within a particular post-92 context i.e. a 'modern' university, similar to technical universities in Europe. Therefore, as a result of the research, four substantive recommendations were produced for BCU to take forward. The first was that all students should be allocated a physical space to carry out their work at the city centre campus, which positions them clearly as a community member and a working priority within the organisation. Secondly, training should be available and made mandatory for supervisors regarding student mental health needs and basic mental health literacy. Thirdly, supervisors should have the opportunity for debriefing outside of their own supervisory teams to discuss student issues, concerns and progress. This would help to 'thicken' the layers of practical support for students and the related institutional learning, knowledge and expertise as part of a broader process of distributive supervision. Finally, it was recommended that a dedicated doctoral student mental health specialist should be recruited to provide training, development and support to both students and supervisors and this should be treated as an immediate institutional employment priority.

6 Vignette 3 – Improving Teaching and Learning through Collaborative Observation

6.1 *Introduction*
Debates about quality and excellence in teaching and learning in HE have featured prominently on the education policy agenda of governments worldwide

in recent years. In the UK, for example, HE providers are increasingly required to demonstrate how they monitor the quality of teaching and what measures they are taking to improve it. However, much policy focus has tended to promote an instrumentalist model of teaching and learning, with teaching staff often perceived as the 'deliverers' of knowledge and skills and students as the 'consumers'. As a counter narrative to this conceptualisation of the teacher-student interrelationship, this vignette discusses the development of an innovative partnership between academic staff and students in a recent project, where students' inclusion is reconceptualised from passive consumer to active collaborator through the shared lens of observation. It explores the conceptual and theoretical framework of a cycle of collaborative observation (CoCO), explaining its rationale, how it differs to conventional observation approaches, along with the methodology devised to introduce and prepare staff and students for working with this approach to observation in an English university.

6.2   Conceptualising the Focus and Methodology of the Project

Improving teaching and learning through collaborative observation was an innovative project undertaken at BCU from 2016 to 2018, funded by the Higher Education Funding Council for England. The project comprised five case studies of undergraduate courses across a single faculty, with each case study including two academic staff and two student participants for each observation cycle. The five case studies included in the project were: (1) Adult Nursing; (2) Child Nursing; (3) Early Childhood Studies; (4) Primary Education and 5) Radiotherapy.

The project used the shared lens of classroom observation as a reciprocal reference point for exploring teaching and learning at course level. The primary aim of the project was to create a sustainable and collaborative model of observation, which would empower students to play an active role in shaping their learning experience and result in the development of a framework for continuous improvement in teaching and learning practices across the programmes involved in the study. As part of the project, we therefore developed our Cycle of Collaborative Observation (CoCO) (Figure 13.2). CoCO provided a common frame of reference for staff and students to collaborate, as well as embodying the thinking and methodology that we wanted to in our approach to improving teaching and learning. We drew on the latest research and practice in the field of observation, learning from the pitfalls of how it has been previously misappropriated as a punitive performance management tool in education systems (e.g. O'Leary & Wood, 2017).

The project was underpinned by the belief that improving student learning requires teachers and students to develop an awareness and understanding

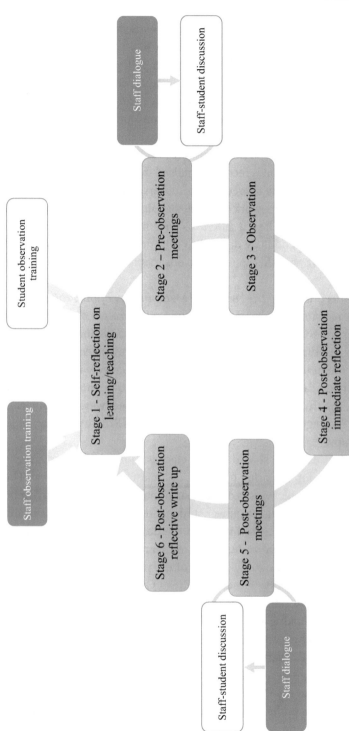

FIGURE 13.2   Cycle of collaborative observation

about learning collaboratively in the context of their programme. Shaped and informed by current research and cutting-edge practice in the field of observation, we proposed an innovative and collaborative model of observing teaching and learning, involving students and staff. Our model was driven by shared values around developing and promoting excellence amongst staff and students. A key feature of this innovative and experimental project was the way in which it aimed to reconceptualise and reconfigure the use of observation as a method to enhance teaching and learning.

The conceptual and methodological framework of our project design started with us reconceptualising and reconfiguring the way in which we planned for the project's participants to engage with observation as a method for studying and enhancing teaching and learning. Severing the umbilical link between observation and its use as a method of assessing teaching and teacher performance was central to this process. We were convinced that unless we were able to remove observation from the assessment context, this would jeopardise our efforts to capture situated examples of authentic teaching and learning and in turn to create a safe, trusting and collaborative environment for reflection and dialogue between staff and students (e.g. O'Leary and Savage, 2019). Similarly, when it came to student involvement, our approach put student voice and their active involvement in informing and shaping teaching and learning at the heart of this innovation. As a counter narrative to the instrumentalist model of teaching and learning with academic staff perceived as the deliverers of knowledge and students as the consumers, this project re-conceptualised teaching and learning as reciprocal social practices that require the involvement of both students and teachers to build a shared contextualised understanding in order to make meaningful improvement.

6.3   Data Collection and Key Findings

Over the course of the two iterations of CoCO (Figure 13.1), students and staff worked through closely alongside each other to co-investigate areas of practice pertinent to their respective programmes. Each case study produced a large volume of rich data, which included initial reflections from all student and staff participants, recordings of the pre- and post-observation meetings, observation field notes, individual reflective write-ups and recordings of evaluation meetings with the project researchers at the end of each cycle of observation. We employed a two-phase approach to the data analysis for this study. Phase one involved each case study team and the project researchers working closely to familiarise themselves with the discrete data generated in each case study and to make sense of each case study's situated data. This was an important step as the data recorded were produced *during* the project in authentic and organic oral exchanges between participants, including observation notes and personal reflections. Phase two involved the project researchers extending the data analysis across all case studies to develop a set of common themes. The two researchers initially analysed the case study data independently, identifying overarching themes that collectively reflected key aspects of student-staff collaboration, which were shared with the staff participants.

Analysis of the rich data gathered during this project revealed that teachers and students learn about teaching and learning by interacting with their peers and with each other, by sharing their insights and experiences in collaborative, cooperative forums. In other words, teaching and learning are inherently socially situated practices. As Strom and Viesca (2020, p. 13) argue, "research activity needs to be situated and local, with a focus on the particular". It therefore makes sense that any attempt to enhance understanding of and improve these practices is best served by allowing its key participants to be part of a collective community in which they are encouraged to engage in a process of dialectic pedagogical knowledge and relationship development. Creating the conditions in which teachers and students have the opportunity to examine their understanding and experiences of teaching and learning and open them up to dialogic exchange is fundamental to developing greater awareness of the strengths and areas for development in their practices. In the context of teaching and learning, approaches like CoCO can help to create the shared spaces in which teachers can come together with their peers and equally with their students to engage in reflexive pedagogical dialogue on their classroom teaching and learning. In turn, this can lead to collective sense making, which can make a valuable contribution to both students and their teachers in understanding and developing their practices.

To conclude this vignette, we ask readers to consider two questions. How can we challenge and replace metrics-based approaches to monitoring and assessing the 'quality' of teaching and learning? How can we create and nurture authentic and sustainable practice that involves students and staff collaboratively generating meaningful teaching and learning experiences?

7   Discussion and Concluding Thoughts

To foster inclusivity and sense of belonging, HE practitioners must be committed (and supported) to create opportunities for sustained and meaningful engagement with difference in their teaching. Our projects into the student experience and mental health suggest that modern universities, with their diverse student cohorts, need to work harder to make new spaces for all students, which allow them to feel more that they belong within and can relate more positively and agentively to HE demands and expectations. Our work on teacher observations challenges the culture of performativity and compliance demanded by the current neoliberal landscape by creating a more collaborative and collegiate system around 'quality' and excellence' in teaching for the staff who actually deliver it. Taken together, these projects offer any university a chance to reconsider how best to deliver quality and excellence for their students in meaningful and practical ways.

As we begin to reclaim our lives from the stranglehold of the pandemic that has regulated how and what we have been able to do over the last two years, we do so with the anticipation of being able to regain a sense of 'normality'. Yet, at the same time, we are even more cognisant now than ever of how the pandemic has created the conditions for us to interrogate and to reassess who we are, how we think and what we do as educators and researchers. Put simply, despite the upheaval and uncertainty, the pandemic has presented us with an opportunity for rethinking and reconfiguring our sense of 'being' and 'doing'. It would be an opportunity missed if we were simply to return to our dependence on the linear systems of metrics-based performance data and the reductionist approaches to learning about and improving teaching and learning that have dominated education internationally in recent decades. Such systems and approaches merely serve to perpetuate the status quo of Western humanist traditions and/or the 'what works' movement in education, which in turn closes down alternative ways of knowing and doing. If we are to embody what it means to be *"response-able"* and *"care-full"* educators and researchers, then we would argue that we need to begin by challenging, resisting and reconceptualising some of the traditional binaries, identities and positionalities of dominant paradigms that exacerbate the status quo.

References

Ahmed, S. (2012). *On being included: Racism and diversity in institutional life.* Duke University Press.

Alexander, C., & Arday, J. (2015). *Aiming higher: Race, inequality and diversity in the academy.* AHRC, Runnymede Trust (Runnymede Perspectives).

Apple, M. W. (2011). Paulo Freire and the tasks of the critical educational scholar/activist. In A. O'Shea & M. O'Brien (Eds.), *Pedagogy, oppression and transformation in a 'post-critical' climate* (pp. 36–50). Bloomsbury.

Aquino, K. C., & Bushell, S. (2020). Device usage and accessible technology needs for post-traditional students in the e-learning environment. *The Journal of Continuing Higher Education, 68*(2), 101–116.

Bayley, A. (2018). Posthumanism, decoloniality and re-imagining pedagogy. *Parallax*, 24(3), 243–253.

Bell, L., & Stevenson, H. (2006). *Educational policy: Process, themes and impact*. Routledge.

Bolton, P., & Hubble, S. (2019). *The post-18 education review (the Augar review) recommendations*. House of Commons Library.

Braidotti, R. (2013). *The posthuman*. Polity Press.

Breeze, M., & Taylor, Y. (2020). *Feminist repetitions in higher education: Interrupting career categories*. Palgrave Macmillan.

Colebrook, C. (2002). *Understanding Deleuze*. Allen & Unwin.

Collini, S. (2012). *What are universities for?* Penguin.

Cotton, T., & Griffiths, M. (2007). Action research, stories and practical philosophy. *Educational Action Research*, 15(4), 545–560.

Crean, M., & Lynch, K. (2011). Resistance, struggle and survival: The university as a site for transformative education. In A. O'Shea & M. O'Brien (Eds.), *Pedagogy, oppression and transformation in a 'post-critical' climate* (pp. 51–68). Bloomsbury.

Donnelly, M., & Gamsu, S. (2018). *Home and away: Social, ethnic and spatial inequalities in student mobility*. The Sutton Trust.

Franklin-Phipps, A., & Rath. C. L. (2018). How to become less deadly: A provocation to the fields of teacher education and educational research. *Parallax*, 24(3), 268–272.

Freire, P. (1972). *Pedagogy of the oppressed* (M. Bergman Ramos, Trans.). Penguin.

Fulford, L. (2020). *Stories from a marginalised majority: An exploration of local live at home students and their experiences of 'student-hood'* [Unpublished EdD thesis]. Faculty of Education, Health and Life Sciences, Birmingham City University.

Haraway, D. (2016). *Staying with the trouble*. Duke University Press.

Harvey, L., & Green, D. (1993). Defining quality. *Assessment and Evaluation in Higher Education*, 18(1), 9–34.

Holdsworth C. (2006). "Don't you think you're missing out, living at home?" Student experiences and residential transitions. *The Sociological Review*, 54(3), 495–519.

Kasworm, C. (2010). Adult learners in a research university: Negotiating undergraduate student identity. *Adult Education Quarterly*, 60(2), 143–160.

Kendall, A., Puttick, M.-R., & Wheatcroft, L. (2021). "I don't want them to feel like we're part of the establishment": Teachers' learning to work with refugee families as entangled becomings. *Professional Development in Education*, 47(2–3), 510–523.

Kershaw, A. (2019, September 27). More than half of young people now going to university, figures show. *The Independent*. Retrieved November 27, 2021, from https://www.independent.co.uk/news/education/education-news/university-students-young-people-over-half-first-time-a9122321.html

Kitching, K. (2011). Taking educational risks with and without guaranteed identities: Freire's 'problem-posing' and Judith Butler's 'troubling'. In A. O'Shea & M. O'Brien

(Eds.), *Pedagogy, oppression and transformation in a 'post-critical' climate* (pp. 102–119). Bloomsbury.

Lefebvre, H. (2002). *Critique of the everyday life, Vol. 2: Foundations for a sociology of the everyday*. Verso.

Lefebvre, H. (2014). *Rhythmanalysis*. Continuum.

Levecque, K., Anseel, F., De Beucklaer, A., Van Det Hayden, J., & Gisle, L. (2017). Work organization and mental health problems in PhD students. *Research Policy, 46*, 868–879.

MacLure, M. (2011). Qualitative inquiry: Where are the ruins? *Qualitative Inquiry, 17*(10), 997–1005.

McCaig, C. (2018). *The marketisation of English higher education*. Emerald Publishing Limited.

McGettigan, A. (2013). *The great university gamble: Money, markets and the future of higher education*. Pluto Press.

NNS. (2021). *National student survey*. Retrieved December 1, 2021, from https://www.thestudentsurvey.com/about-the-nss/

O'Brien, M. (2011). Towards a pedagogy of care and well-being: Restoring the vocation of becoming human through dialogue and relationality. In A. O'Shea & M. O'Brien (Eds.), Pedagogy, *oppression and transformation in a 'post-critical' climate* (pp. 14–35). Bloomsbury.

O'Leary, M., & Savage, S. (2019). Breathing new life into the observation of teaching and learning in higher education: Moving from the performative to the informative. *Professional Development in Education, 46*(1), 145–159.

O'Leary, M., & Wood, P. (2017). Performance over professional learning and the complexity puzzle: Lesson observation in England's further education sector. *Professional Development in Education, 43*(4), 573–591.

Reay, D., Crozier, G., & Clayton, J. (2010). "Fitting in" or "standing out": Working-class students in UK higher education. *British Educational Research Journal, 32*(1), 1–19.

St. Pierre, E., & Pillow, W. (Eds.). (2000). *Working the ruins: Feminist poststructural theory and methods in education*. Routledge.

Strom, K. J., & Mitchell Viesca, K. (2021). Towards a complex framework of teacher learning-practice. *Professional Development in Education, 47*(2–3), 209–224.

Waller, R., Ingram, N., & Ward, M. R. M. (Eds.). (2018). *Higher education and social inequalities: University admissions, experiences, and outcomes*. Routledge.

Wood, P., & O'Leary, M. (2019). Moving beyond teaching excellence: Developing a different narrative for England's higher education sector. *International Journal of Comparative Education and Development, 21*(2), 112–126.